CICERO'S ORATIONS

CICERO'S
ORATIONS

TRANSLATED WITH EXPLANATORY NOTES BY

C. D. YOUNGE

INTRODUCTION BY

CHARLES ANGOFF

NEW YORK · Fine Editions Press · LONDON

*The Special Contents of This Edition © 1957
by Thomas Yoseloff, Inc.
Manufactured in the United States of America*

INTRODUCTION

ORATORY is an ancient and noble art, more often sullied than honored by those who practice it. Because of its very nature, it is frequently employed by unscrupulous seekers for public office, or by advocates in the courts of justice who are more interested in swaying judgment than in championing the right. But also because of its nature, it has been a mighty instrument in the recurring battles, throughout history, for the preservation of the foundations of civilized living.

Oratory at its most sublime and its most eloquent had its birth in the classical world. It was a living force in Athens and in Rome; it determined the direction of their histories for long periods of time; it added a special stamp to their cultures. Indeed, it was, in some regards, the barometer of those cultures. For when free institutions flourished, oratory flourished, too, and when the spirit of independence declined, so did oratory decline. Oratory reached its greatest heights, however, not in times of peace and prosperity but in times of greatest struggle, both internal and external. Orators have ever needed the stimulus of great issues to rise to the pinnacles of impassioned eloquence.

The two most celebrated and most influential orators of the ancient world were Demosthenes in Greece and Cicero in Rome. Had they not lived and labored, the annals of their countries probably would have taken a different direction at one time or another. They had much in common. Both attempted to persuade with logic and with prose rhythm. Both employed their respective languages with refinement. Both were dedicated to the public weal. But while Demosthenes utilized the rapier, Cicero utilized the sword. Demosthenes was concise and parsimonious in his language; Cicero was redundant and opulent. Demosthenes was objective; Cicero was subjective. Demosthenes was profoundly earnest, seldom allowing himself a pleasantry; Cicero was equally serious, but he liked to jest and to display flashes of verbal wit.

John Quincy Adams said: "Cicero is the friend of the soul, whom we can never meet without a gleam of pleasure, from whom we can never part without reluctance." Indeed, there was something truly warm and friendly about Cicero, a man who was fully human, with his share of human failings. Born in 106 B.C. into a noble family, Marcus Tullius Cicero was taken to Rome at an early age, and was then given the benefits of an education in Greece and Asia Minor. He was an orator, statesman, philosopher, lawyer, literary critic. For a time he was the most famous criminal lawyer in Rome, generally serving as counsel for the defense. He rose from the ranks as quaestor in 75 to consul in 63, and, as pro-consul of the province of Cilicia in 51–50, he achieved a fine record as an administrator. He was deeply involved in the bitter conflict against the combination of Caesar, Pompey, and Crassus, a conflict that became so complicated toward the end that he barely knew where he stood: emotionally he inclined toward Pompey, intellectually toward Caesar. He was now beginning to wonder whether the political life was really for him, but the assassination of Caesar propelled him to make one of his most celebrated speeches in behalf of the reconciliation of the various factions. This, apparently against his will, involved him still deeper in politics, and in 43 B.C. he was assassinated by C. Popillius Laenas, who owed his life to Cicero.

As a statesman, Cicero at times vacillated between courage and indecision. Still, he will be remembered for three major achievements: he suppressed the conspiracy of Catiline, and thus won the title of Father of His Country; as an administrator of Cilicia, he set a remarkable example of honest and efficient government; and he was a champion of the constitution against all attempts to set up a dictatorship. Nearly always he could be found on the side of those who were for freedom under law.

More is known about Cicero than about many other ancient statesmen and authors. He left nearly 1,000 letters; 58 orations; 12 philosophical works; 7 rhetorical treatises; and nearly 900 lines of poetry. His most famous orations are the four against Catiline, which lead off the present volume. In these orations Cicero reveals himself in the fullness of his powers as a master of invective. A sample from the Second Oration:

O happy republic, if it can cast forth these dregs of the republic! Even now, when Catiline alone is got rid of, the republic seems to me relieved and refreshed; for what evil or wickedness can be devised or imagined which he did not conceive? What prisoner, what gladiator, what thief, what assassin, what parricide, what forger of wills, what cheat, what debauchee, what spendthrift, what adulterer, what abandoned woman, what corrupter of youth, what profligate, what scoundrel can be found in all Italy, who does not avow that he has been on terms of intimacy with Catiline? What murder has been committed for years without him? What nefarious act of infamy that has not been done by him?

Other fine samples of Cicero's oratory also appear in this book. A legal speech, clear and tremendously moving even now, two thousand years later, may be read in "In Defense of Titus Annius Milo." Milo was convicted and banished, but Cicero's plea for him will be remembered. There is a magnificent tribute to a poet and to the whole literary world in "For Aulus Licinius Archias, the Poet." And if one would see how a master employs the art of ridicule one can hardly do better than to read Cicero's "The Fourth Book of the Second Pleading in the Prosecution of Verres." The case was that of a gross man who had stolen Greek statues and other works of art from temples and private homes, and by the time Cicero is through with him, Verres seems even lower than a swine.

Cicero's poetry and his philosophical disquisitions lend themselves easily to quotation. Particularly is this true of his *De Senectute* (Of Old Age), *De Republica* (Of the Republic), and *De Oratore* and *Orator*, the last two presenting his principles of oratory and literary composition in general. It is, however, his addresses on public issues, in and out of the Roman Senate, that have probably done most to keep Cicero's memory alive. As a philosopher and literary critic, he did remarkably well what others have done better. As an orator in the public forum and in the halls of justice, he achieved an excellence that has not been equalled or even approached by any other man in the past two thousand years, with the possible exception of Demosthenes.

CHARLES ANGOFF

CONTENTS

Introduction *by Charles Angoff*   vii

The First Oration Against Lucius Catilina   1

The Second Oration Against Lucius Catilina   16

The Third Oration Against Lucius Catilina   28

The Fourth Oration Against Lucius Catilina   43

For Aulus Licinius Archias, the Poet   57

In Defense of the Proposed Manilian Law   71

In Behalf of Marcus Claudius Marcellus   100

In Defense of Titus Annius Milo   113

The Fourth Book of the Second Pleading in the
Prosecution of Verres   161

In Defense of Quintus Ligarius   232

THE FIRST ORATION AGAINST LUCIUS CATILINA

Delivered in the Senate

THE ARGUMENT

Lucius Catiline, a man of noble extraction, and who had already
been prætor, had been a competitor of Cicero's for the consulship;
the next year he again offered himself for the office, practising
such excessive and open bribery, that Cicero published a new law
against it, with the additional penalty of ten years' exile; pro-
hibiting likewise all shows of gladiators from being exhibited by
a candidate within two years of the time of his suing for any
magistracy, unless they were ordered by the will of a person de-
ceased. Catiline, who knew this law to be aimed chiefly at him,
formed a design to murder Cicero and some others of the chief
men of the senate, on the day of election, which was fixed for the
twentieth of October. But Cicero had information of his plans,
and laid them before the senate, on which the election was de-
ferred, that they might have time to deliberate on an affair of so
much importance. The day following, when the senate met, he
charged Catiline with having entertained this design, and Catiline's behavior had been so violent, that the senate passed the
decree to which they had occasionally recourse in times of immi-
nent danger from treason or sedition, "Let the consuls take care
that the republic suffers no harm." This decree invested the consuls with absolute power, and suspended all the ordinary forms
of law, till the danger was over. On this Cicero doubled his
guards, introduced some additional troops into the city, and when
the elections came on, he wore a breastplate under his robe for
his protection; by which precaution he prevented Catiline from
executing his design of murdering him and his competitors for
the consulship, of whom Decius Junius Silanus and Lucius Licinius Murena were elected.

Catiline was rendered desperate by this his second defeat, and resolved without further delay to attempt the execution of all his

1

schemes. His greatest hopes lay in Sylla's veteran soldiers, whose cause he had always espoused. They were scattered about in the different districts and colonies of Italy; but he had actually enlisted a considerable body of them in Etruria, and formed them into a little army under the command of Manlius, a centurion of considerable military experience, who was only waiting for his orders. He was joined in his conspiracy by several senators of profligate lives and desperate fortunes, of whom the chiefs were Publius Cornelius Lentulus, Caius Cethegus, Publius Autronius, Lucius Cassius Longinus, Marcus Porcius Lecca, Publius Sylla, Servilius Sylla, Quintus Curius, Lucius Vargunteius, Quintus Annius, and Lucius Bestia. These men resolved that a general insurrection should be raised throughout all Italy; that Catiline should put himself at the head of the troops in Etruria; that Rome should be set on fire in many places at once; and that a general massacre should be made of all the senate, and of all their enemies, of whom none were to be spared but the sons of Pompey, who were to be kept as hostages, and as a check upon their father, who was in command in the east. Lentulus was to be president of their councils, Cassius was to manage the firing of the city, and Cethegus the massacre. But, as the vigilance of Cicero was the greatest obstacle to their success, Catiline desired to see him slain before he left Rome; and two knights, parties to the conspiracy, undertook to visit him early on pretense of business, and to kill him in his bed. The name of one of them was Caius Cornelius.

Cicero, however, had information of all the designs of the conspirators, as by the intrigues of a woman called Fulvia, the mistress of Curius, he had gained him over, and received regularly from him an account of all their operations. He sent for some of the chief men of the city, and informed them of the plot against himself, and even of the names of the knights who were to come to his house, and of the hour at which they were to come. When they did come they found the house carefully guarded, and all admission refused to them. He was enabled also to disappoint an attempt made by Catiline to seize on the town of Præneste, which was a very strong fortress, and would have been of great use to him. The meeting of the conspirators had taken place on the evening of the sixth of November. On the eighth Cicero summoned the senate to meet in the temple of Jupiter in the Capitol, a place which was only used for this purpose on occasions of great danger. (There had been previously several debates on the subject of Catiline's treasons and design of murdering Cicero, and a public reward had actually been offered to the first discoverer of the plot. But Catiline had nevertheless continued to dissemble; had offered to give security for his behavior, and to deliver himself to the custody of any one whom the senate chose to name, even to that of Cicero himself.) Catiline had the boldness to attend this meeting, and all the senate, even his own most particular acquaintance, were so astonished at his impudence that none of them would salute him; the consular senators quitted that part of the house in which he sat, and left the bench empty; and Cicero himself was so provoked at his audacity, that, instead of entering on any formal business, he addressed himself directly to Catiline in the following invective.

I. WHEN, O Catiline, do you mean to cease abusing our patience? How long is that madness of yours still to mock us? When is there to be an end of that unbridled audacity of yours, swaggering about as it does now? Do not the nightly guards placed on the Palatine Hill—do not the watches posted throughout the city—does not the alarm of the people, and the union of all good men—does not the precaution taken of assembling the senate in this most defensible place—do not the looks and countenances of this venerable body here present, have any effect upon you? Do you not feel that your plans are detected? Do you not see that your conspiracy is already arrested and rendered powerless by the knowledge which every one here possesses of it? What is there that you did last night, what the night before—where is it that you were—who was there that you summoned to meet you—what design was there which was adopted by you, with which you think that any one of us is unacquainted?

Shame on the age and on its principles! The senate is aware of these things; the consul sees them; and yet this man lives. Lives! aye, he comes even into the senate. He takes a part in the public deliberations: he is watching and marking down and checking off for slaughter every individual among us. And we, gallant men that we are, think that we are doing our duty to the republic if we keep out of the way of his frenzied attacks.

You ought, O Catiline, long ago to have been led to execution by command of the consul. That destruction which you have been long plotting against us ought to have already fallen on your own head.

What? Did not that most illustrious man, Publius Scipio,[1] the Pontifex Maximus, in his capacity of a private citizen, put to death Tiberius Gracchus, though but slightly undermining the constitution? And shall we, who are the consuls, tolerate Catiline, openly desirous to destroy the whole world with fire and slaughter? For I pass over older instances, such as how Caius Servilius Ahala with his own hand slew Spurius Mælius when plotting a revolution in the state. There was—there was once such virtue in this republic, that brave men would repress mischievous citizens with severer chastisement than the most bitter enemy. For we have a resolution[2] of the senate, a formidable and authoritative decree against you, O Catiline; the wisdom of the republic is not at fault, nor the dignity of this senatorial body. We, we alone,—I say it openly,—we, the consuls, are wanting in our duty.

II. The senate once passed a decree that Lucius Opimius, the consul, should take care that the republic suffered no injury. Not one night elapsed. There was put to death, on some mere suspicion of disaffection, Caius Gracchus, a man whose family had borne the most unblemished reputation for many generations. There was slain Marcus Fulvius, a man of consular rank, and all his children. By a like decree of the senate the safety of the republic was entrusted to Caius Marius[3] and Lucius Valerius, the consuls. Did not the vengeance of the republic, did not execution overtake Lucius Saturninus, a tribune of the people, and Caius Servilius, the prætor, without the delay of one single day? But we, for these twenty days, have been allowing the edge of the senate's authority to grow blunt, as it were. For we are in possession of a similar decree of the senate, but we keep it locked up in its parchment—buried, I may say,

[1] This was Scipio Nasica, who called on the consul Mucius Scævola to do his duty and save the republic: but as he refused to put any one to death without a trial, Scipio called on all the citizens to follow him, and stormed the Capitol, which Gracchus had occupied with his party, and slew many of the partisans of Gracchus, and Gracchus himself.

[2] This resolution was couched in the form "Videant Consules nequid respublica detrimenti capiat;" and it exempted the consuls from all obligation to attend to the ordinary forms of law, and invested them with absolute power over the lives of all the citizens who were intriguing against the republic.

[3] This is the same incident that is the subject of the preceding oration in defense of Rabirius.

in the sheath; and according to this decree you ought, O Catiline, to be put to death this instant. You live,—and you live, not to lay aside, but to persist in your audacity.

I wish, O conscript fathers, to be merciful; I wish not to appear negligent amid such danger to the state; but I do now accuse myself of remissness and culpable inactivity. A camp is pitched in Italy, at the entrance of Etruria, in hostility to the republic; the number of the enemy increases every day; and yet the general of that camp, the leader of those enemies, we see within the walls—ay, and even in the senate,—planning every day some internal injury to the republic. If, O Catiline, I should now order you to be arrested, to be put to death, I should, I suppose, have to fear lest all good men should say that I had acted tardily, rather than that any one should affirm that I acted cruelly. But yet this, which ought to have been done long since, I have good reason for not doing as yet; I will put you to death, then, when there shall be not one person possible to be found so wicked, so abandoned, so like yourself, as not to allow that it has been rightly done. As long as one person exists who can dare to defend you, you shall live; but you shall live as you do now, surrounded by my many and trusty guards, so that you shall not be able to stir one finger against the republic: many eyes and ears shall still observe and watch you, as they have hitherto done, though you shall not perceive them.

III. For wath is there, O Catiline, that you can still expect, if night is not able to veil your nefarious meetings in darkness, and if private houses cannot conceal the voice of your conspiracy within their walls;—if everything is seen and displayed? Change your mind: trust me: forget the slaughter and conflagation you are meditating. You are hemmed in on all sides; all your plans are clearer than the day to us; let me remind you of them. Do you recollect that on the 21st of October I said in the senate, that on a certain day, which was to be the 27th of October, C. Manlius, the satellite and servant of your audacity, would be in arms? Was I mistaken, Catiline, not only in so important, so atrocious, so incredible a fact, but, what is much more remarkable, in the very day? I said also in the senate that you had fixed the massacre of the nobles for the 28th of October, when many chief men of the senate had left Rome, not so much for the sake of saving themselves as of checking your

designs. Can you deny that on that very day you were so
hemmed in by my guards and my vigilance, that you were
unable to stir one finger against the republic; when you said
that you would be content with the flight of the rest, and the
slaughter of us who remained? What? when you made sure
that you would be able to seize Præneste on the first of November by a nocturnal attack, did you not find that that colony
was fortified by my order, by my garrison, by my watchfulness and care? You do nothing, you plan nothing, you think of
nothing which I not only do not hear, but which I do not see
and know every particular of.

IV. Listen while I speak of the night before. You shall now
see that I watch far more actively for the safety than you do
for the destruction of the republic. I say that you came the
night before (I will say nothing obscurely) into the Scythe-
dealers' street, to the house of Marcus Lecca; that many of your
accomplices in the same insanity and wickedness came there
too. Do you dare to deny it? Why are you silent? I will prove it
if you do deny it; for I see here in the senate some men who
were there with you.

O ye immortal Gods, where on earth are we? in what city are
we living? what constitution is ours? There are here,—here in
our body, O conscript fathers, in this the most holy and dignified assembly of the whole world, men who meditate my
death, and the death of all of us, and the destruction of this
city, and of the whole world. I, the consul, see them; I ask them
their opinion about the republic, and I do not yet attack, even
by words, those who ought to be put to death by the sword.
You were, then, O Catiline, at Lecca's that night; you divided
Italy into sections; you settled where every one was to go; you
fixed whom you were to leave at Rome, whom you were to take
with you; you portioned out the divisions of the city for conflagration; you undertook that you yourself would at once leave
the city, and said that there was then only this to delay you,
that I was still alive. Two Roman knights were found to deliver
you from this anxiety, and to promise that very night, before
daybreak, to slay me in my bed. All this I knew almost before
your meeting had broken up. I strengthened and fortified my
house with a stronger guard; I refused admittance, when they

came, to those whom you sent in the morning to salute me, and of whom I had foretold to many eminent men that they would come to me at that time.

V. As, then, this is the case, O Catiline, continue as you have begun. Leave the city at last; the gates are open; depart. That Manlian camp of yours has been waiting too long for you as its general. And lead forth with you all your friends, or at least as many as you can; purge the city of your presence; you will deliver me from a great fear, when there is a wall between me and you. Among us you can dwell no longer—I will not bear it, I will not permit it, I will not tolerate it. Great thanks are due to the immortal gods, and to this very Jupiter Stator, in whose temple we are, the most ancient protector of this city, that we have already so often escaped so foul, so horrible, and so deadly an enemy to the republic. But the safety of the commonwealth must not be too often allowed to be risked on one man. As long as you, O Catiline, plotted against me while I was the consul elect, I defended myself not with a public guard, but by my own private diligence. When, in the next consular comitia, you wished to slay me when I was actually consul, and your competitors also, in the Campus Martius, I checked your nefarious attempt by the assistance and resources of my own friends, without exciting any disturbance publicly. In short, as often as you attacked me, I by myself opposed you, and that, too, though I saw that my ruin was connected with great disaster to the republic. But now you are openly attacking the entire republic.

You are summoning to destruction and devastation the temples of the immortal gods, the houses of the city, the lives of all the citizens; in short, all Italy. Wherefore, since I do not yet venture to do that which is the best thing, and which belongs to my office and to the discipline of our ancestors, I will do that which is more merciful if we regard its rigor, and more expedient for the state. For if I order you to be put to death, the rest of the conspirators will still remain in the republic; if, as I have long been exhorting you, you depart, your companions, those worthless dregs of the republic, will be drawn off from the city too. What is the matter, Catiline? Do you hesitate to do that when I order you which you were already doing

of your own accord? The consul orders an enemy to depart
from the city. Do you ask me, Are you to go into banishment?
I do not order it; but, if you consult me, I advise it.

VI. For what is there, O Catiline, that can now afford you
any pleasure in this city? for there is no one in it, except that
band of profligate conspirators of yours, who does not fear you,
—no one who does not hate you. What brand of domestic baseness is not stamped upon your life? What disgraceful circumstance is wanting to your infamy in your private affairs? From
what licentiousness have your eyes, from what atrocity have
your hands, from what iniquity has your whole body ever abstained? Is there one youth, when you have once entangled him
in the temptations of your corruption, to whom you have not
held out a sword for audacious crime, or a torch for licentious
wickedness?

What? when lately by the death of your former wife you had
made your house empty and ready for a new bridal, did you
not even add another incredible wickedness to this wickedness? But I pass that over, and willingly allow it to be buried
in silence, that so horrible a crime may not be seen to have
existed in this city, and not to have been chastized. I pass over
the ruin of your fortune, which you know is hanging over you
against the ides of the very next month; I come to those things
which relate not to the infamy of your private vices, not to your
domestic difficulties and basness, but to the welfare of the republic and to the lives and safety of us all.

Can the light of this life, O Catiline, can the breath of this
atmosphere be pleasant to you, when you know that there is
not one man of those here present who is ignorant that you, on
the last day of the year, when Lepidus and Tullius were consuls, stood in the assembly armed; that you had prepared your
hand for the slaughter of the consuls and chief men of the
state, and that no reason or fear of yours hindered your crime
and madness, but the fortune of the republic? And I say no
more of these things, for they are not unknown to every one.
How often have you endeavored to slay me, both as consul
elect and as actual consul? how many shots of yours, so aimed
that they seemed impossible to be escaped, have I avoided by
some slight stooping aside, and some dodging, as it were, of
my body? You attempt nothing, you execute nothing, you de-

vise nothing that can be kept hid from me at the proper time;
and yet you do not cease to attempt and to contrive. How often
already has that dagger of yours been wrested from your
hands? how often has it slipped through them by some chance,
and dropped down? and yet you cannot any longer do without
it; and to what sacred mysteries it is consecrated and devoted
by you I know not, that you think it necessary to plunge it in
the body of the consul.

VII. But now, what is that life of yours that you are leading?
For I will speak to you not so as to seem influenced by the
hatred I ought to feel, but by pity, nothing of which is due to
you. You came a little while ago into the senate: in so numerous an assembly, who of so many friends and connections of
yours saluted you? If this in the memory of man never happened to any one else, are you waiting for insults by word of
mouth, when you are overwhelmed by the most irresistible
condemnation of silence? Is it nothing that at your arrival all
those seats were vacated? that all the men of consular rank,
who had often been marked out by you for slaughter, the very
moment you sat down, left that part of the benches bare and
vacant? With what feelings do you think you ought to bear
this? On my honor, if my slaves feared me as all your fellow-
citizens fear you, I should think I must leave my house. Do
not you think you should leave the city? If I saw that I was
even undeservedly so suspected and hated by my fellow-
citizens, I would rather flee from their sight than be gazed at
by the hostile eyes of every one. And do you, who, from the
consciousness of your wickedness, know that the hatred of all
men is just and has been long due to you, hesitate to avoid the
sight and presence of those men whose minds and senses you
offend? If your parents feared and hated you, and if you could
by no means pacify them, you would, I think, depart some-
where out of their sight. Now, your country, which is the common parent of all of us, hates and fears you, and has no other
opinion of you, than that you are meditating parricide in her
case; and will you neither feel awe of her authority, nor defer-
ence for her judgment, no fear of her power?

And she, O Catiline, thus pleads with you, and after a manner silently speaks to you:—There has now for many years been
no crime committed but by you: no atrocity has taken place

10 CICERO'S ORATIONS

without you; you alone unpunished and unquestioned have murdered the citizens, have harassed and plundered the allies; you alone have had power not only to neglect all laws and investigations, but to overthrow and break through them. Your former actions, though they ought not to have been borne, yet I did bear as well as I could; but now that I should be wholly occupied with fear of you alone, that at every sound I should dread Catiline, that no design should seem possible to be entertained against me which does not proceed from your wickedness, this is no longer endurable. Depart, then, and deliver me from this fear; that, if it be a just one, I may not be destroyed; if an imaginary one, that at least I may at last cease to fear.

VIII. If, as I have said, your country were thus to address you, ought she not to obtain her request, even if she were not able to enforce it? What shall I say of your having given yourself into custody? what of your having said, for the sake of avoiding suspicion, that you were willing to dwell in the house of Marcus Lepidus? And when you were not received by him, you dared even to come to me, and begged me to keep you in my house; and when you had received answer from me that I could not possibly be safe in the same house with you, when I considered myself in great danger as long as we were in the same city, you came to Quintus Metellus, the prætor, and being rejected by him, you passed on to your associate, that most excellent man, Marcus Marcellus, who would be, I suppose you thought, most diligent in guarding you, most sagacious in suspecting you, and most bold in punishing you; but how far can we think that man ought to be from bonds and imprisonment who has already judged himself deserving of being given into custody?

Since, then, this is the case, do you hesitate, O Catiline, if you cannot remain here with tranquillity, to depart to some distant land, and to trust your life, saved from just and deserved punishment, to flight and solitude? Make a motion, say you, to the senate, (for that is what you demand,) and if this body votes that you ought to go into banishment, you say that you will obey. I will not make such a motion, it is contrary to my principles, and yet I will let you see what these men think of you. Be gone from the city, O Catiline, deliver the republic from fear; depart into banishment, if that is the word you are waiting for. What now, O Catiline? Do you not perceive, do you not see the silence of these men; they permit it, they say nothing; why wait you for the authority of their words when you see their wishes in their silence?

But had I said the same to this excellent young man, Publius Sextius, or to that brave man, Marcus Marcellus, before this time the senate would deservedly have laid violent hands on me, consul though I be, in this very temple. But as to you, Catiline, while they are quiet they approve, while they permit me to speak they vote, while they are silent they are loud and eloquent. And not they alone, whose authority forsooth is dear to you, though their lives are unimportant, but the Roman knights too, those most honorable and excellent men, and the other virtuous citizens who are now surrounding the senate, whose numbers you could see, whose desires you could know, and whose voices you a few minutes ago could hear,—ay, whose very hands and weapons I have for some time been scarcely able to keep off from you; but those, too, I will easily bring to attend you to the gates if you leave these places you have been long desiring to lay waste.

IX. And yet, why am I speaking? that anything may change your purpose? that you may ever amend your life? that you may meditate flight or think of voluntary banishment? I wish the gods may give you such a mind; though I see, if alarmed at my words you bring your mind to go into banishment, what a storm of unpopularity hangs over me, if not at present, while the memory of your wickedness is fresh, at all events hereafter. But it is worth while to incur that, as long as that is but a private misfortune of my own, and is unconnected with the dangers of the republic. But we cannot expect that you should be concerned at your own vices, that you should fear the penalties of the laws, or that you should yield to the necessities of the republic, for you are not, O Catiline, one whom either shame can recall from infamy, or fear from danger, or reason from madness.

Wherefore, as I have said before, go forth, and if you wish to make me, your enemy as you call me, unpopular, go straight into banishment. I shall scarcely be able to endure all that will be said if you do so; I shall scarcely be able to support my load

of unpopularity if you do go into banishment at the command
of the consul; but if you wish to serve my credit and reputation, go forth with your ill-omened band of profligates; betake
yourself to Manlius, rouse up the abandoned citizens, separate
yourself from the good ones, wage war against your country,
exult in your impious banditti, so that you may not seem to
have been driven out by me and gone to strangers, but to have
gone invited to your own friends.

Though why should I invite you, by whom I know men have
been already sent on to wait in arms for you at the forum
Aurelium; who I know has fixed and agreed with Manlius upon
a settled day; by whom I know that that silver eagle, which I
trust will be ruinous and fatal to you and to all your friends,
and to which there was set up in your house a shrine as it
were of your crimes, has been already sent forward. Need I
fear that you can long do without that which you used to worship when going out to murder, and from whose altars you
have often transferred your impious hand to the slaughter of
citizens?

X. You will go at last where your unbridled and mad desire
has been long hurrying you. And this causes you no grief, but
an incredible pleasure. Nature has formed you, desire has
trained you, fortune has preserved you for this insanity. Not
only did you never desire quiet, but you never even desired
any war but a criminal one; you have collected a band of profligates and worthless men, abandoned not only by all fortune
but even by hope.

Then what happiness will you enjoy! with what delight will
you exult! in what pleasure will you revel! when in so numerous a body of friends, you neither hear nor see one good
man. All the toils you have gone through have always pointed
to this sort of life; your lying on the ground not merely to lie in
wait to gratify your unclean desires, but even to accomplish
crimes; your vigilance, not only when plotting against the
sleep of husbands, but also against the goods of your murdered victims, have all been preparations for this. Now you
have an opportunity of displaying your splendid endurance of
hunger, of cold, of want of everything; by which in a short
time you will find yourself worn out. All this I effected when I
procured your rejection from the consulship, that you should

be reduced to make attempts on your country as an exile, instead of being able to distress it as consul, and that that which had been wickedly undertaken by you should be called piracy rather than war.

XI. Now that I may remove and avert, O conscript fathers, any in the least reasonable complaint from myself, listen, I beseech you, carefully to what I say, and lay it up in your inmost hearts and minds. In truth, if my country, which is far dearer to me than my life,—if all Italy,—if the whole republic were to address me, "Marcus Tullius, what are you doing? will you permit that man to depart whom you have ascertained to be an enemy? whom you see ready to become the general of the war? whom you know to be expected in the camp of the enemy as their chief, the author of all this wickedness, the head of the conspiracy, the instigator of the slaves and abandoned citizens, so that he shall seem not driven out of the city by you, but let loose by you against the city? Will you not order him to be thrown into prison, to be hurried off to execution, to be put to death with the most prompt severity? What hinders you? is it the customs of our ancestors? But even private men have often in this republic slain mischievous citizens.—Is it the laws which have been passed about the punishment of Roman citizens? But in this city those who have rebelled against the republic have never had the rights of citizens.—Do you fear odium with posterity? You are showing fine gratitude to the Roman people which has raised you, a man known only by your own actions, of no ancestral renown, through all the degrees of honor at so early an age to the very highest office, if from fear of unpopularity or of any danger you neglect the safety of your fellow-citizens. But if you have a fear of unpopularity, is that arising from the imputation of vigor and boldness, or that arising from that of inactivity and indecision most to be feared? When Italy is laid waste by war, when cities are attacked and houses in flames, do you not think that you will be then consumed by a perfect conflagration of hatred?"

XII. To this holy address of the republic, and to the feelings of those men who entertain the same opinion, I will make this short answer:—If, O conscript fathers, I thought it best that Catiline should be punished with death, I would not have given the space of one hour to this gladiator to live in. If, forsooth, those excellent men and most illustrious cities not only did not pollute themselves, but even glorified themselves by the blood of Saturninus, and the Gracchi, and Flaccus, and many others of old time, surely I had no cause to fear lest for slaying this parricidal murderer of the citizens any unpopularity should accrue to me with posterity. And if it did threaten me to ever so great a degree, yet I have always been of the disposition to think unpopularity earned by virtue and glory, not unpopularity.

Though there are some men in this body who either do not see what threatens, or dissemble what they do see; who have fed the hope of Catiline by mild sentiments, and have strengthened the rising conspiracy by not believing it; influenced by whose authority many, and they not wicked, but only ignorant, if I punished him would say that I had acted cruelly and tyranically. But I know that if he arrives at the camp of Manlius to which he is going, there will be no one so stupid as not to see that there has been a conspiracy, no one so hardened as not to confess it. But if this man alone were put to death, I know that this disease of the republic would be only checked for a while, not eradicated forever. But if he banishes himself, and takes with him all his friends, and collects at one point all the ruined men from every quarter, then not only will this full-grown plague of the republic be extinguished and eradicated, but also the root and seed of all future evils.

XIII. We have now for a long time, O conscript fathers, lived among these dangers and machinations of conspiracy; but somehow or other, the ripeness of all wickedness, and of this long-standing madness and audacity, has come to a head at the time of my consulship. But if this man alone is removed from this piratical crew, we may appear, perhaps, for a short time relieved from fear and anxiety, but the danger will settle down and lie hid in the veins and bowels of the republic. As it often happens that men afflicted with a severe disease, when they are tortured with heat and fever, if they drink cold water, seem at first to be relieved, but afterwards suffer more and more severely; so this disease which is in the republic, if relieved by the punishment of this man, will only get worse and worse, as the rest will be still alive.

Wherefore, O conscript fathers, let the worthless begone,—

let them separate themselves from the good,—let them collect in one place,—let them, as I have often said before, be separated from us by a wall; let them cease to plot against the consul in his own house,—to surround the tribunal of the city prætor,—to besiege the senate-house with swords,—to prepare brands and torches to burn the city; let it, in short, be written on the brow of every citizen, what are his sentiments about the republic. I promise you this, O conscript fathers, that there shall be so much diligence in us the consuls, so much authority in you, so much virtue in the Roman knights, so much unanimity in all good men, that you shall see everything made plain and manifest by the departure of Catiline,—everything checked and punished.

With these omens, O Catiline, begone to your impious and nefarious war, to the great safety of the republic, to your own misfortune and injury, and to the destruction of those who have joined themselves to you in every wickedness and atrocity. Then do you, O Jupiter, who were consecrated by Romulus with the same auspices as this city, whom we rightly call the stay of this city and empire, repel this man and his companions from your altars and from the other temples,—from the houses and walls of the city,—from the lives and fortunes of all the citizens; and overwhelm all the enemies of good men, the foes of the republic, the robbers of Italy, men bound together by a treaty and infamous alliance of crimes, dead and alive, with eternal punishments.

THE SECOND ORATION AGAINST LUCIUS CATILINA

Addressed to the People

THE ARGUMENT

Catiline did not venture to make any reply to the former speech, but he begged the senate not to be too hasty in believing everything which was said to his prejudice by one who had always been his enemy, as Cicero had; and alleged his high birth, and the stake which he had in the prosperity of the commonwealth, as arguments to make it appear improbable that he should seek to injure it; and called Cicero a stranger, and a new inhabitant of Rome. But the senate interrupted him with a general outcry, calling him traitor and parricide. Upon which, being rendered furious and desperate, he declared aloud what he had before said to Cato, that since he was circumvented and driven headlong by his enemies, he would quench the flame which his enemies were kindling around him in the common ruin. And so he rushed out of the temple. On his arrival at his own house he held a brief conference with the other conspirators, in which it was resolved that he should go at once to the camp of Manlius, and return as speedily as he could at the head of the army which was there awaiting him. Accordingly, that night he left Rome with a small retinue, and made the best of his way towards Etruria. His friends gave out that he had gone into voluntary banishment at Marseilles; and spread that report through the city the next morning, in order to excite odium against Cicero, as having driven him out without any trial or proof of his guilt. But Cicero was aware of his motions, and knew that he had previously sent a quantity of arms, and military ensigns, and especially a silver eagle which he had been used to keep in his own house with a superstitious reverence, because it had been used by the great Marius in his expedition against the Cimbri. However, he thought it desirable to counteract the story of his having gone into exile, and therefore summoned the people into the forum, and made them the following speech.

16

I. At length, O Romans, we have dismissed from the city, or driven out, or, when he was departing of his own accord, we have pursued with words, Lucius Catiline, mad with audacity, breathing wickedness, impiously planning mischief to his country, threatening fire and sword to you and to this city. He is gone, he has departed, he has disappeared, he has rushed out. No injury will now be prepared against these walls within the walls themselves by that monster and prodigy of wickedness. And we have, without controversy, defeated him, the sole general of this domestic war. For now that dagger will no longer hover about our sides, we shall not be afraid in the campus, in the forum, in the senate-house,—ay, and within our own private walls. He was moved from his place when he was driven from the city. Now we shall openly carry on a regular war with an enemy without hindrance. Beyond all question we ruin the man; we have defeated him splendidly when we have driven him from secret treachery into open warfare. But that he has not taken with him his sword red with blood as he intended,— that he has left us alive,—that we wrested the weapon from his hands,—that he has left the citizens safe and the city standing, what great and overwhelming grief must you think that this is to him! Now he lies prostrate, O Romans, and feels himself stricken down and abject, and often casts back his eyes towards this city, which he mourns over as snatched from his jaws, but which seems to me to rejoice at having vomited forth such a pest, and cast it out of doors.

II. But if there be any one of that disposition which all men should have, who yet blames me greatly for the very thing in which my speech exults and triumphs,—namely, that I did not arrest so capital mortal an enemy rather than let him go,—that is not my fault, O citizens, but the fault of the times. Lucius Catiline ought to have been visited with the severest punishment, and to have been put to death long since; and both the customs of our ancestors, and the rigor of my office, and the republic, demanded this of me; but how many, think you, were there who did not believe what I reported? how many who out of stupidity did not think so? how many who even defended him,—how many who, out of their own depravity, favored him? If, in truth, I had thought that, if he were removed, all danger would be removed from you, I would long since have cut off

Lucius Catiline, had it been at the risk, not only of my popularity, but even of my life.

But as I saw that, since the matter was not even then proved
to all of you, if I had punished him with death, as he had deserved, I should be borne down by unpopularity, and so be
unable to follow up his accomplices, I brought the business on
to this point that you might be able to combat openly when
you saw the enemy without disguise. But how exceedingly I
think this enemy to be feared now that he is out of doors, you
may see from this,—that I am vexed even that he has gone
from the city with but a small retinue. I wish he had taken with
him all his forces. He has taken with him Tongillus, with whom
he had been said to have a criminal intimacy, and Publicius,
and Munatius, whose debts contracted in taverns could cause
no great disquietude to the republic. He has left behind him
others—you all know what men they are, how overwhelmed
with debt, how powerful, how noble.

III. Therefore, with our Gallic legions, and with the levies
which Quintus Metellus has raised in the Picenian and Gallic
territory, and with these troops which are every day being got
ready by us, I thoroughly despise that army composed of desperate old men, of clownish profligates, and uneducated spend-
thrifts; of those who have preferred to desert their bail rather
than that army, and which will fall to pieces if I show them
not the battle array of our army, but an edict of the prætor. I
wish he had taken with him those soldiers of his, whom I see
hovering about the forum, standing about the senate-house,
even coming into the senate, who shine with ointment, who
glitter in purple; and if they remain here, remember that that
army is not so much to be feared by us as these men who have
deserted the army. And they are the more to be feared, because
they are aware that I know what they are thinking of, and yet
they are not influenced by it.

I know to whom Apulia has been allotted, who has Etruria,
who the Picenian territory, who the Gallic district, who has
begged for himself the office of spreading fire and sword by
night through the city. They know that all the plans of the
preceding night are brought to me. I laid them before the senate yesterday. Catiline himself was alarmed, and fled. Why do

these men wait? Verily, they are greatly mistaken if they think that former lenity of mine will last forever.

IV. What I have been waiting for, that I have gained,— namely, that you should all see that a conspiracy has been openly formed against the republic; unless, indeed, there be any one who thinks that those who are like Catiline do not agree with Catiline. There is not any longer room for lenity; the business itself demands severity. One thing, even now, I will grant,—let them depart, let them begone. Let them not suffer the unhappy Catiline to pine away for want of them. I will tell them the road. He went by the Aurelian road. If they make haste, they will catch him by the evening. O happy republic, if it can cast forth these dregs of the republic! Even now, when Catiline alone is got rid of, the republic seems to me relieved and refreshed; for what evil or wickedness can be devised or imagined which he did not conceive? What prisoner, what gladiator, what thief, what assassin, what parricide, what forger of wills, what cheat, what debauchee, what spend-thrift, what adulterer, what abandoned woman, what corrupter of youth, what profligate, what scoundrel can be found in all Italy, who does not avow that he has been on terms of intimacy with Catiline? What murder has been committed for years without him? What nefarious act of infamy that has not been done by him?

But in what other man were there ever so many allurements for youth as in him, who both indulged in infamous love for others, and encouraged their infamous affections for himself, promising to some enjoyment of their lust, to others the death of their parents, and not only instigating them to iniquity, but even assisting them in it. But now, how suddenly had he collected, not only out of the city, but even out of the country, a number of abandoned men? No one, not only at Rome, but in every corner of Italy, was overwhelmed with debt whom he did not enlist in this incredible association of wickedness.

V. And, that you may understand the diversity of his pursuits and the variety of his designs, there was no one in any school of gladiators, at all inclined to audacity, who does not avow himself to be an intimate friend of Catiline,—no one on the stage, at all of a fickle and worthless disposition, who does not profess himself his companion. And he, trained in the practice of insult and wickedness, in enduring cold, and hunger, and thirst, and watching, was called a brave man by those fellows, while all the appliances of industry and instruments of virtue were devoted to lust and atrocity.

But if his companions follow him,—if the infamous herd of desperate men depart from the city, O happy shall we be, fortunate will be the republic, illustrious will be the renown of my consulship. For theirs is no ordinary insolence,—no common and endurable audacity. They think of nothing but slaughter, conflagration, and rapine. They have dissipated their patrimonies, they have squandered their fortunes. Money has long failed them, and now credit begins to fail; but the same desires remain which they had in their time of abundance. But if in their drinking and gambling parties they were content with feasts and harlots, they would be in a hopeless state indeed; but yet they might be endured. But who can bear this,—that indolent men should plot against the bravest,—drunkards against the sober,—men asleep against men awake,—men lying at feasts, embracing abandoned women, languid with wine, crammed with food, crowned with chaplets, reeking with ointments, worn out with lust, belch out in their discourse the murder of all good men, and the conflagration of the city?

But I am confident that some fate is hanging over these men, and that the punishment long since due to their iniquity, and worthlessness, and wickedness, and lust, is either visibly at hand or at least rapidly approaching. And if my consulship shall have removed, since it cannot cure them, it will have added, not some brief span, but many ages of existence to the republic. For there is no nation for us to fear,—no king who can make war on the Roman people. All foreign affairs are tranquilized, both by land and sea, by the valor of one man. Domestic war alone remains. The only plots against us are within our own walls,—the danger is within,—the enemy is within. We must war with luxury, with madness, with wickedness. For this war, O citizens, I offer myself as the general. I take on myself the enmity of profligate men. What can be cured, I will cure, by whatever means it may be possible. What must be cut away, I will not suffer to spread, to the ruin of the republic. Let them depart, or let them stay quiet; or if they remain in the city and in the same disposition as at present, let them expect what they deserve.

VI. But there are men, O Romans, who say that Catiline has been driven by me into banishment. But if I could do so by a word, I would drive out those also who say so. Forsooth, that timid, that excessively bashful man could not bear the voice of the consul; as soon as he was ordered to go into banishment, he obeyed, he was quiet. Yesterday, when I had been all but murdered at my own house, I convoked the senate in the temple of Jupiter Stator; I related the whole affair to the conscript fathers; and when Catiline came thither, what senator addressed him? who saluted him? who looked upon him not so much even as an abandoned citizen, as an implacable enemy? Nay the chiefs of that body left that part of the benches to which he came naked and empty.

On this I, that violent consul, who drive citizens into exile by a word, asked of Catiline whether he had been at the nocturnal meeting at Marcus Lecca's, or not; when that most audacious man, convicted by his own conscience, was at first silent. I related all the other circumstances; I described what he had done that night, where he had been, what he had arranged for the next night, how the plan of the whole war had been laid down by him. When he hesitated, when he was convicted, I asked why he hesitated to go whither he had been long preparing to go; when I knew that arms, that the axes, the fasces, and trumpets, and military standards, and that silver eagle to which he had made a shrine in his own house, had been sent on, did I drive him into exile who I knew had already entered upon war? I suppose Manlius, that centurion who has pitched his camp in the Fæsulan district, has proclaimed war against the Roman people in his own name; and that camp is not now waiting for Catiline as its general, and he, driven forsooth into exile, will go to Marseilles, as they say, and not to that camp.

VII. O the hard lot of those, not only of those who govern, but even of those who save the republic. Now, if Lucius Catiline, hemmed in and rendered powerless by my counsels, by my toils, by my dangers, should on a sudden become alarmed, should change his designs, should desert his friends, should abandon his design of making war, should change his path from this course of wickedness and war, and betake himself to flight and exile, he will not be said to have been deprived by me of the arms of his audacity, to have been astounded and terrified by my diligence, to have been driven from his hope and from his enterprise, but, uncondemned and innocent, to have been driven into banishment by the consul by threats and violence; and there will be some who will seek to have him thought not worthless but unfortunate, and me considered not a most active consul, but a most cruel tyrant. I am not unwilling, O Romans, to endure this storm of false and unjust unpopularity as long as the danger of this horrible and nefarious war is warded off from you. Let him be said to be banished by me as long as he goes into banishment; but, believe me, he will not go. I will never ask of the immortal gods, O Romans, for the sake of lightening my own unpopularity, for you to hear that Lucius Catiline is leading an army of enemies, and is hovering about in arms; but yet in three days you will hear it. And I much more fear that it will be objected to me some day or other, that I have let him escape, rather than that I have banished him. But when there are men who say he has been banished because he has gone away, what would these men say if he had been put to death?

Although those men who keep saying that Catiline is going to Marseilles do not complain of this so much as they fear it; for there is not one of them so inclined to pity, as not to prefer that he should go to Manlius rather than to Marseilles. But he, if he had never before planned what he is now doing, yet would rather be slain while living as a bandit, than live as an exile; but now, when nothing has happened to him contrary to his own wish and design,—except, indeed, that he has left Rome while we are alive,—let us wish rather that he may go into exile than complain of it.

VIII. But why are we speaking so long about one enemy, and about that enemy who now avows that he is one; and whom I now do not fear, because, as I have always wished, a wall is between us; and are saying nothing about those who dissemble, who remain at Rome, who are among us? Whom, indeed, if it were by any means possible, I should be anxious not so much to chastise as to cure, and to make friendly to the republic; nor, if they will listen to me, do I quite know why that may not be. For I will tell you, O Romans, of what classes of men those forces are made up, and then, if I can, I will apply to each the medicine of my advice and persuasion.

There is one class of them, who, with enormous debts have still greater possessions, and who can by no means be detached from their affection to them. Of these men the appearance is most respectable, for they are wealthy, but their intention and their cause are most shameless. Will you be rich in lands, in houses, in money, in slaves, in all things, and yet hesitate to diminish your possessions to add to your credit? What are you expecting? War? What! in the devastation of all things, do you believe that your own possessions will be held sacred? do you expect an abolition of debts? They are mistaken who expect that from Catiline. There may be schedules made out, owing to my exertions, but they will be only catalogues of sale. Nor can those who have possessions be safe by any other means; and if they had been willing to adopt this plan earlier, and not, as is very foolish, to struggle on against usury with the profits of their farms, we should have them now richer and better citizens. But I think these men are the least of all to be dreaded, because they can either be persuaded to abandon their opinions, or if they cling to them, they seem to me more likely to form wishes against the republic than to bear arms against it.

IX. There is another class of them, who, although they are harassed by debt, yet are expecting supreme power; they wish to become masters. They think that when the republic is in confusion they may gain those honors which they despair of when it is in tranquillity. And they must, I think, be told the same as every one else,—to despair of obtaining what they are aiming at; that in the first place, I myself am watchful for, am present to, am providing for the republic. Besides that, there is a high spirit in the virtuous citizens, great unanimity, great numbers, and also a large body of troops. Above all that, the immortal gods will stand by and bring aid to this invincible nation, this most illustrious empire, this most beautiful city, against such wicked violence. And if they had already got that which they with the greatest madness wish for, do they think that in the ashes of the city and blood of the citizens, which in their wicked and infamous hearts they desire, they will become consuls and dictators and even kings? Do they not see that they are wishing for that which, if they were to obtain it, must be given up to some fugitive slave, or to some gladiator?

There is a third class, already touched by age, but still vigorous from constant exercise; of which class is Manlius himself, whom Catiline is now succeeding. These are men of those colonies which Sylla established at Fæsulæ, which I know to be composed, on the whole, of excellent citizens and brave men; but yet these are colonists, who, from becoming possessed of unexpected and sudden wealth, boast themselves extravagantly and insolently; these men, while they build like rich men, while they delight in farms, in litters, in vast families of slaves, in luxurious banquets, have incurred such great debts, that, if they would be saved, they must raise Sylla from the dead; and they have even excited some countrymen, poor and needy men, to entertain the same hopes of plunder as themselves. And all these men, O Romans, I place in the same class of robbers and banditti. But, I warn them, let them cease to be mad, and to think of proscriptions and dictatorships; for such a horror of these times is ingrained into the city, that not even men, but it seems to me that even the very cattle would refuse to bear them again.

X. There is a fourth class, various, promiscuous and turbulent; who indeed are now overwhelmed; who will never recover themselves; who, partly from indolence, partly from managing their affairs badly, partly from extravagance, are embarrassed by old debts; and worn out with bail bonds, and judgments, and seizures of their goods, are said to be betaking themselves in numbers to that camp both from the city and the country. These men I think not so much active soldiers as lazy insolvents; who, if they cannot stand at first, may fall, but falls so, that not only the city but even their nearest neighbors know nothing of it. For I do not understand why, if they cannot live with honor, they should wish to die shamefully; or why they think they shall perish with less pain in a crowd, than if they perish by themselves.

There is a fifth class, of parricides, assassins, in short of all infamous characters, whom I do not wish to recall from Catiline, and indeed they cannot be separated from him. Let them perish in their wicked war, since they are so numerous that a prison cannot contain them.

There is a last class, last not only in number but in the sort of men and in their way of life; the especial body-guard of Catiline, of his levying; ay, the friends of his embraces and of his bosom; whom you see with carefully combed hair, glossy, beardless, or with well-trimmed beards; with tunics with sleeves, or reaching to the ancles; clothed with veils, not with robes; all the industry of whose life, all the labor of whose watchfulness, is expended in suppers lasting till daybreak.

In these bands are all the gamblers, all the adulterers, all the unclean and shameless citizens. These boys, so witty and delicate, have learnt not only to love and to be loved, not only to sing and to dance, but also to brandish daggers and to administer poisons; and unless they are driven out, unless they die, even should Catiline die, I warn you that the school of Catiline would exist in the republic. But what do those wretches want? Are they going to take their wives with them to the camp? How can they do without them, especially in these nights? and how will they endure the Apennines, and these frosts, and this snow? unless they think that they will bear the winter more easily because they have been in the habit of dancing naked at their feasts. O war much to be dreaded, when Catiline is going to have his body-guard of prostitutes!

XI. Array now, O Romans, against these splendid troops of Catiline, your guards and your armies; and first of all oppose to that worn-out and wounded gladiator your consuls and generals; then against that banished and enfeebled troop of ruined men lead out the flower and strength of all Italy: instantly the cities of the colonies and municipalities will match the rustic mounds of Catiline; and I will not condescend to compare the rest of your troops and equipments and guards with the want and destitution of that highwayman. But if, omitting all these things in which we are rich and of which he is destitute,—the senate, the Roman knights, the people, the city, the treasury, the revenues, all Italy, all the provinces, foreign nations,—if, I say, omitting all these things, we choose to compare the causes themselves which are opposed to one another, we may understand from that alone how thoroughly prostrate they are. For on the one side are fighting modesty, on the other wantonness; on the one chastity, on the other uncleanness; on the one honesty, on the other fraud; on the one piety, on the other wickedness; on the one consistency, on the other insanity; on the one honor, on the other baseness; on the one continence, on the other lust; in short, equity, temperance, fortitude, prudence, all the virtues contend against iniquity with luxury, against indolence, against rashness, against all the vices; lastly, abundance contends against destitution, good plans against baffled designs, wisdom against madness, well-founded hope against universal despair. In a contest and war of this sort, even if the zeal of men were to fail, will not the immortal gods compel such numerous and excessive vices to be defeated by these most eminent virtues?

XII. And as this is the case, O Romans, do ye, as I have said before, defend your house with guards and vigilance. I have taken care and made arrangements that there shall be sufficient protection for the city without distressing you and without any tumult. All the colonists and citizens of your municipal towns, being informed by me of this nocturnal sally of Catiline, will easily defend their cities and territories; the gladiators which he thought would be his most numerous and most trusty band, although they are better disposed than part of the patricians, will be held in check by our power. Quintus Metellus, whom I, making provision for this, sent on to the Gallic and Picenian territory, will either overwhelm the man, or will prevent all his motions and attempts; but with respect to the arrangement of all other matters, and maturing and acting on our plans, we shall consult the senate, which, as you are aware, is convened.

Now once more I wish those who have remained in the city, and who, contrary to the safety of the city and of all of you, have been left in the city by Catiline, although they are enemies, yet because they were born citizens, to be warned again and again by me. If my lenity has appeared to any one too remiss, it has been only waiting that that might break out which was lying hid. As to the future, I cannot now forget that this is my country, that I am the consul of these citizens; that I must either live with them, or die for them. There is no guard at the gate, no one plotting against their path; if any one wishes to go, he can provide for himself; but if any one stirs in the city, and if I detect not only any action, but any attempt or design against the country, he shall feel that there are in this city vigilant consuls, eminent magistrates, a brave senate, arms, and prisons; which our ancestors appointed as the avengers of nefarious and convicted crimes.

XIII. And all this shall be so done, O Romans, that affairs of the greatest importance shall be transacted with the least possible disturbance; the greatest dangers shall be avoided without any tumult; an internal civil war the most cruel and terrible in the memory of man, shall be put an end to by me alone in the robe of peace acting as general and commander-in-chief. And this I will so arrange, O Romans, that if it can be by any means managed, even the most worthless man shall not suffer the punishment of his crimes in this city. But if the violence of open audacity, if danger impending over the republic drives me of necessity from this merciful disposition, at all events I will manage this, which seems scarcely even to be hoped for in so great and so treacherous a war, that no good man shall fall, and that you may all be saved by the punishment of a few.

And I promise you this, O Romans, relying neither on my own prudence, nor on human counsels, but on many and manifest intimations of the will of the immortal gods; under whose guidance I first entertained this hope and this opinion; who are now defending their temples and the houses of the city, not afar off, as they were used to, from a foreign and distant enemy, but here on the spot, by their own divinity and present help. And you, O Romans, ought to pray to and implore them to defend from the nefarious wickedness of abandoned citizens, now that all the forces of all enemies are defeated by land and sea, this city which they have ordained to be the most beautiful and flourishing of all cities.

THE THIRD ORATION AGAINST LUCIUS CATILINA

CATILINA

Addressed to the People

THE ARGUMENT

While Cicero was addressing the preceding speech to the people, a debate was going on in the senate of which we have no account. In the meanwhile Catiline, after staying a few days on the road to raise the country as he passed along, where his agents had been previously busy among the people, proceeded to Manlius's camp with the fasces and all the ensigns of military command displayed before him. Upon this news the senate immediately declared him and Manlius public enemies; they offered pardon to all his followers who should return to their duty by a certain day; and ordered the consuls to make new levies, and that Antonius should follow Catiline with his army, and Cicero remain behind to protect the city.

In the meantime Lentulus, and the other conspirators who remained behind, were proceeding with their designs. And among other steps, they decided on endeavoring to tamper with some ambassadors from the Allobroges,[1] who were at that moment within the city, as the Allobroges were supposed not to be very well affected to the Roman power. At first these ambassadors appear to have willingly given ear to their proposals; but after a while they began to consider the difficulty of the business proposed to them, and the danger which would ensue to their state if it failed after they had become implicated in it; and accordingly they revealed the business to Quintus Fabius Sanga, the patron of their city, who communicated it to Cicero. Cicero desired the ambassadors to continue to listen to the proposals of the conspirators, till they had become fully acquainted with the extent of the plot, and till they were able to furnish him with full evidence against the actors in it; and by his suggestion they required the conspirators to furnish them with credentials to show to their countrymen.

---

[1] The Allobroges occupied the districts of Dauphiné and Savoy.

This was thought reasonable by Lentulus and his party, and they accordingly appointed a man named Vulturcius to accompany them, who was to introduce them to Catiline on their road, in order to confirm the agreement, and to exchange pledges with him, and Lentulus also furnished them with a letter to Catiline under his own hand and seal, though not signed. Cicero being privately informed of all these particulars, concerted with the ambassadors the time and manner of their leaving Rome by night, and had them arrested on the Mulvian bridge, about a mile from the city, with these letters and papers in their possession. This was all done, and they brought as prisoners to Cicero's house early in the morning.

Cicero immediately summoned the senate; and at the same time he sent for Lentulus, Cethegus, and others of the conspirators who were more especially implicated, such as Gabinius and Statilius, who all came immediately to his house, being ignorant of the discovery that had taken place. Being informed also that a quantity of arms had been provided by Cethegus for the purpose of the conspiracy, he orders Caius Sulpicius, one of the prætors, to search his house, and he did so, and found a great number of swords and daggers ready cleaned and fit for use.

He then proceeds to meet the senate in the Temple of Concord, with the ambassadors and conspirators in custody. He relates the whole affair to them, and introduces Vulturcius to be examined before them. Cicero, by the order of the senate, promises him pardon and reward if he reveals what he knew. On which he confesses everything; tells them that he had letters from Lentulus to Catiline to urge him to avail himself of the assistance of the slaves, and to lead his army with all expedition against Rome; in order, when the city had been set on fire and the massacre commenced, that he might be able to intercept and destroy those who fled.

Then the ambassadors were examined, who declared that they had received letters to the chief men of their nation from Lentulus, Cethegus, and Statilius; and that they, and Lucius Cassius also, begged them to send a body of cavalry into Italy, and that Lentulus assured them, from the Sibylline books, that he was the third[2] Cornelius who was destined to reign at Rome. The letters were produced and opened. On the sight of them the conspirators respectively acknowledged them to be theirs, and Lentulus was even so conscience-stricken that he confessed his whole crime.

The senate passed a vote acknowledging the services of Cicero in the most ample terms, and voted that Lentulus should be deposed from his office of prætor, and, with all the other conspirators,

[2] Cinna and Sylla had been the two former Cornelii.

committed to safe custody. Cicero, after the senate adjourned, proceeded to the forum and gave an account to the people of everything which had passed, both in regard to the steps that he had taken to detect the whole conspiracy, and to convict the conspirators; and also of what had taken place in the senate, and of the votes and resolutions which that body had just passed.

While the prisoners were before the senate he had copies of their examinations and confessions taken down, and dispersed through Italy and all the provinces. This happened on the third of December.

I. You SEE this day, O Romans, the republic, and all your lives, your goods, your fortunes, your wives and children, this home of most illustrious empire, this most fortunate and beautiful city, by the great love of the immortal gods for you, by my labors and counsels and dangers, snatched from fire and sword, and almost from the very jaws of fate, and preserved and restored to you.

And if those days on which we are preserved are not less pleasant to us, or less illustrious, than those on which we are born, because the joy of being saved is certain, the good fortune of being born uncertain, and because we are born without feeling it, but we are preserved with great delight; ay, since we have, by our affection and by our good report, raised to the immortal gods that Romulus who built this city, he, too, who has preserved this city, built by him, and embellished as you see it, ought to be held in honor by you and your posterity; for we have extinguished flames which were almost laid under and placed around the temples and shrines, and houses and walls of the whole city; we have turned the edge of swords drawn against the republic, and have turned aside their points from your throats. And since all this has been displayed in the senate, and made manifest, and detected by me, I will now explain it briefly, that you, O citizens, that are as yet ignorant of it, and are in suspense, may be able to see how great the danger was, how evident and by what means it was detected and arrested. First of all, since Catiline, a few days ago, burst out of the city, when he had left behind the companions of his wickedness, the active leaders of this infamous war, I have continually watched and taken care, O Romans, of the means by which we might be safe amid such great and such carefully concealed treachery.

II. Further, when I drove Catiline out of the city (for I do not fear the unpopularity of this expression, when that is more to be feared that I should be blamed because he has departed alive), but then when I wished him to be removed, I thought either that the rest of the band of conspirators would depart with him, or that they who remained would be weak and powerless without him.

And I, as I saw that those whom I knew to be inflamed with the greatest madness and wickedness were among us, and had remained at Rome, spent all my nights and days in taking care to know and see what they were doing, and what they were contriving; that, since what I said would, from the incredible enormity of the wickedness, make less impression on your ears, I might so detect the whole business that you might with all your hearts provide for your safety, when you saw the crime with your own eyes. Therefore, when I found that the ambassadors of the Allobroges had been tampered with by Publius Lentulus, for the sake of exciting a Transalpine war and commotion in Gaul, and that they, on their return to Gaul, had been sent with letters and messages to Catiline on the same road, and that Vulturcius had been added to them as a companion, and that he too had had letters given him for Catiline, I thought that an opportunity was given me of contriving what was most difficult, and which I was always wishing the immortal gods might grant, that the whole business might be manifestly detected not by me alone, but by the senate also, and by you.

Therefore, yesterday I summoned Lucius Flaccus and C. Pomtinus, the prætors, brave men and well-affected to the republic. I explained to them the whole matter, and showed them what I wished to have done. But they, full of noble and worthy sentiments towards the republic, without hesitation, and without any delay, undertook the business, and when it was evening, went secretly to the Mulvian bridge, and there so distributed themselves in the nearest villas, that the Tiber and the bridge was between them. And they took to the same place, without any one having the least suspicion of it, many brave men, and I had sent many picked young men of the prefecture of Reate, whose assistance I constantly employ in the protection of the republic, armed with swords. In the meantime, about the end of the third watch, when the ambassadors of the Allobroges, with a great retinue and Vulturcius with them, began to come upon the Mulvian bridge, an attack is made upon them; swords are drawn both by them and by our people; the matter was understood by the prætors alone, but was unknown to the rest.

III. Then, by the intervention of Pomtinus and Flaccus, the fight which had begun was put an end to; all the letters which were in the hands of the whole company are delivered to the prætors with the seals unbroken; the men themselves are arrested and brought to me at daybreak. And I immediately summoned that most worthless contriver of all this wickedness, Gabinius, as yet suspecting nothing; after him, P. Statilius is sent for, and after him Cethegus; but Lentulus was a long time in coming,—I suppose, because, contrary to his custom, he had been up a long time the night before, writing letters.

But when those most noble and excellent men of the whole city, who, hearing of the matter, came in crowds to me in the morning, thought it best for me to open the letters before I related the matter to the senate, lest, if nothing were found in them, so great a disturbance might seem to have been caused to the state for nothing, I said I would never so act as shrink from referring matter of public danger to the public council. In truth if, O Romans, these things which had been reported to me had not been found in them, yet I did not think I ought, in such a crisis of the republic, to be afraid of the imputation of over-diligence. I quickly summoned a full senate, as you saw; and meantime, without any delay, by the advice of the Allobroges, I sent Caius Sulpicius the prætor, a brave man, to bring whatever arms he could find in the house of Cethegus, whence he did bring a great number of swords and daggers.

IV. I introduced Vulturcius without the Gauls. By the command of the senate, I pledged him the public faith for his safety. I exhorted him fearlessly to tell all he knew. Then, when he had scarcely recovered himself from his great alarm, he said: that he had messages and letters for Catiline, from Publius Lentulus, to avail himself of the guard of the slaves, and to come towards the city with his army as quickly as possible; and that was to be done with the intention that, when they had set fire to the city on all sides, as it had been arranged and distributed, and had made a great massacre of the citizens, he might be at hand to catch those who fled, and to join himself to the leaders within the city. But the Gauls being introduced, said that an oath had been administered to them, and letters given them by Publius Lentulus, Cethegus, and Statilius, for their nation; and that they had been enjoined by them, and by Lucius Cassius, to send cavalry into Italy as early as possible; that infantry should not be wanting; and that Lentulus had assured him, from the Sibylline oracles and the answers of soothsayers, that he was that third Cornelius to whom the kingdom and sovereignty over this city was fated to come; that Cinna and Sylla had been before him; and that he had also said that was the year destined to the destruction of this city and empire, being the tenth year after the acquittal of the virgins, and the twentieth after the burning of the Capitol. But they said there had been this dispute between Cethegus and the rest,—that Lentulus and others thought it best that the massacre should take place and the city be burnt at the Saturnalia, but that Cethegus thought it too long to wait.

V. And, not to detain you, O Romans, we ordered the letters to be brought forward which were said to have been given them by each of the men. First, I showed his seal to Cethegus; he recognized it: we cut the thread; we read the letter. It was written with his own hand: that he would do for the senate and people of the Allobroges what he had promised their ambassadors; and that he begged them also to do what their ambassadors had arranged. Then Cethegus, who a little before had made answer about the swords and daggers which had been found in his house, and had said that he had always been fond of fine arms, being stricken down and dejected at the reading of his letters, convicted by his own conscience, became suddenly silent. Statilius, being introduced, owned his handwriting and his seal. His letters were read, of nearly the same tenor: he confessed it. Then I showed Lentulus his letters, and asked him whether he recognized the seal? He nodded assent. But it is, said I, a well-known seal;—the likeness of your grandfather, a most illustrious man, who greatly loved his country and his fellow-citizens; and it, even though silent, ought to have called you back from such wickedness.

Letters are read of the same tenor to the senate and people of the Allobroges. I offered him leave, if he wished to say anything of these matters: and at first he declined to speak; but a little afterwards, when the whole examination had been gone through and concluded, he rose. He asked the Gauls what he had had to do with them? why they had come to his house? and he asked Vulturcius too. And when they had answered him briefly and steadily, under whose guidance they had come to him, and how often; and when they asked him whether he had said nothing to them about the Sibylline oracles, then he on a sudden, mad with wickedness, showed how great was the power of conscience; for though he might have denied it, he suddenly, contrary to every one's expectation, confessed it: so not only did his genius and skill in oratory, for which he was always eminent, but even, through the power of his manifest and detected wickedness, that impudence, in which he surpassed all men, and audacity deserted him.

But Vulturcius on a sudden ordered the letters to be produced and opened which he said had been given to him for Catiline, by Lentulus. And though Lentulus was greatly agitated at that, yet he acknowledged his seal and his handwriting; but the letter was anonymous, and ran thus:—"Who I am you will know from him whom I have sent to you: take care to behave like a man, and consider to what place you have proceeded, and provide for what is now necessary for you: take care to associate to yourself the assistance of every one, even of the powerless." Then Gabinius being introduced, when at first he had begun to answer impudently, at last denied nothing of those things which the Gauls alleged against him. And to me, indeed, O Romans, though the letters, the seals, the handwriting, and the confession of each individual seemed most certain indications and proofs of wickedness, yet their color, their eyes, their countenance, their silence, appeared more certain still; for they stood so stupefied, they kept their eyes so fixed on the ground, at times looking stealthily at one another, that they appeared now not so much to be informed against by others as to be informing against themselves.

VI. Having produced and divulged these proofs, O Romans,

I consulted the senate what ought to be done for the interests of the republic. Vigorous and fearless opinions were delivered by the chief men, which the senate adopted without any variety; and since the decree of the senate is not yet written out, I will relate to you from memory, O citizens, what the senate has decreed. First of all, a vote of thanks to me is passed in the most honorable words, because the republic has been delivered from the greatest dangers by my valor and wisdom, and prudence. Then Lucius Flaccus and Caius Pomtinus, the prætors, are deservedly and rightly praised, because I had availed myself of their brave and loyal assistance. And also, praise is given to that brave man, my colleague, because he had removed from his counsels, and from the counsels of the republic, those who had been accomplices in this conspiracy. And they voted that Publius Lentulus, when he had abdicated the prætorship, should be given into custody; and also, that Caius Cethegus, Lucius Statilius, Publius Gabinius, who were all present, should be given into custody: and the same decree was passed against Lucius Cassius, who had begged for himself the office of burning the city; against Marcus Caparius, to whom it had been proved that Apulia had been allotted for the purpose of exciting disaffection among the shepherds; against Publius Furius, who belongs to the colonies which Lucius Sylla led to Fæsulæ, against Quintus Manlius Chilo, who was always associated with this man Furius in his tampering with the Allobroges; against Publius Umbrenus, a freedman, by whom it was proved that the Gauls were originally brought to Gabinius.

And the senate, O citizens, acted with such lenity, that, out of so great a conspiracy, and such a number and multitude of domestic enemies, it thought that since the republic was saved, the minds of the rest might be restored to a healthy state by the punishment of nine most abandoned men. And also a supplication[3] was decreed in my name, (which is the first time

---

[3] A supplication was a solemn thanksgiving to the gods, decreed by the senate, when all the temples were opened and the statues of the gods placed in public upon couches (*pulvinaria*), to which the people offered up their thanksgivings and prayers. It was usually decreed on the intelligence arriving of any great victory, and the number of days which it was to last was proportioned to the importance of the victory. It was

since the building of the city that such an honor has ever been
paid to a man in a civil capacity,) to the immortal gods, for
their singular kindness. And it was decreed in these words,
"because I had delivered the city from conflagration, the citizens from massacre, and Italy from war." And if this supplication be compared with others, O citizens, there is this difference between them,—that all others have been appointed
because of the successes of the republic; this one alone for its
preservation. And that which was the first thing to be done,
has been done and executed; for Publius Lentulus, though,
being convicted by proofs and by his own confession, by the
judgment of the senate he had lost not only the rights of a
prætor, but also those of a citizen, still resigned his office; so
that, though Caius Marcius, that most illustrious of men, had
no scruples about putting to death Caius Glaucius the prætor,
against whom nothing had been decreed by name, still we are
relieved from that scruple in the case of Publius Lentulus, who
is now a private individual.

VII. Now, since, O citizens, you have the nefarious leaders
of this most wicked and dangerous war taken prisoners and in
your grasp, you ought to think that all the resources of Catiline,—all his hopes and all his power, now that these dangers
of the city are warded off, have fallen to pieces. And, indeed,
when I drove him from the city, I foresaw in my mind, O citizens, that if Catiline were removed, I had no cause to fear
either the drowsiness of Publius Lentulus, or the fat of Lucius
Cassius, or the mad rashness of Cassius Cethegus. He alone
was to be feared of all these men, and that, only as long as he
was within the walls of the city. He knew everything, he had
access to everybody. He had the skill and the audacity to address, to tempt, and to tamper with every one. He had acuteness suited to crime; and neither tongue nor hand ever failed
to support that acuteness. Already he had men he could rely
on, chosen and distributed for the execution of all other business; and when he had ordered anything to be done, he did

generally regarded as a prelude to a triumph. Of course, from what has
been said, it must have been usually confined to generals; who laid aside
the *toga* on leaving the city to assume the command of the army, and
assumed the *paludamentum*, or military robe.

not think it was done on that account. There was nothing to
which he did not personally attend and see to,—for which he
did not watch and toil. He was able to endure cold, thirst, and
hunger.

Unless I had driven this man, so active, so ready, so audacious, so crafty, so vigilant in wickedness, so industrious in
criminal exploits, from his plots within the city to the open
warfare of the camp, (I will express my honest opinion, O
citizens,) I should not easily have removed from your necks
so vast a weight of evil. He would not have determined on the
Saturnalia[4] to massacre you,—he would not have announced
the destruction of the republic, and even the day of its doom
so long beforehand,—he would never have allowed his seal
and his letters, the undeniable witnesses of his guilt, to be
taken, which now, since he is absent, has been so done that no
larceny in a private house has ever been so thoroughly and
clearly detected as this vast conspiracy against the republic.
But if Catiline had remained in the city to this day, although,
as long as he was so, I met all his designs and withstood them;
yet, to say the least, we should have had to fight with him, and
should never, while he remained as an enemy in the city, have
delivered the republic from such dangers, with such ease, such
tranquillity, and such silence.

VIII. Although all these things, O Romans, have been so
managed by me, that they appear to have been done and provided for by the order and design of the immortal gods; and
as we may conjecture this because the direction of such
weighty affairs scarcely appears capable of having been carried out by human wisdom; so, too, they have at this time so
brought us present aid and assistance, that we could almost
behold them without eyes. For to say nothing of those things,
namely, the firebrands seen in the west in the night time, and
the heat of the atmosphere,—to pass over the falling of thunder-
bolts and the earthquakes,—to say nothing of all the other por-
tents which have taken place in such numbers during my consulship, that the immortal gods themselves have been seeming

[4] The Saturnalia was a feast of Saturn at which extraordinary licence
and indulgence was allowed to all the slaves; it took place at the end of
December, while this speech of Cicero was delivered early in November.

to predict what is now taking place; yet, at all events, this which I am about to mention, O Romans, must be neither passed over nor omitted.

For you recollect, I suppose, when Cotta and Torquatus were consuls, that many towers in the Capitol were struck with lightning, when both the images of the immortal gods were moved, and the statutes of many ancient men were thrown down, and the brazen tablets on which the laws were written were melted. Even Romulus, who built this city, was struck, which, you recollect, stood in the Capitol, a gilt statue, little and suckling, and clinging to the teats of the wolf. And when at this time the soothsayers were assembled out of all Etruria, they said that slaughter, and conflagration, and the overthrow of the laws, and civil and domestic war, and the fall of the whole city and empire was at hand, unless the immortal gods, being appeased in every possible manner, by their own power turned aside, as I may say, the very fates themselves.

Therefore, according to their answers, games were celebrated for ten days, nor was anything omitted which might tend to the appeasing of the gods. And they enjoined also that we should make a greater statue of Jupiter, and place it in a lofty situation, and (contrary to what had been done before) turn it towards the east. And they said that they hoped that if that statue which you now behold looked upon the rising of the sun, and the forum, and the senate-house, then those designs which were secretly formed against the safety of the city and empire would be brought to light, so as to be able to be thoroughly seen by the senate and by the Roman people. And the consuls ordered it to be so placed; but so great was the delay in the work, that it was never set up by the former consuls, nor by us before this day.

IX. Here who, O Romans, can there be so obstinate against the truth, so headstrong, so void of sense, as to deny that all these things which we see, and especially this city, is governed by the divine authority and power of the immortal gods? Forsooth, when this answer had been given,—that massacre, and conflagration, and ruin was prepared for the republic; and that, too, by profligate citizens, which, from the enormity of the wickedness, appeared incredible to some people, you found that it had not only been planned by wicked citizens, but had

even been undertaken and commenced. And is not this fact so
present that it appears to have taken place by the express will
of the good and mighty Jupiter, that, when this day, early in
the morning, both the conspirators and their accusers were
being led by my command through the forum to the Temple
of Concord, at that very time the statue was being erected?
And when it was set up, and turned towards you and towards
the senate, the senate and you yourselves saw everything
which had been planned against the universal safety brought
to light and made manifest.

And on this account they deserve even greater hatred and
greater punishment, for having attempted to apply their fatal
and wicked fire, not only to your houses and homes, but even
to the shrines and temples of the Gods. And if I were to say
that it was I who resisted them, I should take too much to myself, and ought not to be borne. He—he, Jupiter, resisted them.
He determined that the Capitol should be safe, he saved these
temples, he saved this city, he saved all of you. It is under the
guidance of the immortal gods, O Romans, that I have cherished the intention and desires which I have, and have arrived
at such undeniable proofs. Surely, that tampering with the
Allobroges would never have taken place, so important a
matter would never have been so madly entrusted, by Lentulus and the rest of our internal enemies, to strangers and
foreigners, such letters would never have been written, unless
all prudence had been taken by the immortal gods from such
terrible audacity. What shall I say? That Gauls, men from a
state scarcely at peace with us, the only nation existing which
seems both to be able to make war on the Roman people, and
not to be unwilling to do so,—that they should disregard the
hope of empire and of the greatest success voluntarily offered
to them by patricians, and should prefer your safety to their
own power—do you not think that that was caused by divine
interposition? especially when they could have destroyed us,
not by fighting, but by keeping silence.

X. Wherefore, O citizens, since a supplication has been decreed at all the altars, celebrate those days with your wives and
children; for many just and deserved honors have been often
paid to the immortal gods, but juster ones never. For you have
been snatched from a most cruel and miserable destruction,

and you have been snatched from it without slaughter, without bloodshed, without an army, without a battle. You have conquered in the garb of peace, with me in the garb of peace for your only general and commander.

Remember, O citizens, all civil dissensions, and not only those which you have heard of, but these also which you yourselves remember and have seen. Lucius Sylla crushed Publius Sulpicius;[5] he drove from the city Caius Marius the guardian of this city; and of many other brave men some he drove from the city, and some he murdered. Cnæus Octavius the consul drove his colleague by force of arms out of the city; all this place was crowded with heaps of carcases and flowed with the blood of citizens; afterwards Cinna and Marius got the upper hand; and then most illustrious men were put to death, and the lights of the state were extinguished. Afterwards Sylla avenged the cruelty of this victory; it is needless to say with what a diminution of the citizens, and with what disasters to the republic. Marcus Lepidus disagreed with that most eminent and brave man Quintus Catulus. His death did not cause as much grief to the republic as that of the others.

And these dissensions, O Romans, were such as concerned not the destruction of the republic, but only a change in the constitution. They did not wish that there should be no republic, but that they themselves should be the chief men in that which existed; nor did they desire that the city should be burnt, but that they themselves should flourish in it. And yet all those dissensions, none of which aimed at the destruction of the republic, were such that they were to be terminated not by a reconciliation and concord, but only by internecine war among the citizens. But in this war alone, the greatest and most cruel in the memory of man,—a war such as even the countries of the barbarians have never waged with their own tribes,— a war in which this law was laid down by Lentulus, and Cati-

[5] Sulpicius procured a law to be passed for taking the command against Mithridates from Sylla and giving it to Marius; Sylla came to Rome with his army and slew Sulpicius, when Marius fled to Africa. Sylla made Octavius and Cinna consuls, who quarreled after he was gone, and Cinna went over to the party of Marius, who returned to Rome. Lepidus and Catulus were consuls the year after the death of Sylla, and they quarreled because Lepidus wished to rescind all the acts of Sylla. Lepidus was defeated, fled to Sardinia, and died there.

line, and Cassius, and Cethegus, that every one, who could live in safety as long as the city remained in safety, should be considered as an enemy,—in this war I have so managed matters, O Romans, that you should all be preserved in safety; and though your enemies had thought that only such a number of the citizens would be left as had held out against an interminable massacre, and only so much of the city as the flames could not devour, I have preserved both the city and the citizens unhurt and undiminished.

XI. And for these exploits, important as they are, O Romans, I ask from you no reward of virtue, no badge of honor, no monument of my glory, beyond the everlasting recollection of this day. In your minds I wish all my triumphs, all my decorations of honor, the monuments of my glory, the badges of my renown, to be stored and laid up. Nothing voiceless can delight me, nothing silent,—nothing, in short, such as even those who are less worthy can obtain. In your memory, O Romans, my name shall be cherished, in your discourses it shall grow, in the monuments of your letters it shall grow old and strengthen; and I feel assured that the same day which I hope will be for everlasting, will be remembered forever, so as to tend both to the safety of the city and the recollection of my consulship; and that it will be remembered that there existed in this city at the same time two citizens, one of whom limited the boundaries of your empire only by the regions of heaven, not by those of the earth, while the other preserved the abode and home of that same empire.

XII. But since the fortune and condition of those exploits which I have performed is not the same with that of those men who have directed foreign wars—because I must live among those whom I have defeated and subdued, they have left their enemies either slain or crushed,—it is your business, O Romans, to take care, if their good deeds are a benefit to others, that mine shall never be an injury to me. For that the wicked and profligate designs of audacious men shall not be able to injure you, I have taken care; it is your business to take care that they do not injure me. Although, O Romans, no injury can be done to me by them,—for there is a great protection in the affection of all good men, which is procured for me forever; there is great dignity in the republic, which will always silently defend me; there is great power in conscience, and those who neglect it, when they desire to attack me will destroy themselves.

There is moreover that disposition in me, O Romans, that I not only will yield to the audacity of no one, but that I always voluntarily attack the worthless. And if all the violence of domestic enemies being warded off from you turns itself upon me alone, you will have to take care, O Romans, in what condition you wish those men to be for the future, who for your safety have exposed themselves to unpopularity and to all sorts of dangers. As for me, myself, what is there which now can be gained by me for the enjoyment of life, especially when neither in credit among you, nor in the glory of virtue, do I see any higher point to which I can be desirous to climb?

That indeed I will take care of, O Romans, as a private man to uphold and embellish the exploits which I have performed in my consulship: so that, if there has been any unpopularity incurred in preserving the republic, it may injure those who envy me, and may tend to my glory. Lastly, I will so behave myself in the republic as always to remember what I have done, and to take care that they shall appear to have been done through virtue, and not by chance. Do you, O Romans, since it is now night, worship that Jupiter, the guardian of this city and of yourselves, and depart to your homes; and defend those homes, though the danger is now removed, with guard and watch as you did last night. That you shall not have to do so long, and that you shall enjoy perpetual tranquillity, shall, O Romans, be my care.

THE FOURTH ORATION AGAINST LUCIUS CATILINA

Delivered in the Senate

THE ARGUMENT

The night after the events mentioned in the argument to the preceding oration, Cicero's wife Terentia, with the vestal virgins, was performing at home the mystic rites of the Bona Dea, while Cicero was deliberating with his friends on the best mode of punishing the conspirators. Terentia interrupted their deliberations by coming in to inform them of a prodigy which had just happened; that after the sacrifice in which she had been engaged was over, the fire revived spontaneously; on which the vestal virgins had sent her to him, to inform him of it, and to bid him pursue what he was then thinking of and intending for the good of his country, since the goddess had given this sign that she was watching over his safety and glory.

The next day the senate ordered public rewards to the ambassadors and to Vulturcius; and showed signs of intending to proceed with extreme rigor against the conspirators, when, on a sudden, rumors arose of plots having been formed by the slaves of Lentulus and Cethegus for their master's rescue; which obliged Cicero to double all the guards, and determined him to prevent any repetition of such attempts by bringing before the senate without delay the question of the punishment of the prisoners. On which account he summoned the senate to meet the next morning.

There were many difficulties in the matter. Capital punishments were unusual and very unpopular at Rome. And there was an old law of Porcius Lecca, a tribune of the people, which granted to all criminals who were capitally condemned an appeal to the people; and also a law had been passed, since his time, by Caius Gracchus, to prohibit the taking away the life of any citizen without a formal hearing before the people. And these considerations had so much weight with some of the senators, that they absented themselves from the senate during this debate, in order to have no share in sentencing prisoners of such high rank to death. The debate was opened by Silanus, the consul elect, who declared his opinion, that those in custody, and those also who should be taken subsequently, should all be put to death. Every one who followed him agreed with him, till Julius Cæsar, the prætor elect (who has been often suspected of having been, at least to some extent, privy to the conspiracy,) rose, and in an elaborate speech proposed that they should not be put to death, but that their estates should be confiscated, and they themselves kept in perpetual confinement. Cato opposed him with great earnestness. But some of Cicero's friends appeared inclined to Cæsar's motion, thinking it a safer measure for Cicero himself; but when Cicero perceived this, he rose himself, and discussed the opinions both of Silanus and Cæsar in the following speech, which decided the senate to vote for their condemnation. And as soon as the vote had passed, Cicero went immediately from the senate house, took Lentulus from the custody of his kinsman Lentulus Spinther, and delivered him to the executioner. The other conspirators, Cethegus, Statilius, Gabinius, etc., were in like manner conducted to execution by the prætors; and Cicero was conducted home to his house in triumph by the whole body of the senate and by the knights, the whole multitude following him, and saluting him as their deliverer.

I. I SEE, O conscript fathers, that the looks and eyes of you all are turned towards me; I see that you are anxious not only for your own danger and that of the republic, but even, if that be removed, for mine. Your good-will is delightful to one amid evils, and pleasing amid grief; but I entreat you, in the name of the immortal gods, lay it aside now, and, forgetting my safety, think of yourselves and of your children. If, indeed, this condition of the consulship has been allotted to me, that I should bear all bitterness, all pains and tortures, I will bear them not only bravely but even cheerfully, provided that by my toils dignity and safety are procured for you and for the Roman people.

I am that consul, O conscript fathers, to whom neither the forum in which all justice is contained, nor the Campus Martius,[1] consecrated to the consular assemblies, nor the senate

---

[1] The Campus Martius was consecrated or restored to Mars after the expulsion of the Tarquins; the comitia centuriata at which all magistrates were created were held there.

house, the chief assistance of all nations, nor my own home, the common refuge of all men, nor my bed devoted to rest, in short, not even this seat of honor, this curule chair, has ever been free from the danger of death, or from plots and treachery. I have been silent about many things, I have borne much, I have conceded much, I have remedied many things with some pain to myself, amid the alarm of you all. Now if the immortal gods have determined that there shall be this end to my consulship, that I should snatch you, O conscript fathers, and the Roman people from miserable slaughter, your wives and children and the vestal virgins from most bitter distress, the temples and shrines of the gods, and this most lovely country of all of us, from impious flames, all Italy from war and devastation; then, whatever fortune is laid up for me by myself, it shall be borne. If, indeed, Publius Lentulus, being led on by soothsayers, believed that his name was connected by destiny with the destruction of the republic, why should not I rejoice that my consulship has taken place almost by the express appointment of fate for the preservation of the republic?

II. Wherefore, O conscript fathers, consult the welfare of yourselves, provide for that of the republic; preserve yourselves, your wives, your children, and your fortunes; defend the name and safety of the Roman people; cease to spare me, and to think of me. For, in the first place, I ought to hope that all the gods who preside over this city will show me gratitude in proportion as I deserve it; and in the second place, if anything does happen to me, I shall fall with a contented and prepared mind; and, indeed, death cannot be disgraceful to a brave man, nor premature to one of consular rank, nor miserable to a wise man. Not that I am a man of so iron a disposition as not to be moved by the grief of a most dear and affectionate brother now present, and by the tears of all these men by whom you now see me surrounded. Nor does my fainting wife, my daughter prostrate with fear, and my little son whom the republic seems to me to embrace as a sort of hostage for my consulship, the son-in-law, who, awaiting the end of that day, is now standing in my sight, fail often to recall my mind to my home. I am moved by all these circumstances, but in such a direction as to wish that they all may be safe together with you, even if some violence overwhelms me, rather than that both they and we should perish together with the republic.

Wherefore, O conscript fathers, attend to the safety of the republic; look round upon all the storms which are impending, unless you guard against them. It is not Tiberius Gracchus, who wished to be made a second time a tribune of the people; it is not Caius Gracchus, who endeavored to excite the partisans of the agrarian law; it is not Lucius Saturninus, who slew Memmius, who is now in some danger, who is now brought before the tribunal of your severity. They are now in your hands who withstood all Rome, with the object of bringing conflagration on the whole city, massacre on all of you, and of receiving Catiline; their letters are in your possession, their seals, their handwriting, and the confession of each individual of them; the Alloborges are tampered with, the slaves are excited, Catiline is sent for; the design is actually begun to be put in execution, that all should be put to death, so that no one should be left even to mourn the name of the republic, and to lament over the downfall of so mighty a dominion.

III. All these things the witnesses have informed you of, the prisoners have confessed, you by many judgments have already decided; first, because you have thanked me in unprecedented language, and have passed a vote that the conspiracy of abandoned men has been laid open by my virtue and diligence; secondly, because you have compelled Publius Lentulus to abdicate the prætorship; again, because you have voted that he and the others about whom you have decided should be given into custody; and above all, because you have decreed a supplication in my name, an honor which has never been paid to anyone before acting in a civil capacity; last of all, because yesterday you gave most ample rewards to the ambassadors of the Allobroges and to Titus Vulturcius; all which acts are such that they, who have been given into custody by name, without any doubt seem already condemned by you.

But I have determined to refer the business to you as a fresh matter, O conscript fathers, both as to the fact, what you think of it, and as to the punishment, what you vote. I will state what it behoves the consul to state. I have seen for a long time great madness existing in the republic, and new designs being formed, and evil passions being stirred up, but I

never thought that so great, so destructive a conspiracy as this
was being meditated by citizens. Now to whatever point your
minds and opinions incline, you must decide before night. You
see how great a crime has been made known to you; if you
think that but few are implicated in it you are greatly mistaken; this evil has spread wider than you think; it has spread
not only throughout Italy, but it has even crossed the Alps,
and creeping stealthily on, it has already occupied many of the
provinces; it can by no means be crushed by tolerating it, and
by temporising with it; however you determine on chastising
it, you must act with promptitude.

IV. I see that as yet there are two opinions. One that of
Decius Silanus, who thinks that those who have endeavored
to destroy all these things should be punished with death; the
other, that of Caius Cæsar, who objects to the punishment of
death, but adopts the most extreme severity of all other punishment. Each acts in a manner suitable to his own dignity and to
the magnitude of the business with the greatest severity. The
one thinks that it is not right that those, who have attempted
to deprive all of us and the whole Roman people of life, to
destroy the empire, to extinguish the name of the Roman
people, should enjoy life and the breath of heaven common
to us all, for one moment; and he remembers that this sort of
punishment has often been employed against worthless citizens in this republic. The other feels that death was not appointed by the immortal gods for the sake of punishment, but
that it is either a necessity of nature, or a rest from toils and
miseries; therefore wise men have never met it unwillingly,
brave men have often encountered it even voluntarily. But
imprisonment, and that too perpetual, was certainly invented
for the extraordinary punishment of nefarious wickedness;
therefore he proposes that they should be distributed among
the municipal towns. This proposition seems to have in it injustice if you command it, difficulty if you request it; however
let it be so decreed if you like.

For I will undertake, and, as I hope, I shall find one who will
not think it suitable to his dignity to refuse what you decide
on for the sake of the universal safety. He imposes besides a
severe punishment on the burgesses of the municipal town if
any of the prisoners escape; he surrounds them with the most

terrible guard, and with everything worthy of the wickedness of abandoned men. And he proposes to establish a decree that no one shall be able to alleviate the punishment of those whom he is condemning by a vote of either the senate or the people. He takes away even hope, which alone can comfort men in their miseries; besides this, he votes that their goods should be confiscated; he leaves life alone to these infamous men, and if he had taken that away, he would have relieved them by one pang of many tortures of mind and body, and of all the punishment of their crimes. Therefore, that there might be some dread in life to the wicked, men of old have believed that there were some punishments of that sort appointed for the wicked in the shades below; because in truth they perceived that if this were taken away death itself would not be terrible.

V. Now, O conscript fathers, I see what is my interest; if you follow the opinion of Caius Cæsar, (since he has adopted this path in the republic which is accounted the popular one,) perhaps since he is the author and promoter of this opinion, the popular violence will be less to be dreaded by me; if you adopt the other opinion, I know not whether I am not likely to have more trouble; but still let the advantage of the republic outweigh the consideration of my danger. For we have from Caius Cæsar, as his own dignity and as the illustrious character of his ancestors demanded, a vote as a hostage of his lasting good-will to the republic; it has been clearly seen how great is the difference between the lenity of demagogues, and a disposition really attached to the interests of the people. I see that of those men who wish to be considered attached to the people one man is absent, that they may not seem forsooth to give a vote about the lives of Roman citizens. He only three days ago gave Roman citizens into custody, and decreed me a supplication, and voted most magnificent rewards to the witnesses only yesterday. It is not now doubtful to anyone what he, who voted for the imprisonment of the criminals, congratulation to him who had detected them, and rewards to those who had proved the crime, thinks of the whole matter, and of the cause. But Caius Cæsar considers that the Sempronian[2]

[2] The Sempronian law was proposed by Caius Gracchus, B. C. 123, and enacted that the people only should decide respecting the life or civil condition of a citizen. It is alluded to also in the oration Pro Rabir

law was passed about Roman citizens, but that he who is an enemy of the republic can by no means be a citizen; and moreover that the very proposer of the Sempronian law suffered punishment by the command of the people. He also denies that Lentulus, a briber and a spendthrift, after he has formed such cruel and bitter plans about the destruction of the Roman people, and the ruin of this city, can be called a friend of the people. Therefore this most gentle and merciful man does not hesitate to commit Publius Lentulus to eternal darkness and imprisonment, and establishes a law to all posterity that no one shall be able to boast of alleviating his punishment, or hereafter to appear a friend of the people to the destruction of the Roman people. He adds also the confiscation of their goods, so that want also and beggary may be added to all the torments of mind and body.

VI. Wherefore, if you decide on this you give me a companion in my address, dear and acceptable to the Roman people; or if you prefer to adopt the opinion of Silanus, you will easily defend me and yourselves from the reproach of cruelty, and I will prevail that it shall be much lighter. Although, O conscript fathers, what cruelty can there be in chastising the enormity of such excessive wickedness? For I decide from my own feeling. For so may I be allowed to enjoy the republic in safety in your company, as I am not moved to be somewhat vehement in this cause by any severity of disposition, (for who is more mercifulness than I am?) but rather by a singular humanity and mercifulness. For I seem to myself to see this city, the light of the world, and the citadel of all nations, falling on a sudden by one conflagration. I see in my mind's eye miserable and unburied heaps of cities in my buried country; the sight of Cethegus and his madness raging amid your slaughter is ever present to my sight. But when I have set before myself Lentulus reigning, as he himself confesses that he had hoped was his destiny, and this Gabinius arrayed in the purple, and Catiline arrived with his army, then I shudder at the lamentation of matrons, and the flight of virgins and of boys, and the insults of the vestal virgins; and because these

c. 4, where Cicero says, "Caius Gracchus passed a law that no decision should be come to about the life of a Roman citizen without your command," speaking to the *Quirites*.

things appear to me exceedingly miserable and pitiable, therefore I show myself severe and rigorous to those who have
wished to bring about this state of things. I ask, forsooth, if
any father of a family, supposing his children had been slain
by a slave, his wife murdered, his house burnt were not to inflict on his slaves the severest possible punishment, would he
appear element and merciful, or most inhuman, and cruel? To
me he would seem unnatural and hard-hearted who did not
soothe his own pain and anguish by the pain and torture of the
criminal. And so we, in the case of these men who desired to
murder us, and our wives, and our children,—who endeavored
to destroy the houses of every individual among us, and also
the republic, the home of all,—who designed to place the nation of the Allobroges on the relics of this city, and on the
ashes of the empire destroyed by fire;—if we are very rigorous,
we shall be considered merciful; if we are very rigorous, we
shall be considered merciful; if we choose to be lax, we must
endure the character of the greatest cruelty, to the damage of
our country and our fellow-citizens.

Unless, indeed, Lucius[3] Cæsar, a thoroughly brave man, and
of the best disposition towards the republic, seemed to any
one to be too cruel three days ago, when he said that the
husband of his own sister, a most excellent woman, (in his
presence and in his hearing,) ought to be deprived of life,—
when he said that his grandfather had been put to death by
command of the consul, and his youthful son, sent as an ambassador by his father, had been put to death in prison. And what
deed had they done like these men? had they formed any plan
for destroying the republic? At that time great corruption was
rife in the republic, and there was the greatest strife between
parties. And, at that time, the grandfather of this Lentulus, a
most illustrious man, put on his armor and pursued Gracchus;
he even received a severe wound that there might be no
diminution of the great dignity of the republic. But this man,
his grandson, invited the Gauls to overthrow the foundations

---

[3] The brother-in-law of Lucius Cæsar was Marcus Fulvius, whose death
at the command of Opimius the consul, is referred to in the 2d cap. 1st
Cat. He sent his son to the consul to treat for his surrender, whom
Opimius sent back the first time, and forbade to return to him, when he
did return, he put him to death.

of the republic; he stirred up the slaves, he summoned Catiline, he distributed us to Cethegus to be massacred, and the rest of the citizens to Gabinius to be assassinated, the city he allotted to Cassius to burn, and the plundering and devastating of all Italy he assigned to Catiline. You fear, I think, lest in the case of such unheard-of and abominable wickedness you should seem to decide anything with too great severity; when we ought much more to fear lest by being remiss in punishing we should appear cruel to our country, rather than appear by the severity of our irritation too rigorous to its most bitter enemies.

VII. But, O conscript fathers, I cannot conceal what I hear; for sayings are bruited about, which come to my ears, of those men who seem to fear that I may not have force enough to put in execution the things which you determine on this day. Everything is provided for, and prepared, and arranged, O conscript fathers, both by my exceeding care and diligence, and also by the still greater zeal of the Roman people for the retaining of their supreme dominion, and for the preserving of the fortunes of all. All men of all ranks are present, and of all ages; the forum is full, the temples around the forum are full, all the approaches to this place and to this temple are full. For this is the only cause that has ever been known since the first foundation of the city, in which all men were of one and the same opinion—except those, who, as they saw they must be ruined, preferred to perish in company with all the world rather than by themselves.

These men I except, and I willingly set them apart from the rest; for I do not think that they should be classed in the number of worthless citizens, but in that of the most bitter enemies. But, as for the rest; O ye immortal gods! in what crowds, with what zeal, with what virtue do they agree in defense of the common dignity and safety. Why should I here speak of the Roman knights? who yield to you the supremacy in rank and wisdom, in order to vie with you in love for the republic,—whom this day and this cause now reunite with you in alliance and unanimity with your body, reconciled after a disagreement of many years. And if we can preserve forever in the republic this union now established in my consulship, I pledge myself to you that no civil and domestic calamity can hereafter reach any part of the republic. I see that the tribunes of the treasury—excellent men—have united with similar zeal in defense of the republic, and all the notaries.[4] For as this day had by chance brought them in crowds to the treasury, I see that they were diverted from an anxiety for the money due to them, from an expectation of their capital, to a regard for the common safety. The entire multitude of honest men, even the poorest, is present; for who is there to whom these temples, the sight of the city, the possession of liberty,—in short, this light and this soil of his, common to us all, is not both dear and pleasant and delightful?

VIII. It is worth while, O conscript fathers, to know the inclinations of the freedmen; who, having by their good fortune obtained the right of citizens, consider this to be really their country, which some who have been born here, and born in the highest rank, have considered to be not their own county, but a city of enemies. But why should I speak of men of this body whom their private fortunes, whom their common republic, whom, in short, that liberty which is most delightful has called forth to defend the safety of their country? There is no slave who is only in an endurable condition of slavery who does not shudder at the audacity of citizens, who does not desire that these things may stand, who does not contribute all the good-will that he can, and all that he dares, to the common safety.

Wherefore, if this consideration moves any one, that it has been heard that some tool of Lentulus is running about the shops,—is hoping that the minds of some poor and ignorant men may be corrupted by bribery; that, indeed, has been attempted and begun, but no one has been found either so wretched in their fortune or so abandoned in their inclination as not to wish the place of their seat and work and daily gain, their chamber and their bed, and, in short, the tranquil course of their lives, to be still preserved to them. And far the greater part of those who are in the shops,—ay, indeed, (for that is the more correct way of speaking), the whole of this class is of all

---

[4] The notaries at Rome were in the pay of the state; they were chiefly employed in making up the public accounts. In the time of Cicero it seems to have been lawful for any one to obtain the office of *scriba* by purchase, (see Cic. in Verr. ii. 79,) and freedman and their sons frequently availed themselves of this privilege.

the most attached to tranquillity; their whole stock, forsooth, their whole employment and livelihood, exists by the peaceful intercourse of the citizens, and is wholly supported by peace. And if their gains are diminished whenever their shops are shut, what will they be when they are burnt? And, as this is the case, O conscript fathers, the protection of the Roman people is not wanting to you; do you take care that you do not seem to be wanting to the Roman people.

IX. You have a consul preserved out of many dangers and plots, and from death itself, not for his own life, but for your safety. All ranks agree for the preservation of the republic with heart and will, with zeal, with virtue, with their voice. Your common country, besieged by the hands and weapons of an impious conspiracy, stretches forth her hands to you as a suppliant; to you she recommends herself, to you she recommends the lives of all the citizens, and the citadel, and the Capitol, and the altars of the household gods, and the eternal unextinguishable fire of Vesta, and all the temples of all the gods, and the altars and the walls and the houses of the city. Moreover, your own lives, those of your wives and children, the fortunes of all men, your homes, your hearths, are this day interested in your decision.

You have a leader mindful of you, forgetful of himself—an opportunity which is not always given to men; you have all ranks, all individuals, the whole Roman people, (a thing which in civil transactions we see this day for the first time,) full of one and the same feeling. Think with what great labor this our dominion was founded, by what virtue this our liberty was established, by what kind favor of the gods our fortunes were aggrandized and ennobled, and how nearly one night destroyed them all. That this may never hereafter be able not only to be done, but not even to be thought of, you must this day take care. And I have spoken thus, not in order to stir you up who almost outrun me myself, but that my voice, which ought to be the chief voice in the republic, may appear to have fulfilled the duty which belongs to me as consul.

X. Now, before I return to the decision, I will say a few words concerning myself. As numerous as is the band of conspirators,—and you see that it is very great,—so numerous a multitude of enemies do I see that I have brought upon myself.

But I consider them base and powerless and despicable and abject. But if at any time that band shall be excited by the wickedness and madness of anyone, and shall show itself more powerful than your dignity and that of the republic, yet, O conscript fathers, I shall never repent of my actions and of my advice. Death, indeed, which they perhaps threaten me with, is prepared for all men; such glory during life as you have honored me with by your decrees no one has ever attained to. For you have passed votes of congratulation to others for having governed the republic successfully, but to me alone for having saved it.

Let Scipio be thought illustrious, he by whose wisdom and valor Hannibal was compelled to return into Africa, and to depart from Italy. Let the second Africanus be extolled with conspicuous praise, who destroyed two cities most hostile to this empire, Carthage and Numantia. Let Lucius Paullus be thought a great man, he whose triumphal car was graced by Perses, previously a most powerful and noble monarch. Let Marius be held in eternal honor, who twice delivered Italy from siege, and from the fear of slavery. Let Pompey be preferred to them all—Pompey, whose exploits and whose virtues are bounded by the same districts and limits as the course of the sun. There will be, forsooth, among the praises of these men, some room for my glory, unless haply it be a greater deed to open to us provinces whither we may fly than to take care that those who are at a distance may, when conquerors, have a home to return to.

Although in one point the circumstances of foreign triumph are better than those of domestic victory; because foreign enemies, either if they be crushed become one's servants, or if they be received into the state, think themselves bound to us by obligation; but those of the number of citizens who become depraved by madness and once begin to be enemies to their country,—those men, when you have defeated their attempts to injure the republic, you can neither restrain by force nor conciliate by kindness. So that I see that an eternal war with all wicked citizens has been undertaken by me; which, however, I am confident can easily be driven back from me and mine by your aid, and by that of all good men, and by the memory of

such great dangers, which will remain, not only among this
people which has been saved, but in the discourse and minds of
all nations forever. Nor, in truth, can any power be found
which will be able to undermine and destroy your union with
the Roman knights, and such unanimity as exists among all
good men.

XI. As, then, this is the case, O conscript fathers, instead of
my military command,—instead of the army,—instead of the
province[5] which I have neglected, and the other badges of
honor which have been rejected by me for the sake of protecting the city and your safety,—in place of the ties of clientship
and hospitality with citizens in the provinces, which, however,
by my influence in the city, I study to preserve with as
much toil as I labor to acquire them,—in place of all these
things, and in reward for my singular zeal in your behalf, and
for this diligence in saving the republic which you behold, I
ask nothing of you but the recollection of this time and of my
whole consulship. And as long as that is fixed in your minds, I
shall think I am fenced round by the strongest wall. But if the
violence of wicked men shall deceive and overpower my expectations, I recommend to you my little son, to whom, in
truth, it will be protection enough, not only for his safety, but
even for his dignity, if you recollect that he is the son of him
who has saved all these things at his own single risk.

Wherefore, O conscript fathers, determine with care, as you
have begun, and boldly, concerning your own safety, and that
of the Roman people, and concerning your wives and children;
concerning your altars and your hearths, your shrines and
temples; concerning the houses and homes of the whole city;
concerning your dominion, your liberty, and the safety of Italy
and the whole republic. For you have a consul who will not
hesitate to obey our decrees, and who will be able, as long as he

[5] Cicero, in order to tempt Antonius to aid him in counteracting the
treasonable designs of Catiline, had given up to him the province of
Macedonia, which had fallen to his own lot; and having accepted that
of Cisalpine Gaul in exchange for it, he gave that also to Quintus Metellus; being resolved to receive no emolument, directly or indirectly, from
his consulship.

lives, to defend what you decide on, and of his own power to execute it.[6]

[6] This speech was spoken, and the criminals executed, on the fifth of December. But Catiline was not yet entirely overcome. He had with him in Etruria two legions,—about twelve thousand men; of which, however, not above one quarter were regularly armed. For some time bey marches and countermarches he eluded Antonius, but when the news reached his army of the fate of the rest of the conspirators, it began to desert him in great numbers. He attempted to escape into Gaul, but found himself intercepted by Metellus, who had been sent thither by Cicero with three legions. Antonius is supposed not to have been disinclined to connive at his escape, if he had not been compelled as it were by his questor Sextus and his lieutenant Petreius to force him to a battle, in which, however, Antonius himself, being ill of the gout, did not take the command, which devolved on Petreius, who after a severe action destroyed Catiline and his whole army, of which every man is said to have been slain in the battle.

FOR AULUS LICINIUS ARCHIAS, THE POET

THE ARGUMENT

Archias was a Greek poet, a native of Antioch, who came to Rome in the train of Lucullus, when Cicero was a child. He assumed the names of Aulus and Licinius, the last out of compliment to the Luculli, and Cicero had been for some time a pupil of his, and had retained a great regard for him. A man of the name of Gracchus now prosecuted him as a false pretender to the rights of a Roman citizen, according to the provisions of the *lex Papiria*. But Cicero contends that he is justified by that very law, for Archias before coming to Rome had stayed at Heraclea, a confederate city, and had been enrolled as a Heraclean citizen; and in the *lex Papiria* it was expressly provided that those who were on the register of any confederate city as its citizens, if they were residing in Italy at the time the law was passed, and if they made a return of themselves to the prætor within sixty days, were to be exempt from its operation. However, the greatest part of this oration is occupied, not in legal arguments, but in a panegyric on Archias, who is believed to have died soon afterwards; and he must have been a very old man at the time that it was spoken, as it was nearly forty years previously that he had first come to Rome.

I. IF THERE BE any natural ability in me, O judges,—and I know how slight that is; or if I have any practice as a speaker, —and in that line I do not deny that I have some experience; or if I have any method in my oratory, drawn from my study of the liberal sciences, and from that careful training to which I admit that at no part of my life have I ever been disinclined; certainly, of all those qualities, this Aulus Licinius is entitled to be among the first to claim the benefit from me as his peculiar right. For as far as ever my mind can look back upon the space of time that is past, and recall the memory of its earliest youth, tracing my life from that starting-point, I see that Archias was the principal cause of my undertaking, and the principal means of my mastering, those studies. And, if this voice of mine, formed by his encouragement and his precepts, has at times been the instrument of safety to others, undoubtedly we ought, as far as lies in our power, to help and save the very man from whom we have received that gift which has enabled us to bring help to many and salvation to some. And lest anyone should, perchance, marvel at this being said by me, as the chief of his ability consists in something else, and not in this system and practise of eloquence, he must be told that even we ourselves have never been wholly devoted to this study. In truth, all the arts which concern the civilizing and humanizing of men, have some link which binds them together, and are, as it were, connected by some relationship to one another.

II. And, that it may not appear marvelous to anyone of you, that I, in a formal proceeding like this and in a regular court of justice, when an action is being tried before a prætor of the Roman people, a most eminent man, and before most impartial judges, before such an assembly and multitude of people as I see around me, employ this style of speaking, which is at variance, not only with the ordinary usages of courts of justice, but with the general style of forensic pleading; I entreat you in this cause to grant me this indulgence, suitable to this defendant, and as I trust not disagreeable to you,—the indulgence, namely, of allowing me, when speaking in defense of a most sublime poet and most learned man, before this concourse of highly-educated citizens, before this most polite and accomplished assembly, and before such a prætor as him who is presiding at this trial, to enlarge with a little more freedom than usual on the study of polite literature and refined arts, and, speaking in the character of such a man as that, who, owing to the tranquillity of his life and the studies to which he has devoted himself, has but little experience of the dangers of a court of justice, to employ a new and unusual style of oratory. And if I feel that that indulgence is given and allowed me by you, I will soon cause you to think that this Aulus Licinius is a man who not only, now that he is a citizen, does not deserve to be expunged from the list of citizens, but that he is worthy, even if he were not one, of being now made a citizen.

III. For when first Archias grew out of childhood, and out of the studies of those arts by which young boys are gradually trained and refined, he devoted himself to the study of writing. First of all at Antioch, (for he was born there, and was of high rank there,) formerly an illustrious and wealthy city, and the seat of learned men and of liberal sciences; an there it was his lot speedily to show himself superior to all in ability and credit. Afterwards, in the other parts of Asia, and over all Greece, his arrival was so talked of wherever he came, that the anxiety with which he was expected was even greater than the fame of his genius; but the admiration which he excited when he had arrived, exceeded even the anxiety with which he was expected. Italy was at that time full of Greek science and of Greek systems, and these studies were at that time cultivated in Latium with greater zeal than they now are in the same towns; and here too at Rome, on account of the tranquil state of the republic at that time, they were far from neglected. Therefore, the people of Tarentum, and Rhegium, and Neapolis, presented him with the freedom of the city and with other gifts; and all men who were capable of judging of genius thought him deserving of their acquaintance and hospitality. When, from this great celebrity of his, he had become known to us though absent, he came to Rome, in the consulship of Marius and Catulus. It was his lot to have those men as his first consuls, the one of whom could supply him with the most illustrious achievements to write about, the other could give him, not only exploits to celebrate, but his ears and judicious attention. Immediately the Luculli, though Archias was as yet but a youth,[1] received him in their house. But it was not only to his

[1] The Latin is *prætextatus*. Before he had exchanged the *prætexta* for the *toga virilis*. It has generally been thought that the age at which this exchange was made was seventeen, but Professor Long, the highest possible authority on all subjects of Latin literature, and especially on Roman law, says, (Smith, Dict. Ant. v. *Impubes*,) "The *toga virilis* was assumed at the Liberalia in the month of March; and though no age appears to have been positively fixed for the ceremony, it probably took place, as a generale rule, on the feast which next followed the completion of the fourteenth year, though it is certain that the completion of the fourteenth year was not always the time observed." Even supposing Archias to have been seventeen, it appears rather an early age for him to have established such a reputation as Cicero speaks of, and perhaps, as not being at that time a Roman citizen, he probably did not wear the *prætexta* at all; the expression is not to be taken literally, but we are merely to understand generally that he was quite a young man.

genius and his learning but also to his natural disposition and virtue, that it must be attributed that the house which was the first to be opened to him in his youth, is also the one in which he lives most familiarly in his old age. He at that time gained the affection of Quintus Metellus, that great man who was the conqueror of Numidia, and his son Pius. He was eagerly listened to by Marcus Æmilius; he associated with Quintus Catulus,—both with the father and the sons. He was highly respected by Lucius Crassus; and as for the Luculli, and Drusus, and the Octavii, and Cato, and the whole family of the Hortensii, he was on terms of the greatest possible intimacy with all of them, and was held by them in the greatest honor. For not only did every one cultivate his acquaintance who wished to learn or to hear anything, but even every one pretended to have such a desire.

IV. In the meantime, after a sufficiently long interval, having gone with Lucius Lucullus into Sicily, and having afterwards departed from that province in the company of the same Lucullus, he came to Heraclea. And as that city was one which enjoyed all the rights of a confederate city to their full extent, he became desirous of being enrolled as a citizen of it. And, being thought deserving of such a favor for his own sake, when aided by the influence and authority of Lucullus, he easily obtained it from the Heracleans. The freedom of the city was given him in accordance with the provisions of the law of Silvanus and Carbo: "If any men had been enrolled as citizens of the confederate cities, and if, at the time that the law was passed, they had a residence in Italy, and if within sixty days they had made a return of themselves to the prætor." As he had now had a residence at Rome for many years, he returned himself as a citizen, to the prætor, Quintus Metellus, his most intimate friend. If we have nothing else to speak about except the rights of citizenship and the law, I need say no more. The cause is over. For which of all these statements, O Gratius, can be invalidated? Will you deny that he was enrolled, at the time I speak of, as a citizen of Heraclea? There is a man present of the very highest authority, a most scrupulous and truthful man, Lucius Lucullus, who will tell you not that he thinks it, but that he knows it; not that he has heard of it, but that he saw it; not even that he was present when it was done, but that he actually did it himself. Deputies from Heraclea are present, men of the highest rank; they have come expressly on account of this trial, with a commission from their city, and to give evidence on the part of their city; and they say that he was enrolled as a Heraclean. On this you ask for the public registers of the Heracleans, which we all know were destroyed in the Italian war, when the register office was burnt. It is ridiculous to say nothing to the proofs which we have, but to ask for proofs which it is impossible for us to have; to disregard the recollection of men, and to appeal to the memory of documents; and when you have the conscientious evidence of a most honorable man, the oath and good faith of a most respectable municipality, to reject those things which cannot by any possibility be tampered with, and to demand documentary evidence, though you say at the same moment that that is constantly played tricks with. "But he had no residence at Rome." What, not he who for so many years before the freedom of the city was given to him, had established the abode of all his property and fortunes at Rome? "But he did not return himself." Indeed he did and in that return which alone obtains with the college of prætors the authority of a public document.

V. For as the returns of Appius were said to have been kept carelessly, and as the trifling conduct of Gabinius, before he was convicted, and his misfortune after his condemnation, had taken away all credit from the public registers, Metellus, the most scrupulous and moderate of all men, was so careful, that he came to Lucius Lentulus, the prætor, and to the judges, and said that he was greatly vexed at an erasure which appeared in one name. In these documents, therefore, you will see no erasure affecting the name of Aulus Licinius. And as this is the case, what reason have you for doubting about his citizenship, especially as he was enrolled as a citizen of other cities also? In truth, as men in Greece were in the habit of giving rights of citizenship to many men of very ordinary qualifications, and endowed with no talents at all, or with very moderate ones, without any payment, it is likely, I suppose, that the Rhegians, and Locrians, and Neapolitans, and Tarentines should have been unwilling to give to this man, enjoying the highest possible reputation for genius, what they were in the habit of giving even to theatrical artists. What, when other men, who not

only after the freedom of the city had been given, but even
after the passing of the Papian law, crept somehow or other
into the registers of those municipalities, shall he be rejected
who does not avail himself of those other lists in which he is
enrolled, because he always wished to be considered a Heraclean? You demand to see our own censor's returns. I suppose
no one knows that at the time of the last census he was with
that most illustrious general, Lucius Lucullus, with the army;
that at the time of the preceding one he was with the same man
when he was in Asia as questor; and that in the census before
that, when Julius and Crassus were censors, no regular account of the people was taken. But, since the census does not
confirm the right of citizenship, but only indicates that he, who
is returned in the census, did at that time claim to be considered as a citizen, I say that, at that time, when you say, in your
speech for the prosecution, that he did not even himself consider that he had any claim to the privileges of a Roman citizen, he more than once made a will according to our laws, and
he entered upon inheritances left him by Roman citizens; and
he was made honorable mention of by Lucius Lucullus, both
as prætor and as consul, in the archives kept in the treasury.

VI. You must rely wholly on what arguments you can find.
For he will never be convicted either by his own opinion of his
case, or by that which is formed of it by his friends.

You ask us, O Gratius, why we are so exceedingly attached
to this man. Because he supplies us with food whereby our
mind is refreshed after this noise in the forum, and with rest
for our ears after they have been wearied with bad language.
Do you think it possible that we could find a supply for our
daily speeches, when discussing such a variety of matters unless we were to cultivate our minds by the study of literature;
or that our minds could bear being kept so constantly on the
stretch if we did not relax them by that same study? But I confess that I am devoted to those studies; let others be ashamed
of them if they have buried themselves in books without being
able to produce anything out of them for the common advantage, or anything which may bear the eyes of men and the
light. But why need I be ashamed, who for many years have
lived in such a manner as never to allow my own love of tranquillity to deny me to the necessity or advantage of another,

or my fondness for pleasure to distract, or even sleep to delay my attention to such claims? Who then can reproach me, or who has any right to be angry with me, if I allow myself as much time for the cultivation of these studies as some take for the performance of their own business, or for celebrating days of festival and games, or for other pleasures, or even for the rest and refreshment of mind and body, or as others devote to early banquets, to playing at dice, or at ball? And this ought to be permitted to me, because by these studies my power of speaking and those faculties are improved, which, as far as they do exist in me, have never been denied to my friends when they have been in peril. And if that ability appears to anyone to be but moderate, at all events I know whence I derive those principles which are of the greatest value. For if I had not persuaded myself from my youth upwards, both by the precepts of many masters and by much reading, that there is nothing in life greatly to be desired, except praise and honor, and that while pursuing those things all tortures of the body, all dangers of death and banishment are to be considered but of small importance, I should never have exposed myself, in defense of your safety, to such numerous and arduous contests, and to these daily attacks of profligate men. But all books are full of such precepts, and all the sayings of philosophers, and all antiquity is full of precedents teaching the same lesson, but all these things would lie buried in darkness, if the light of literature and learning were not applied to them. How many images of the bravest men, carefully elaborated, have both the Greek and Latin writers bequeathed to us, not merely for us to look at and gaze upon, but also for our imitation! And I, always keeping them before my eyes as examples for my own public conduct, have endeavored to model my mind and views by continually thinking of those excellent men.

VII. Some one will ask, "What? were those identical great men, whose virtues have been recorded in books, accomplished in all that learning which you are extolling so highly?" It is difficult to assert this of all of them; but still I know what answer I can make to that question: I admit that many men have existed of admirable disposition and virtue, who, without learning, by the almost divine instinct of their own mere nature, have been, of their own accord, as it were, moderate and wise

man. I even add this, that very often nature without learning
has had more to do with leading men to credit and to virtue,
than learning when not assisted by a good natural disposition.
And I also contend, that when to an excellent and admirable
natural disposition there is added a certain system and training
of education, then from that combination arises an extraordinary perfection of character; such as is seen in that god-like
man, whom our fathers saw in their time, Africanus; and in
Caius Lælius and Lucius Furius, most virtuous and moderate
man; and in that most excellent man, the most learned man of
his time, Marcus Cato the elder; and all these men, if they had
been to derive no assistance from literature in the cultivation
and practise of virtue, would never have applied themselves
to the study of it. Though, even if there were no such great advantage to be reaped from it, and if it were only pleasure that
is sought from these studies, still I imagine you would consider
it a most reasonable and liberal employment of the mind: for
other occupations are not suited to every time, nor to every age
or place; but these studies are the food of youth, the delight of
old age; the ornament of prosperity, the refuge and comfort of
adversity; a delight at home, and no hindrance abroad; they
are companions by night, and in travel, and in the country.

VIII. And if we ourselves were not able to arrive at these advantages, nor even taste them with our senses, still we ought
to admire them, even when we saw them in others. Who of us
was of so ignorant and brutal a disposition as not lately to be
grieved at the death of Roscius? who, though he was an old
man when he died, yet, on account of the excellence and
beauty of his art, appeared to be one who on every account
ought not to have died. Therefore, had he by the gestures of
his body gained so much of our affections, and shall we disregard the incredible movements of the mind, and the rapid
operations of genius? How often have I seen this man Archias,
O judges,—(for I will take advantage of your kindness, since
you listen to me so attentively while speaking in this unusual
manner,)—how often have I seen him, when he had not written
a single word, repeat extempore a great number of admirable
verses on the very events which were passing at the moment!
How often have I seen him go back, and describe the same
thing over again with an entire change of language and ideas!

And what he wrote with care and with much thought, that I have seen admired to such a degree, as to equal the credit of even the writings of the ancients. Should not I, then, love this man? should I not admire him? should not I think it my duty to defend him in every possible way? And, indeed, we have constantly heard from men of the greatest eminence and learning, that the study of other sciences was made up of learning, and rules, and regular method; but that a poet was such by the unassisted work of nature, and was moved by the vigor of his own mind, and was inspired, as it were, by some divine wrath. Wherefore rightly does our own great Ennius call poets holy; because they seem to be recommended to us by some especial gift, as it were, and liberality of the gods. Let then, judges, this name of poet, this name which no barbarians even have ever disregarded, be holy in your eyes, men of cultivated minds as you all are. Rocks and deserts reply to the poet's voice; savage beasts are often moved and arrested by song; and shall we, who have been trained in the pursuit of the most virtuous acts, refuse to be swayed by the voice of poets? The Colophonians say that Homer was their citizen; the Chians claim him as theirs; the Salaminians assert their right to him; but the men of Smyrna loudly assert him to a citizen of Smyrna, and they have even raised a temple to him in their city. Many other places also fight with one another for the honor of being his birth-place.

IX. They, then, claim a stranger, even after his death, because he was a poet; shall we reject this man while he is alive, a man who by his own inclination and by our laws does actually belong to us? especially when Archias has employed all his genius with the utmost zeal in celebrating the glory and renown of the Roman people? For when a young man, he touched on our wars against the Cimbri, and gained the favor even of Caius Marius himself, a man who was tolerably proof against this sort of study. For there was no one so disinclined to the Muses as not willingly to endure that the praise of his labors should be made immortal by means of verse. They say that the great Themistocles, the greatest man that Athens produced, said, when some one asked him what sound or whose voice he took the greatest delight in hearing, "The voice of that by whom his own exploits were best celebrated." Therefore,

the great Marius was also exceedingly attached to Lucius
Plotius, because he thought that the achievement which he had
performed could be celebrated by his genius. And the whole
Mithridatic war, great and difficult as it was, and carried on
with so much diversity of fortune by land and sea, has been
related at length by him; and the books in which that is sung
of, not only make illustrious Lucius Lucullus, that most gallant
and celebrated man, but they do honor also to the Roman
people. For, while Lucullus was general, the Roman people
opened Pontus, though it was defended both by the resources
of the king and by the character of the country itself. Under
the same general the army of the Roman people, with no very
great numbers, routed the countless hosts of the Armenians.
It is the glory of the Roman people that, by the wisdom of that
same general, the city of the Cyzicenes, most friendly to us,
was delivered and preserved from all the attacks of the kind,
and from the very jaws as it were of the whole war. Ours is the
glory which will be forever celebrated, which is derived from
the fleet of the enemy which was sunk after its admirals had
been slain, and from the marvellous naval battle off Tenedos:
those trophies belong to us, those monuments are ours, those
triumphs are ours. Therefore, I say that the men by whose
genius these exploits are celebrated, make illustrious at the
same time the glory of the Roman people. Our countryman,
Ennius, was dear to the elder Africanus; and even on the tomb
of the Scipios his effigy is believed to be visible, carved in the
marble. But undoubtedly it is not only the men who are themselves praised who are done honor to by those praises, but the
name of the Roman people also is adorned by them. Cato, the
ancestor of this Cato, is extolled to the skies. Great honor is
paid to the exploits of the Roman people. Lastly, all those great
men, the Maximi, the Marcelli, and the Fulvii, are done honor
to, not without all of us having also a share in the panegyric.

X. Therefore our ancestors received the man who was the
cause of all this, a man of Rudiæ, into their city as a citizen;
and shall we reject from our city a man of Heraclea, a man
sought by many cities, and made a citizen of ours by these very
laws?

For if anyone thinks that there is a smaller gain of glory derived from Greek verses than from Latin ones, he is greatly

mistaken, because Greek poetry is read among all nations, Latin is confined to its own natural limits, which are narrow enough. Wherefore, if those achievements which we have performed are limited only by the bounds of the whole world, we ought to desire that, wherever our vigor and our arms have penetrated, our glory and our fame should likewise extend. Because, as this is always an ample reward for those people whose achievements are the subject of writings, so especially is it the greatest inducement to encounter labors and dangers to all men who fight for themselves for the sake of glory. How many historians of his exploits is Alexander the Great said to have had with him; and he, when standing on Cape Sigeum at the grave of Achilles, said,—"O happy youth, to find Homer as the panegyrist of your glory!" And he said the truth; for, if the Iliad had not existed, the same tomb which covered his body would have also buried his renown. What, did not our own Magnus, whose valor has been equal to his fortune, present Theophanes the Mitylenæan, a relater of his actions, with the freedom of the city in an assembly of the soldiers? And those brave men, our countrymen, soldiers and country-bred men as they were, still being moved by the sweetness of glory, as if they were to some extent partakers of the same renown, showed their approbation of that action with a great shout. Therefore, I suppose, if Archias were not a Roman citizen according to the laws, he could not have contrived to get presented with the freedom of the city by some general! Sylla, when he was giving it to the Spaniards and Gauls, would, I suppose, have refused him if he had asked for it! a man whom we ourselves saw in the public assembly, when a bad poet of the common people had put a book in his hand, because he had made an epigram on him with every other verse too long, immediately ordered some of the things which he was selling at the moment to be given him as a reward, on condition of not writing anything more about him for the future. Would not he who thought the industry of a bad poet still worthy of some reward, have sought out the genius, and excellence, and copiousness in writing of this man? What more need I say? Could he not have obtained the freedom of the city from Quintus Metellus Pius, his own most intimate friend, who gave it to many men, either by his own request, or by the intervention of

the Luculli? especially when Metellus was so anxious to have
his own deeds celebrated in writing, that he gave his attention
willingly to poets born even at Cordova, whose poetry had a
very heavy and foreign flavor.

XI. For this should not be concealed, which cannot possibly
be kept in the dark, but it might be avowed openly: we are
all influenced by a desire of praise, and the best men are the
most especially attracted by glory. Those very philosophers
even in the books which they write about despising glory, put
their own names on the title-page. In the very act of record-
ing their contempt for renown and notoriety, they desire to
have their own names known and talked of. Decimus Brutus,
that most excellent citizen and consummate general, adorned
the approaches to his temples and monuments with the verses
of Attius. And lately that great man Fulvius, who fought with
the Ætolians, having Ennius for his companion, did not hesitate to devote the spoils of Mars to the Muses. Wherefore, in
a city in which generals, almost in arms, have paid respect to
the name of poets and to the temples of the Muses, these
judges in the garb of peace ought not to act in a manner in-
consistent with the honor of the Muses and the safety of poets.

And that you may do that the more willingly, I will now
reveal my own feelings to you, O judges, and I will make a
confession to you of my own love of glory,--too eager perhaps,
but still honorable. For this man has in his verses touched upon
and begun the celebration of the deeds which we in our consulship did in union with you, for the safety of this city and
empire, and in defense of the life of the citizens and of the
whole republic. And when I had heard his commencement,
because it appeared to me to be a great subject and at the same
time an agreeable one, I encouraged him to complete his work.
For virtue seeks no other reward for its labors and its dangers
beyond that of praise and renown; and if that be denied to it,
what reason is there, O judges, why in so small and brief a
course of life as is allotted to us, we should impose such labors
on ourselves? Certainly, if the mind had no anticipations of
posterity, and if it were to confine all its thoughts within the
same limits as those by which the space of our lives is bounded,
it would neither break itself with such severe labors, nor
would it be tormented with such cares and sleepless anxiety,

nor would it so often have to fight for its very life. At present there is a certain virtue in every good man, which night and day stirs up the mind with the stimulus of glory, and reminds it that all mention of our name will not cease at the same time with our lives, but that our fame will endure to all posterity.

XII. Do we all who are occupied in the affairs of the state, and who are surrounded by such perils and dangers in life, appear to be so narrow-minded, as, though to the last moment of our lives we have never passed one tranquil or easy moment, to think that everything will perish at the same time as ourselves? Ought we not, when many most illustrious men have with great care collected and left behind them statues and images, representations not of their minds but of their bodies, much more to desire to leave behind us a copy of our counsels and of our virtues, wrought and elaborated by the greatest genius? I thought, at the very moment of performing them, that I was scattering and disseminating all the deeds which I was performing, all over the world for the eternal recollection of nations. And whether that delight is to be denied to my soul after death, or whether, as the wisest men have thought, it will affect some portion of my spirit, at all events, I am at present delighted with some such idea and hope.

Preserve then, O judges, a man of such virtue as that of Archias, which you see testified to you not only by the worth of his friends, but by the length of time during which they have been such to him; and of such genius as you ought to think is his, when you see that it has been sought by most illustrious men. And his cause is one which is approved of by the benevolence of the law, by the authority of his munici-pality, by the testimony of Lucullus, and by the documentary evidence of Metellus. And as this is the case, we do entreat you, O judges, if there may be any weight attached, I will not say to human, but even to divine recommendation in such important matters, to receive under your protection that man who has at all times done honor to your generals and to the exploits of the Roman people,—who even in these recent perils of our own, and in your domestic dangers, promises to give an eternal testimony of praise in our favor, and who forms one of that band of poets who have at all times and in all nations been considered and called holy, so that he may seem relieved by your humanity, rather than overwhelmed by your severity.

The things which, according to my custom, I have said briefly and simply, O judges, I trust have been approved by all of you. Those things which I have spoken, without regarding the habits of the forum or judicial usage, both concerning the genius of the man and my own zeal in his behalf, I trust have been received by you in good part. That they have been so by him who presides at this trial, I am quite certain.

IN DEFENSE OF THE PROPOSED MANILIAN LAW

THE ARGUMENT

In the year B. C. 67, Aulus Gabinius had obtained the passing of a decree by which Pompey was invested for three years with the supreme command over all the Mediterranean, and over all the coasts of that sea, to a distance of four hundred furlongs from the sea. And in this command he had acted with great vigor and with complete success; destroying all the pirates' strongholds, and distributing the men themselves as colonists among the inland towns of Asia Minor and Greece. After this achievement he did not return to Rome, but remained in Asia, making various regulations for the towns which he had conquered.

During this period Lucullus had been prosecuting the war against Mithridates, and proceeding gradually in the reduction of Pontus; he had penetrated also into Mesopotamia, but had subsequently been distressed by seditions in his army, excited by Clodius, his brother-in-law; and these seditions had given fresh courage to Mithridates, who had fallen on Caius Triarius, one of his lieutenants, and routed his army with great slaughter. At the time that Pompey commenced his campaign against the pirates, the consul Marcus Aquillius Glabrio was sent to supersede Luculles in his command; but he was perfectly incompetent to oppose Mithridates, who seemed likely with such an enemy to recover all the power of which Lucullus had deprived him. So in the year B. C. 66, while Glabrio was still in Bithynia, and Pompey in Asia Minor, Caius Manilius, a tribune of the people, brought forward a proposition, that, in addition to the command which Pompey already possessed, he should be invested with unlimited power in Bithynia, Pontus, and Armenia, for the purpose of conducting the war against Mithridates. The measure was strongly opposed by Catulus and by Hortensius, but it was supported by Cæsar, and by Cicero in the following speech, which is the first which he ever addressed to the people; and the proposition was carried.

71

I. ALTHOUGH, O Romans, your numerous assembly has always seemed to me the most agreeable body that anyone can address, and this place, which is most honorable to plead in, has also seemed always the most distinguished place for delivering an oration in, still I have been prevented from trying this road to glory, which has at all times been entirely open to every virtuous man, not indeed by my own will, but by the system of live which I have adopted from my earliest years. For as hitherto I have not dared, on account of my youth, to intrude upon the authority of this place, and as I considered that no arguments ought to be brought to this place except such as were the fruit of great ability, and worked up with the greatest industry, I have thought it fit to devote all my time to the necessities of my friends. And accordingly, this place has never been unoccupied by men who were defending your cause, and my industry, which has been virtuously and honestly employed about the dangers of private individuals, has received its most honorable reward in your approbation. For when, on account of the adjournment of the comitia, I was three times elected the first prætor by all the centuries, I easily perceived, O Romans, what your opinion of me was, and what conduct you enjoined, to others. Now, when there is that authority in me which you, by conferring honors on me, have chosen that there should be, and all that facility in pleading which almost daily practise in speaking can give a vigilant man who has habituated himself to the forum, at all events, if I have any authority, I will employ it before those who have given it to me; and if I can accomplish anything by speaking, I will display it to those men above all others, who have thought fit, by their decision, to confer honors on that qualification. And, above all things, I see that I have reason to rejoice on this account, that, since I am speaking in this place, to which I am so entirely unaccustomed, I have a cause to advocate in which eloquence can hardly fail anyone; for I have to speak of the eminent and extraordinary virtue of Cnæus Pompey; and it is harder for me to find out how to end a discourse on such a subject, than how to begin one. So that what I have to seek for is not so much a variety of arguments, as moderation in employing them.

II. And, that my oration may take its origin from the same

source from which all this cause is to be maintained; an important war, and one perilous to your revenues and to your allies, is being waged against you by two most powerful kings, Mithridates and Tigranes. One of these having been left to himself, and the other having been attacked, thinks that an opportunity offers itself to him to occupy all Asia. Letters are brought from Asia every day to Roman knights, most honorable men, who have great property at stake, which is all employed in the collection of your revenues; and they, in consequence of the intimate connection which I have with their order, have come to me and entrusted me with the task of pleading the cause of the republic, and warding off danger from their private fortunes. They say that many of the villages of Bithynia, which is at present a province belonging to you, have been burnt; that the kingdom of Ariobarzanes, which borders on those districts from which you derive a revenue, is wholly in the power of the enemy; that Lucullus, after having performed great exploits, is departing from that war; that it is not enough that whoever succeeds him should be prepared for the conduct of so important a war; that one general is demanded and required by all men, both allies and citizens, for that war; that he alone is feared by the enemy, and that no one else is.

You see what the case is; now consider what you ought to do. It seems to me that I ought to speak in the first place of the sort of war that exists; in the second place, of its importance; and lastly, of the selection of a general. The kind of war is such as ought above all others to excite and inflame your minds to a determination to persevere in it. It is a war in which the glory of the Roman people is at stake; that glory which has been handed down to you from your ancestors, great indeed in everything, but most especially in military affairs. The safety of our friends and allies is at stake, in behalf of which your ancestors have waged many most important wars. The most certain and the largest revenues of the Roman people are at stake; and if they be lost, you will be at a loss for the luxuries of peace, and the sinews of war. The property of many citizens is at stake, which you ought greatly to regard, both for your own sake, and for that of the republic.

III. And since you have at all times been covetous of glory

and greedy of praise beyond all other nations, you have to wipe out that stain, received in the former Mithridatic War, which has now fixed itself deeply and eaten its way into the Roman name, the stain arising from the fact that he, who in one day marked down by one order, and one single letter, all the Roman citizens in all Asia, scattered as they were over so many cities, for slaughter and butchery, has not only never yet suffered any chastisement worthy of his wickedness, but now, twenty-three years after that time, is still a king, and a king in such a way that he is not content to hide himself in Pontus, or in the recesses of Cappadocia, but he seeks to emerge from his hereditary kingdom, and to range among your revenues, in the broad light of Asia. Indeed up to this time your generals have been contending with the king so as to carry off tokens of victory rather than actual victory. Lucius Sylla has triumphed, Lucius Murena has triumphed over Mithridates, two most gallant men: and most consummate generals; but yet they have triumphed in such a way that he, though routed and defeated, was still king. Not but what praise is to be given to those generals for what they did. Pardon must be conceded to them for what they left undone; because the republic recalled Sylla from that war into Italy, and Sylla recalled Murena.

IV. But Mithridates employed all the time, which he had left to him, not in forgetting the old war, but in preparing for a new one; and, after he had built and equipped very large fleets, and had got together mighty armies from every nation he could, and had pretended to be preparing war against the tribes of the Bosphorus, his neighbors, sent ambassadors and letters as far as Spain to those chiefs with whom we were at war at the time, in order that, as you would by that means have war waged against you in the two parts of the world the furthest separated and most remote of all from one another, by two separate enemies warring against you with one uniform plan, you, hampered by the double enmity, might find that you were fighting for the empire itself. However, the danger on one side, the danger from Sertorius and from Spain, which had much the most solid foundation and the most formidable strength, was warded off by the divine wisdom and extraordinary valor of Cnæus Pompeius. And on the other side of the empire, affairs were so managed by Lucius Lucullus, that most illustrious of men, that the beginning of all those achievements in those countries, great and eminent as they were, deserve to be attributed not to his good fortune but to his valor; but the latter events which have taken place lately, ought to be imputed not to his fault, but to his ill-fortune. However, of Lucullus I will speak hereafter, and I will speak, O Romans, in such a manner, that his true glory shall not appear to be at all disparaged by my pleading, nor, on the other hand, shall any undeserved credit seem to be given to him. At present, when we are speaking of the dignity and glory of your empire, since that is the beginning of my oration, consider what feelings you think you ought to entertain.

V. Your ancestors have often waged war on account of their merchants and seafaring men having been injuriously treated. What ought to be your feelings when so many thousand Roman citizens have been put to death by one order and at one time? Because their ambassadors had been spoken to with insolence, your ancestors determined that Corinth, the light of all Greece, should be destroyed. Will you allow that king to remain unpunished, who has murdered a lieutenant of the Roman people of consular rank, having tortured him with chains and scourging, and every sort of punishment? They would not allow the freedom of Roman citizens to be diminished; will you be indifferent to their lives being taken? They avenged the privileges of our embassy when they were violated by a word; will you abandon an ambassador who has been put to death with every sort of cruelty? Take care lest, as it was a most glorious thing for them, to leave you such wide renown and such a powerful empire, it should be a most discreditable thing for you, not to be able to defend and preserve that which you have received. What more shall I say? Shall I say, that the safety of our allies is involved in the greatest hazard and danger? King Ariobarzanes has been driven from his kingdom, an ally and friend of the Roman people; two kings are threatening all Asia, who are not only most hostile to you, but also to your friends and allies. And every city throughout all Asia, and throughout all Greece, is compelled by the magnitude of the danger to put its whole trust in the expectation of your assistance. They do not dare to beg of you any particular general, especially since you have sent them another, nor do they think that they can do this without extreme danger. They see and feel this, the same thing which you too see and feel,—that there is one man in whom all qualities are in the highest perfection, and that he is near, (which circumstance makes it seem harder to be deprived of him,) by whose mere arrival and name, although it was a maritime war for which he came, they are nevertheless aware that the attacks of the enemy were retarded and repressed. They then, since they cannot speak freely, silently entreat you to think them (as you have thought your allies in the other provinces) worthy of having their safety recommended to such a man; and to think them worthy even more than others, because we often send men with absolute authority into such a province as theirs, of such character, that, even if they protect them from the enemy, still their arrival among the cities of the allies is not very different from an invasion of the enemy. They used to hear of him before, now they see him among them; a man of such moderation, such mildness, such humanity, that those seem to be the happiest people among whom he remains for the longest time.

VI. Wherefore, if on account of their allies, though they themselves had not been roused by any injuries, your ancestors waged war against Antiochus, against Philip, against the Ætolians, and against the Carthaginians; with how much earnestness ought you, when you yourselves have been provoked by injurious treatment, to defend the safety of the allies, and at the same time, the dignity of your empire? especially when your greatest revenues are at stake. For the revenues of the other provinces, O Romans, are such that we can scarcely derive enough from them for the protection of the provinces themselves. But Asia is so rich and so productive, that in the fertility of its soil, and in the variety of its fruits, and in the vastness of its pasture lands, and in the multitude of all those things which are matters of exportation, it is greatly superior to all other countries. Therefore, O Romans, this province, if you have any regard for what tends to your advantage in time of war, and to your dignity in time of peace, must be defended by you, not only from all calamity, but from all fear of calamity. For in other matters when calamity comes on one, then damage is sustained; but in the case of revenues, not only the arrival of evil, but the bare dread of it, brings disaster. For when the troops of the enemy are not far off, even though no actual irruption takes place, still the flocks are abandoned, agriculture is relinquished, the sailing of merchants is at an end. And accordingly, neither from harbor dues, nor from tenths, nor from the tax on pasture lands, can any revenue be maintained. And therefore it often happens that the produce of an entire year is lost by one rumor of danger, and by one alarm of war. What do you think ought to be the feelings of those who pay us tribute, or of those who get it in, and exact it, when two kings with very numerous armies are all but on the spot? when one inroad of cavalry may in a very short time carry off the revenue of a whole year? when the publicans think that they retain the large households of slaves, which they have in the saltworks, in the fields, in the harbors, and custom-houses, at the greatest risk? Do you think that you can enjoy these advantages unless you preserve those men who are productive to you, free not only, as I said before, from calamity, but even from the dread of calamity?

VII. And even this must not be neglected by you, which I had proposed to myself as the last thing to be mentioned, when I was to speak of the kind of war, for it concerns the property of many Roman citizens; whom you, as becomes your wisdom, O Romans, must regard with the most careful solicitude. The publicans,[1] most honorable and accomplished men, have taken all their resources and all their wealth into that province; and their property and fortunes ought, by themselves, to be an object of your especial care. In truth, if we have always considered the revenues as the sinews of the republic, certainly we shall be right if we call that order of men which collects them, the prop and support of all the other orders. In the next place clever and industrious men, of all the other orders of the state, are some of them actually trading themselves in Asia, and you ought to show a regard for their interests in their absence; and others of them have large sums invested in that province. It will, therefore, become your humanity to protect a large number of those citizens from misfortune; it will be-

---

[1] It has been said before that the publicans were taken almost exclusively from the equestrian order.

come your wisdom to perceive that the misfortune of many
citizens cannot be separated from the misfortune of the republic. In truth, firstly, it is of but little consequence for you
afterwards to recover for the publicans revenues which have
been once lost; for the same men have not afterwards the same
power of contracting for them, and others have not the inclination, through fear. In the next place that which the same Asia,
and that same Mithridates taught us, at the beginning of the
Asiatic war, that, at all events, we, having learnt by disaster,
ought to keep in our recollection. For we know that then, when
many had lost large fortunes in Asia, all credit failed at Rome,
from payments being hindered. For it is not possible for many
men to lose their property and fortunes in one city, without
drawing many along with them into the same vortex of disaster. But do you now preserve the republic from this misfortune; and believe me, (you yourselves see that it is the
case,) this credit, and this state of the money-market which
exists at Rome and in the forum, is bound up with, and is
inseparable from, those fortunes which are invested in Asia.
Those fortunes cannot fall without credit here being under-
mined by the same blow, and perishing along with them. Consider, then, whether you ought to hesitate to apply yourselves
with all zeal to that war, in which the glory of your name, the
safety of your allies, your greatest revenues, and the fortunes
of numbers of your citizens, will be protected at the same
time as the republic.

VIII. Since I have spoken of the description of war, I will
now say a few words about its magnitude. For this may be
said of it,—that it is a kind of war so necessary, that it must
absolutely be waged, and yet not one of such magnitude as
to be formidable. And in this we must take the greatest care
that those things do not appear to you contemptible which
require to be most diligently guarded against. And that all
men may understand that I give Lucius Lucullus all the praise
that is due to a gallant man, and most wise[2] man, and to a

[2] The Latin is, "forti *viro*, et sapientissimo *homini*," and this opposition
of *vir* and *homo* is not uncommon in Cicero's orations. "*Homo* is nearly
synonymous with *vir*, but with this distinction, that *homo* is used of a
man considered as an intellectual and moral being,—namely, where personal qualities are to be denoted; whereas *vir* signifies a man in his relations to the state."—Biddle, Lat. Dict. v. *Homo*.

most consummate general, I say that when he first arrived in Asia, the forces of Mithridates were most numerous, well appointed, and provided with every requisite; and that the finest city in Asia, and the one, too, that was most friendly to us, the city of Cyzicus, was besieged by the king in person, with an enormous army, and that the siege had been pressed most vigorously, when Lucius Lucullus, by his valor, and perseverance, and wisdom, relieved it from the most extreme danger. I say that he also, when general, defeated and destroyed that great and well-appointed fleet, which the chiefs of Sertorius's party were leading against Italy with furious zeal; I say besides, that by him numerous armies of the enemy were destroyed in several battles, and that Pontus was opened to our legions, which before his time had been closed against the Roman people on every side; and that Sinope and Amisus, towns in which the king had palaces, adorned and furnished with every kind of magnificence, and many other cities of Pontus and Cappadocia, were taken by his mere approach and arrival near them; that the king himself was stripped of the kingdom possessed by his father and his grandfather, and forced to betake himself as a suppliant to other kings and other nations; and that all these great deeds were achieved without any injury to the allies of the Roman people, or any diminution of its revenues. I think that this is praise enough;—such praise that you must see, O Romans, that Lucius Lucullus has not been praised as much from this rostrum by anyone of these men who are objecting to this law and arguing against our cause.

IX. Perhaps now it will be asked, how, when all this has been already done, there can be any great war left behind. I will explain this, O Romans; for this does not seem an unreasonable question. At first Mithridates fled from his kingdom, as Medea is formerly said to have fled from the same region of Pontus; for they say that she, in her flight, strewed about the limbs of her brother in those places along which her father was likely to pursue her, in order that the collection of them, dispersed as they were, and the grief which would afflict his father, might delay the rapidity of his pursuit. Mithridates, flying in the same manner, left in Pontus the whole of the vast quantity of gold and silver, and of beautiful things which he had inherited from his ancestors, and which he himself had collected and brought into his own kingdom, having obtained them by plunder in the former war from all Asia. While our men were diligently occupied in collecting all this, the king himself escaped out of their hands. And so grief retarded the father of Medea in his pursuit, but delight delayed our men. In this alarm and flight of his, Tigranes, the king of Armenia, received him, encouraged him while despairing of his fortunes, gave him new spirit in his depression, and recruited with new strength his powerless condition. And after Lucius Lucullus arrived in his kingdom, very many tribes were excited to hostilities against our general. For those nations which the Roman people never had thought either of attacking in war or tampering with, had been inspired with fear. There was, besides, a general opinion which had taken deep root, and had spread over all the barbarian tribes in those districts, that our army had been led into those countries with the object of plundering a very wealthy and most religiously worshiped temple. And so, many powerful nations were roused against us by a fresh dread and alarm. But our army, although it had taken a city of Tigranes's kingdom, and had fought some successful battles, still was out of spirits at its immense distance from Rome, and its separation from its friends. At present I will not say more; for the result of these feelings of theirs was, that they were more anxious for a speedy return home than for any further advance into the enemies' country. But Mithridates had by this time strengthened his army by reinforcements of those men belonging to his own dominions who had assembled together, and by large promiscuous forces belonging to many other kings and tribes. And we see that this is almost invariably the case, that kings when in misfortune easily induce many to pity and assist them, especially such as are either kings themselves, or who live under kingly power, because to them the name of king appears something great and sacred. And accordingly he, when conquered, was able to accomplish what, when he was in the full enjoyment of his powers, he never dared even to wish for. For when he had returned to his kingdom, he was not content (though that had happened to him beyond all his hopes) with again setting his foot on that land after he had been expelled from it; but he even volunteered an attack on your army, flushed as it was with glory and victory. Allow me, in this place, O Romans, (just as poets do who write of Roman affairs,) to pass over our disaster, which was so great that it came to Lucius Lucullus's ears, not by means of a messenger despatched from the scene of action, but through the report of common conversation. At the very time of this misfortune,—of this most terrible disaster in the whole war, Lucius Lucullus, who might have been able, to a great extent, to remedy the calamity, being compelled by your orders, because you thought, according to the old principle of your ancestors, that limits ought to be put to length of command, discharged a part of his soldiers who had served their appointed time, and delivered over part to Glabrio. I pass over many things designedly; but you yourselves can easily conjecture how important you ought to consider that war which most powerful kings are uniting in,—which disturbed nations are renewing,—which nations, whose strength is unimpaired, are undertaking, and which a new general of yours has to encounter after a veteran army has been defeated.

X. I appear to have said enough to make you see why this war is in its very nature unavoidable, in its magnitude dangerous. It remains for me to speak of the general who ought to be selected for that war, and appointed to the management of such important affairs.

I wish, O Romans, that you had such an abundance of brave and honest men, that it was a difficult subject for your deliberations, whom you thought most desirable to be appointed to the conduct of such important affairs, and so vast a war. But now, when there is Cnæus Pompeius alone, who has exceeded in valor, not only the glory of these men who are now alive, but even all recollections of antiquity, what is there that, in this case, can raise a doubt in the mind of anyone? For I think that these four qualities are indispensable in a great general,— knowledge of military affairs, valor, authority and good fortune. Who, then, ever was, or ought to have been, better acquainted with military affairs than this man? who, the moment that he left school and finished his education as a boy, at a time when there was a most important war going on, and most active enemies were banded against us, went to his father's army and to the discipline of the camp; who, when scarcely out of his boyhood, became a soldier of a consummate general,—when entering on manhood, became himself the general of a mighty army; who has been more frequently engaged with the enemy, than anyone else has ever disputed with an adversary; who has himself, as general, conducted more wars than other men have read of; who has subdued more provinces than other men have wished for; whose youth was trained to the knowledge of military affairs, not by the precepts of others, but by commanding himself,—not by the disasters of war, but by victories,—not by campaigns, but by triumphs. In short, what description of war can there be in which the fortune of the republic has not given him practise? Civil war, African war, Transalpine war, Spanish war, promiscuous war of the most warlike cities and nations, servile war, naval war, every variety and diversity of wars and of enemies, has not only been encountered by this one man, but encountered victoriously; and these exploits show plainly that there is no circumstance in military practise which can elude the knowledge of this man.

XI. But now, what language can be found equal to the valor of Cnæus Pompeius? What statement can anyone make which shall be either worthy of him, or new to you, or unknown to anyone? For those are not the only virtues of a general which are usually thought so,—namely, industry in business, fortitude amid dangers, energy in acting, rapidity in executing, wisdom in foreseeing; which all exist in as great perfection in that one man as in all the other generals put together whom we have either seen or heard of. Italy is my witness, which that illustrious conqueror himself, Lucius Sylla, confessed had been delivered by this man's valor and ready assistance. Sicily is my witness, which he released when it was surrounded on all sides by many dangers, not by the dread of his power, but by the promptitude of his wisdom. Africa is my witness, which, having been overwhelmed by numerous armies of enemies, overflowed with the blood of those same enemies. Gaul is my witness, through which a road into Spain was laid open to our legions by the destruction of the Gauls. Spain is my witness, which has repeatedly seen our many enemies there defeated and subdued by this man. Again and again, Italy is my witness, which, when it was weighed down by the disgraceful and perilous servile war, entreated aid from this man, though he was at a distance; and that war, having dwindled down and wasted away at the expectation of Pompeius, was destroyed and buried by his arrival. But now, also every coast, all foreign nations and countries, all seas, both in their open waters and in every bay, and creek, and harbor, are my witnesses. For during these last years, what place in any part of the sea had so strong a garrison as to be safe from him? what place was so much hidden as to escape his notice? Who ever put to sea without being aware that he was committing himself to the hazard of death or slavery, either from storms or from the sea being crowded with pirates? Who would ever have supposed that a war of such extent, so mean, so old a war, a war so extensive in its theatre and so widely scattered, could have been terminated by all our generals put together in one year, or by one general in all the years of his life? In all these later years what province have you had free from pirates? what revenue has been safe? what ally have you been able to protect? to whom have your fleets been any defense? How many islands do you suppose have been deserted? how many cities of the allies do you think have been either abandoned out of fear of the pirates, or have been taken by them?

XII. But why do I speak of distant events? It was—it was, indeed, formerly—a characteristic of the Roman people to carry on its wars at a distance from home, and to defend by the bulwarks of its power not its own homes, but the fortunes of its allies. Need I say, that the sea has during all these latter years been closed against your allies, when even our own armies never ventured to cross over from Brundusium, except in the depth of winter? Need I complain that men who were coming to you from foreign nations were taken prisoners, when even the ambassadors of the Roman people were forced to be ransomed? Need I say, that the sea was not safe for merchants, when twelve axes[3] came into the power of the pirates? Need I mention, how Cnidus, and Colophon, and Samos, most noble cities, and others too in countless numbers, were taken by them, when you know that your own harbors, and those har-

---

[3] The Scholiast says that a consul named Milienus (whose name, however, does not appear in the Fasti) was taken prisoner by the pirates, and sold with his ensigns of office. The axes mean his fasces.

bors too from which you derive, as it were, your very life and
breath, were in the power of the pirates? Are you ignorant
that the harbor of Caieta, that illustrious harbor, when full of
ships, was plundered by the pirates under the very eyes of the
prætor? and that from Misenum, the children of the very man
who had before that waged war against the pirates in that
place, were carried off by the pirates? For why should I complain of the disaster of Ostia, and of that stain and blot on the
republic, when almost under your very eyes, that fleet which
was under the command of a Roman consul was taken and
destroyed by the pirates? O ye immortal gods! could the incredible and godlike virtue of one man in so short a time bring
so much light to the republic, that you who had lately been
used to see a fleet of the enemy before the mouth of the Tiber,
should now hear that there is not one ship belonging to the
pirates on this side of the Atlantic? And although you have
seen with what rapidity these things were done, still that rapidity ought not to be passed over by me in speaking of them.
—For who ever, even if he were only going for the purpose
of transacting business or making profits, contrived in so short
a time to visit so many places, and to perform such long journeys, with as great celerity as Cnæus Pompeius has performed
his voyage, bearing with him the terrors of war as our general?
He, when the weather could hardly be called open for sailing, went to Sicily, explored the coasts of Africa; from thence
he came with his fleet to Sardinia, and these three great grana-
ries of the republic he fortified with powerful garrisons and
fleets; when, leaving Sardinia, he came to Italy, having secured the two Spains and Cisalpine Gaul with garrisons and
ships. Having sent vessels also to the coast of Illyricum, and
to every part of Achaia and Greece, he also adorned the two
seas of Italy with very large fleets, and very sufficient garrisons; and he himself going in person, added all Cilicia to the
dominions of the Roman people, on the forty-ninth day after
he set out from Brundusium. All the pirates who were anywhere to be found, were either taken prisoners and put to
death, or else had surrendered themselves voluntarily to the
power and authority of this one man. Also, when the Cretans
had sent ambassadors to implore his mercy even into Pam-
phylia to him, he did not deny them hopes of being allowed

to surrender, and he exacted hostages from them. And thus Cnæus Pompeius at the end of winter prepared, at the beginning of spring undertook, and by the middle of summer terminated, this most important war, which had lasted so long, which was scattered in such distant and such various places, and by which every nation and country was incessantly distressed.

XIII. This is the godlike and incredible virtue of that general. What more shall I say? How many and how great are his other exploits which I began to mention a short time back; for we are not only to seek for skill in war in a consummate and perfect general, but there are many other eminent qualities which are the satellites and companions of this virtue. And first of all, how great should be the incorruptibility of generals! How great should be their moderation in everything! how perfect their good faith! How universal should be their affability! how brilliant their genius! how tender their humanity! And let us briefly consider to what extent these qualities exist in Cnæus Pompeius. For they are all of the highest importance, O Romans, but yet they are to be seen and ascertained more by comparison with the conduct of others than by any display which they make of themselves. For how can we rank a man among generals of any class at all, if centurionships[4] are sold, and have been constantly sold in his army? What great or honorable thoughts can we suppose that that man cherishes concerning the republic, who has either distributed the money which was taken from the treasury for the conduct of the war among the magistrates, out of ambition[5] to keep his province, or, out of avarice, has left it behind him at Rome, invested for his own advantage? Your murmurs show, O Romans, that you recognize, in my description, men who have done these things. But I name no one, so that no one can be angry with me, without making confession beforehand of his own malpractices. But who is there who is ig-

[4] The Scholiast says that Cicero is here hinting at Glabrio the consul, or at the younger Marius.

[5] Lucullus is supposed to be meant here, as it is said that he had employed large sums in soliciting the votes of influential men, so as to be left in command of the province of Asia, in which he had amassed enormous riches.

norant what terrible distresses our armies suffer wherever they
go, through this covetousness of our generals? Recollect the
marches which, during these latter years, our generals have
made in Italy, through the lands and towns of the Roman citizens; then you will more easily imagine what is the course
pursued among foreign nations. Do you think that of late years
more cities of the enemy have been destroyed by the arms of
your soldiers, or more cities of your own allies by their winter
campaigns? For that general who does not restrain himself
can never restrain his army; nor can he be strict in judging
others who is unwilling for others to be strict in judging him.
Do we wonder now that this man should be so far superior
to all others, when his legions arrived in Asia in such order
that not only no man's hand in so numerous an army, but not
even any man's footstep was said to have done the least injury to any peaceful inhabitant? But now we have daily rumors
—ay, and letters too—brought to Rome about the way in which
the soldiers are behaving in their winter quarters; not only is
no one compelled to spend money on the entertainment of the
troops, but he is not permitted to do so, even if he wish. For
our ancestors thought fit that the houses of our allies and
friends should be a shelter to our soldiers from the winter,
not a theatre for the exercise of their avarice.

XIV. Come now, consider also what moderation he has displayed in other matters also. How was it, do you suppose, that
he was able to display that excessive rapidity, and to perform
that incredible voyage? For it was no unexampled number of
rowers, no hitherto unknown skill in navigation, no new winds,
which bore him so swiftly to the most distant lands; but those
circumstances which are wont to delay other men did not delay him. No avarice turned him aside from his intended route
in pursuit of some plunder or other; no lust led him away in
pursuit of pleasure; no luxury allured him to seek its delights;
the illustrious reputation of no city tempted him to make its
acquaintance; even labor did not turn him aside to seek rest.
Lastly, as for the statues, and pictures, and other embellish-
ments of Greek cities, which other men think worth carrying
away, he did not think them worthy even of a visit from him.
And, therefore, every one in those countries looks upon Cnæus
Pompeius as some one descended from heaven, not as some

one sent out from this city. Now they begin to believe that
there really were formerly Romans of the same moderation;
which hitherto has seemed to foreign nations a thing incredible, a false and ridiculous tradition. Now the splendor of your
dominion is really brilliant in the eyes of those nations. Now
they understand that it was not without reason that, when we
had magistrates of the same moderation, their ancestors preferred being subject to the Roman people to being themselves
lords of other nations. But now the access of all private individuals to him is so easy, their complaints of the injuries received from others are so little checked, that he who in dignity
is superior to the noblest men, in affability seems to be on a
par with the meanest. How great his wisdom is, how great his
authority and fluency in speaking,—and that too is a quality
in which the dignity of a general is greatly concerned,—you, O
Romans, have often experienced yourselves in this very place.
But how great do you think his good faith must have been
towards your allies, when the enemies of all nations have
placed implicit confidence in it? His humanity is such that it
is difficult to say, whether the enemy feared his valor more
when fighting against him, or loved his mildness more when
they had been conquered by him. And will anyone doubt, that
this important war ought to be entrusted to him, who seems
to have been born by some especial design and favor of the
gods for the express purpose of finishing all the wars which
have existed in their own recollection?

XV. And since authority has great weight in conducting
wars, and in discharging the duties of military command, it
certainly is not doubtful to anyone that in that point this same
general is especially preeminent. And who is ignorant that it
is of great importance in the conduct of wars, what opinion
the enemy, and what opinion the allies have of your generals,
when we know that men are not less influenced in such serious
affairs, to despise, or fear, or hate, or love a man by common
opinion and common report, than by sure grounds and principles? What name, then, in the whole world has ever been
more illustrious than his? whose achievements have ever been
equal to his? And, what gives authority in the highest degree,
concerning whom have you ever passed such numerous and
such honorable resolutions? Do you believe that there is any-

where in the whole world any place so desert that the renown
of that day has not reached it, when the whole Roman people, the forum being crowded, and all the adjacent temples
from which this place can be seen being completely filled,—
the whole Roman people, I say, demanded Cnæus Pompeius
alone as their general in the war in which the common interests
of all nations were at stake? Therefore, not to say more on the
subject, nor to confirm what I say by instances of others as to
the influence which authority has in war, all our instances of
splendid exploits in war must be taken from this same Cnæus
Pompeius. The very day that he was appointed by you commander-in-chief of the maritime war, in a moment such a
cheapness of provisions ensued, (though previously there had
been a great scarcity of corn, and the price had been exceedingly high,) owing to the hope conceived of one single
man, and his high reputation, as could scarcely have been
produced by a most productive harvest after a long period of peace. Now, too, after the disaster which befell us in
Pontus, from the result of that battle, of which, sorely against
my will, I just now reminded you, when our allies were in a
state of alarm, when the power and spirits of our enemies had
risen, and the province was in a very insufficient state of defense, you would have entirely lost Asia, O Romans, if the
fortune of the Roman people had not, by some divine interposition, brought Cnæus Pompeius at that particular moment
into those regions. His arrival both checked Mithridates, elated
with his unusual victory, and delayed Tigranes, who was
threatening Asia with a formidable army. And can anyone
doubt what he will accomplish by his valor, when he did so
much by his authority and reputation? or how easily he will
preserve our allies and our revenues by his power and his
army, when he defended them by the mere terror of his name?

XVI. Come, now; what a great proof does this circumstance
afford us of the influence of the same man on the enemies of
the Roman people, that all of them, living in countries so far
distant from us and from each other, surrendered themselves
to him alone in so short a time? that the ambassadors of the
Cretans, though there was at the time a general [6] and an army

[6] Metellus, afterwards called Creticus, from his victory over the Cretans.

of ours in their island, came almost to the end of the world
to Cnæus Pompeius, and said, all the cities of the Cretans were
willing to surrender themselves to him? What did Mithridates
himself do? Did he not send an ambassador into Spain to the
same Cnæus Pompeius? a man whom Pompeius has always
considered an ambassador, but who that party, to whom it has
always been a source of annoyance that he was sent to him
particularly, have contended was sent as a spy rather than
as an ambassador. You can now, then, O Romans, form an
accurate judgment how much weight you must suppose that
this authority of his—now, too, that it has been further in-
creased by many subsequent exploits, and by many com-
mendatory resolutions of your own—will have with those kings
and among foreign nations.

It remains for me timidly and briefly to speak of his good
fortune, a quality which no man ought to boast of in his own
case, but which we may remember and commemorate as hap-
pening to another, just as a man may extol the power of the
gods. For my judgment is this, that very often commands have
been conferred upon, and armies have been entrusted to
Maximus, to Marcellus, to Scipio, to Marius, and to other great
generals, not only on account of their valor, but also on account
of their good fortune. For there has been, in truth, in the case
of some most illustrious men, good fortune added as some
contribution of the gods to their honor and glory, and as a
means of performing mighty achievements. But concerning
the good fortune of this man of whom we are now speaking, I
will use so much moderation as not to say that good fortune
was actually placed in his power, but I will so speak as to
appear to remember what in past, to have good hope of what
is to come; so that my speech may, on the one hand, not appear to the immortal gods to be arrogant, nor, on the other
hand, to be ungrateful. Accordingly, I do not intend to mention, O Romans, what great exploits he has achieved both at
home and in war, by land and by sea, and with what invariable
felicity he has achieved them; how, not only the citizens have
always consented to his wishes,—the allies complied with them,
—the enemy obeyed them, but how even the winds and
weather have seconded them. I will only say this, most briefly,

—that no one has ever been so impudent as to dare in silence
to wish for so many and such great favors as the immortal
gods have showered upon Cnæus Pompeius. And that this
favor may continue his, and be perpetual, you, O Romans,
ought to wish and pray (as, indeed, you do), both for the
sake of the common safety and prosperity, and for the sake
of the man himself.

Wherefore, as the war is at the same time so necessary that
it cannot be neglected, so important that it must be conducted
with the greatest care; and since you have it in your power
to appoint a general to conduct it, in whom there is the most
perfect knowledge of war, the most extraordinary valor, the
most splendid personal influence, and the most eminent good
fortune, can you hesitate, O Romans, to apply this wonderful
advantage which is offered you and given you by the immortal
gods, to the preservation and increase of the power of the republic?

XVII. But, if Cnæus Pompeius were a private individual
at Rome at this present time, still he would be the man who
ought to be selected and sent out to so great a war. But now,
when to all the other exceeding advantages of the appointment, this opportunity is also added,—that he is in those very
countries already,—that he has an army with him,—that there
is another army there which can at once be made over to him
by those who are in command of it,—why do we delay? or
why do we not, under the guidance of the immortal gods
themselves, commit this royal war also to him to whom all the
other wars in those parts have been already entrusted to the
greatest advantage, to the very safety of the republic?

But to be sure, that most illustrious man, Quintus Catulus,
a man most honestly attached to the republic, and loaded with
your kindness in a way most honorable to him; and also
Quintus Hortensius, a man endowed with the highest qualities of honor, and fortune, and virtue, and genius, disagree to
this proposal. And I admit that their authority has in many
instances had the greatest weight with you, and that it ought
to have the greatest weight; but in this cause, although you
are aware that the opinions of many very brave and illustrious
men are unfavorable to us, still it is possible for us, disregard-

ing those authorities, to arrive at the truth by the circumstances of the case and by reason. And so much the more easily, because those very men admit that everything which has been said by me up to this time is true,—that the war is necessary, that it is an important war, and that all the requisite qualifications are in the highest perfection in Cnæus Pompeius. What, then, does Hortensius say? "That if the whole power must be given to one man, Pompeius alone is most worthy to have it; but that, nevertheless, the power ought not to be entrusted to one individual." That argument, however, has now become obsolete, having been refuted much more by facts than by words. For you, also, Quintus Hortensius, said many things with great force and fluency (as might be expected from your exceeding ability, and eminent facility as an orator) in the senate against that brave man, Aulus Gabinius, when he had brought forward the law about appointing one commander-in-chief against the pirates; and also from this place where I now stand, you made a long speech against that law. What then? By the immortal gods, if your authority had had greater weight with the Roman people than the safety and real interests of the Roman people itself, should we have been this day in possession of our present glory, and of the empire of the whole earth? Did this, then, appear to you to be dominion, when it was a common thing for the ambassadors, and prætors, and questors of the Roman people to be taken prisoners? when we were cut off from all supplies, both public and private, from all our provinces? when all the seas were so closed against us, that we could neither visit any private estate of our own, nor any public domain beyond the sea?

XVIII. What city ever was there before this time,—I speak not of the city of the Athenians, which is said formerly to have had a sufficiently extensive naval dominion; nor of that of the Carthaginians, who had great power with their fleet and maritime resources; nor of those of the Rhodians, whose naval discipline and naval renown has lasted even to our recollection,— but was there ever any city before this time so insignificant, if it was only a small island, as not to be able by its own power to defend its harbors, and its lands, and some part of its country and maritime coast? But, forsooth, for many years before the Gabinian law was passed, the Roman people, whose name, till within our own memory, remained invincible in naval battles, was deprived not only of a great, aye, of much the greatest part of its usefulness, but also of its dignity and dominion. We, whose ancestors conquered with our fleets Antiochus the king, and Perses, and in every naval engagement defeated the Carthaginians, the best practised and best equipped of all men in maritime affairs; we could now in no place prove ourselves equal to the pirates. We, who formerly had not only all Italy in safety, but who were able by the authority of our empire to secure the safety of all our allies in the most distant countries, so that even the island of Delos, situated so far from us in the Ægean sea, at which all men were in the habit of touching with their merchandise and their freights, full of riches as it was, little and unwalled as it was, still was in no alarm; we, I say, were cut off, not only from our provinces, and from the sea-coast of Italy, and from our harbors, but even from the Appian road; and at this time, the magistrates of the Roman people were not ashamed to come up into this very rostrum where I am standing, which your ancestors had bequeathed to you adorned with nautical trophies, and the spoils of the enemy's fleet.

XIX. When you opposed that law, the Roman people, O Quintus Hortensius, thought that you, and the others who held the same opinion with you, delivered your sentiments in a bold and gallant spirit. But still, in a matter affecting the safety of the commonwealth, the Roman people preferred consulting its own feelings of indignation to your authority. Accordingly, one law, one man, and one year, delivered us not only from that misery and disgrace, but also caused us again at length to appear really to be the masters of all nations and countries by land and sea. And on this account the endeavor to detract, shall I say from Gabinius, or from Pompeius, or (what would be truer still) from both? appears to me particularly unworthy; being done in order that Aulus Gabinius might not be appointed lieutenant to Cnæus Pompeius, though he requested and begged it. Is he who begs for a particular lieutenant in so important a war unworthy to obtain any one whom he desires, when all other generals have taken whatever lieu-

tenants they chose, to assist them in pillaging the allies and
plundering the provinces? or ought he, by whose law safety
and dignity has been given to the Roman people, and to all
nations, to be prevented from sharing in the glory of that
commander and that army, which exists through his wisdom
and was appointed at his risk? Was it allowed to Caius Falcid-
ius, to Quintus Metellus, to Quintus Cælius Laterensis, and to
Cnæus Lentulus, all of whom I name to do them honor, to be
lieutenants the year after they had been tribunes of the people; and shall men be so exact in the case of Gabinius alone,
who, in this war which is carried on under the provisions of
the Gabinian law, and in the case of this commander and this
army which he himself appointed with your assistance, ought
to have the first right of any one? And concerning whose appointment as lieutenant I hope that the consuls will bring forward a motion in the senate; and if they hesitate, or are unwilling to do so, I undertake to bring it forward myself; nor,
O Romans, shall the hostile edict of any one deter me from
relying on you and defending your privileges and your kindness. Nor will I listen to anything except the interposition of
the tribunes; and as to that, those very men who threaten it,
will, I apprehend, consider over and over again what they
have a right to do. In my own opinion, O Romans, Aulus Gabinius alone has a right to be put by the side of Cnæus Pompeius as a partner of the glory of his exploits in the maritime
war; because the one, with the assistance of your votes, gave
to that man alone the task of undertaking that war, and the
other, when it was entrusted to him, undertook it and terminated it.

XX. It remains for me to speak of the authority and opinion
of Quintus Catulus; who, when he asked of you, if you thus
placed all your dependence on Cnæus Pompeius, in whom you
would have any hope, if anything were to happen to him, received a splendid reward for his own virtue and worth, when
you all, with almost one voice, cried out that you would, in
that case, put your trust in him. In truth he is such a man,
that no affair can be so important, or so difficult, that he cannot manage it by his wisdom, or defend it by his integrity, or
terminate it by his valor. But, in this case, I entirely differ

from him; because, the less certain and the less lasting the
life of man is, the more ought the republic to avail itself of
the life and valor of any admirable man, as long as the immortal gods allow it to do so. But let no innovation be established contrary to the precedents and principles of our ancestors.—I will not say, at this moment, that our ancestors in
peace always obeyed usage, but in war were always guided
by expediency, and always accommodated themselves with
new plans to the new emergencies of the times. I will not say
that two most important wars, the Punic war and the Spanish
war, were put an end to by one general; that two most powerful cities, which threatened the greatest danger to this empire
—Carthage and Numantia, were destroyed by the same Scipio.
I will not remind you that it was but lately determined by you
and by your ancestors, to rest all the hopes of the empire on
Caius Marius, so that the same man conducted the war against
Jugurtha, and against the Cimbri, and against the Teutones.
But recollect, in the case of Cnæus Pompeius himself, with
reference to whom Catulus objects to having any new regulations introduced, how many new laws have been made with
the most willing consent of Quintus Catulus.

XXI. For what can be so unprecedented as for a young man
in a private capacity to levy an army at a most critical time of
the republic? He levied one.—To command it? He did command it. To succeed gloriously in his undertaking? He did succeed. What can be so entirely contrary to usage, as for a very
young man, whose age[7] fell far short of that required for the
rank of a senator, to have a command and an army entrusted

[7] "As regards the age at which a person might become a senator, we
have no express statement for the time of the republic, although it appears to have been fixed by some custom or law, as the *ætas senatoria* is
frequently mentioned, especially during the latter period of the republic;
but we may by induction discover the probable age. We know that according to the law of the tribune Villius the age fixed for the questorship
was thirty-one. Now as it might happen that a questor was made a senator immediately after the expiration of his office, we may presume that
the earliest age at which a man could become a senator was thirty-two.
Augustus at last fixed the senatorial age at twenty-five, which appears to
have remained unaltered throughout the time of the empire."—Smith,
Dict. Ant. p. 851, v. *Senatus*.

to him? to have Sicily committed to his care, and Africa, and the war which was to be carried on there? He conducted himself in these provinces with singular blamelessness, dignity, and valor; he terminated a most serious war in Africa, and brought away, his army victorious. But what was ever so unheard-of as for a Roman knight to have a triumph? But even that circumstance the Roman people not only saw, but they thought that it deserved to be thronged to and honored with all possible zeal. What was ever so unusual, as, when there were two most gallant and most illustrious consuls, for a Roman knight to be sent as proconsul to a most important and formidable war? He was so sent—on which occasion, indeed, when some one in the senate said that a private individual ought not to be sent as proconsul, Lucius Philippus is reported to have answered, that if he had his will he should be sent not for one consul, but for both the consuls. Such great hope was entertained that the affairs of the republic would be prosperously managed by him, that the charge which properly belonged to the two consuls was entrusted to the valor of one young man. What was ever so extraordinary as for a man to be released from all laws by a formal resolution of the senate, and made consul before he was of an age to undertake any other magistracy according to the laws? What could be so incredible, as for a Roman knight to celebrate a second triumph in pursuance of a resolution of the senate? All the unusual circumstances which in the memory of man have ever happened to all other men put together, are not so many as these which we see have occurred in the history of this one man. And all these instances, numerous, important, and novel as they are, have all occurred in the case of the same man, taking their rise in the authority of Quintus Catulus himself, and by that of other most honorable men of the same rank.

XXII. Wherefore, let them take care that it is not considered a most unjust and intolerable thing, that their authority in matters affecting the dignity of Cnæus Pompeius should hitherto have been constantly approved of by you, but that your judgment and the authority of the Roman people in the case of the same man, should be disregarded by them. Especially when the Roman people can now, of its own right, defend its own

authority with respect to this man against all who dispute it,—
because, when those very same men objected, you chose him
alone of all men to appoint to the management of the war
against the pirates. If you did this at random, and had but little
regard for the interests of the republic, then they are right to
endeavor to guide your party spirit by their wisdom; but if you
at that time showed more foresight in the affairs of the state
than they did: if you, in spite of their resistance, by yourselves
conferred dignity on the empire, safety on the whole world;
then at last let those noble men confess that both they and all
other men must obey the authority of the universal Roman
people. And in this Asiatic and royal war, not only is that military valor required, which exists in a singular degree in Cnæus
Pompeius, but many other great virtues of mind are also demanded. It is difficult for your commander-in-chief in Asia,
Cilicia, Syria, and all the kingdoms of the inland nations, to behave in such a manner as to think of nothing else but the
enemy and glory. Then, even if there be some men moderate
and addicted to the practice of modesty and self-government,
still, such is the multitude of covetous and licentious men, that
no one thinks that these are such men. It is difficult to tell you,
O Romans, how great our unpopularity is among foreign nations, on account of the injurious and licentious behavior of
those whom we have of late years sent among them with military command. For, in all those countries which are now under
our dominion, what temple do you think has had a sufficient
holy reputation, what city has been sufficiently sacred, what
private house has been sufficiently closed and fortified, to be
safe from them? They seek out wealthy and splendid cities to
find pretense for making war on them for the sake of plundering them. I would willingly argue this with those most eminent
and illustrious men, Quintus Catulus and Quintus Hortensius,
for they know the distresses of the allies, they see their calamities, they hear their complaints. Do you think that you are
sending an army in defense of your allies against their enemies,
or rather, under pretense of the existence of enemies, against
your allies and friends themselves? What city is there in Asia
which can stand the ferocity and arrogance, I will not say of
the army, of a commander-in-chief, or of a lieutenant, but of
even the brigade of one single military tribune?

XXIII. So that even if you have any one who may appear able to cope in terms of advantage with the king's armies, still, unless he be also a man who can keep his hands, and eyes, and desires from the treasures of the allies, from their wives and children, from the ornaments of their temples and cities, from the gold and jewels of the king, he will not be a fit person to be sent to this Asiatic and royal war. Do you think that there is any city there peacefully inclined towards us which is rich? Do you think that there is any rich city there, which will appear to those men to be peacefully inclined towards us? The sea-coast, O Romans, begged for Cnæus Pompeius, not only on account of his renown for military achievements, but also because of the moderation of his disposition. For it saw that it was not the Roman people that was enriched every year by the public money, but only a few individuals, and that we did nothing more by the name of our fleets beyond sustaining losses, and so covering ourselves with additional disgrace. But now, are these men, who think that all these honors and offices are not to be conferred on one person, ignorant with what desires, with what hope of retrieving past losses, and on what conditions, these men go to the provinces? As if Cnæus Pompeius did not appear great in our eyes, not only on account of his own positive virtues, but by a comparison with the vices of others. And, therefore, do not you doubt to entrust everything to him alone, when he has been found to be the only man for many years whom the allies are glad to see come to their cities with an army. And if you think that our side of the argument, O Romans, should be confirmed by authorities, you have the authority of Publius Servilius, a man of the greatest skill in all wars, and in affairs of the greatest importance, who has performed such mighty achievements by land and sea, that, when you are deliberating about war, no one's authority ought to have more weight with you. You have the authority of Caius Curio, a man who has received great kindnesses from you, who has performed great exploits, who is endued with the highest abilities and wisdom; and of Cnæus Lentulus, in whom all of you know there is (as, indeed, there ought to be from the ample honors which you have heaped upon him) the most eminent wisdom, and the greatest dignity of character; and of Caius Cassius, a man of extraordinary integrity, and valor, and

virtue. Consider, therefore, whether, we do not seem by the authority of these men to give a sufficient answer to the speeches
of those men who differ from us.

XXIV. And as this is the case, O Caius Mamilius, in the first
place, I exceedingly praise and approve of that law of yours,
and of your purpose, and of your sentiments. And in the second
place, I exhort you, having the approbation of the Roman
people, to persevere in those sentiments, and not to fear the
violence or threats of any one. And, first of all, I think you have
the requisite courage and perseverance; and, secondly, when
we see such a multitude present displaying such zeal in our
cause as we now see displayed for the second time, in appointing the same man to the supreme command, how can we doubt
in the matter, or question our power of carrying our point? As
for me, all the zeal, and wisdom, and industry, and ability of
which I am possessed, all the influence which I have through
the kindness shown for me by the Roman people, and through
my power as prætor, as also, through my reputation for authority, good faith, and virtue, all of it I pledge to you and the
Roman people, and devote to the object of carrying this resolution. And I call all the gods to witness, and especially those
who preside over this place and temple, who see into the minds
of all those who apply themselves to affairs of state, that I am
not doing this at the request of any one, nor because I think
to conciliate the favor of Cnæus Pompeius by taking this side,
nor in order, through the greatness of any one else, to seek for
myself protection against dangers, or aids in the acquirement
of honors; because, as for dangers, we shall easily repel them,
as a man ought to do, protected by our own innocence; and as
for honors, we shall not gain them by the favor of any men, nor
by anything that happens in this place, but by the same labori-
ous course of life which I have hitherto adopted, if your favor-
able inclination assist me. Wherefore, whatever I have undertaken in this cause, O Romans, I assure you that I have undertaken wholly for the sake of the republic; and I am so far from
thinking that I have gained by it the favor of any influential
man, that I know, on the other hand, that I have brought on
myself many enmities, some secret, some undisguised, which I
never need have incurred, and which yet will not be mischiev-

ous to you. But I have considered that I, invested with my present honors, and loaded with so many kindnesses from you, ought to prefer your inclination, and the dignity of the republic, and the safety of our provinces and allies, to all considerations of my own private interest.

IN BEHALF OF MARCUS CLAUDIUS
MARCELLUS

THE ARGUMENT

Marcus Claudius Marcellus was descended from the most illustrious
families at Rome, and had been consul with Servius Sulpicius
Rufus; in which office he had given great offense to Cæsar by
making a motion in the senate to deprive him of his command;
and in the civil war he espoused the side of Pompeius, and had
been present at the battle of Pharsalia, after which he retired to
Lesbos. But after some time the whole senate interceded with
Cæsar to pardon him, and to allow him to return to his country.
And when he yielded to their entreaties, Cicero made the following speech, thanking Cæsar for his magnanimity; though he had,
as he says himself, (Ep. Fam. iv. 4,) determined to say nothing;
but he was afraid that if he continued silent Cæsar would inter-
pret it as a proof that he despaired of the republic.

Cæsar, though he saw the senate unanimous in their petition for
Marcellus, yet had the motion for his pardon put to the vote, and
called for the opinion of every individual senator on it. Cicero
appears at this time to have believed that Cæsar intended to
restore the republic, as he mentions in his letters, (Ep. Fam. xiii.
68.)

I. This day, O conscript fathers, has brought with it an end to
the long silence in which I have of late indulged; not out of
any fear, but partly from sorrow, partly from modesty; and at
the same time it has revived in me my ancient habit of saying
what my wishes and opinions are. For I cannot by any means
pass over in silence such great humanity, such unprecedented
and unheard-of clemency, such moderation in the exercise of
supreme and universal power, such incredible and almost god-
like wisdom. For now that Marcus Marcellus, O conscript
fathers, has been restored to you and the republic, I think that

not only his voice and authority are preserved and restored to you and to the republic, but my own also.

For I was concerned, O conscript fathers, and most exceedingly grieved, when I saw such a man as he is, who had espoused the same cause which I myself had, not enjoying the same good fortune as myself; nor was I able to persuade myself to think it right or fair that I should be going on in my usual routine, while that rival and imitator of my zeal and labors, who had been a companion and comrade of mine throughout, was separated from me. Therefore, you, O Caius Cæsar, have reopened to me my former habits of life, which were closed up, and you have raised, as it were, a standard to all these men, as a sort of token to lead them to entertain hopes of the general welfare of the republic. For it was seen by me before in many instances, and especially in my own, and now it is clearly understood by everybody, since you have granted Marcus Marcellus to the senate and people of Rome, in spite of your recollection of all the injuries you have received at his hands, that you prefer the authority of this order and the dignity of the republic to the indulgence of your own resentment or your own suspicions.

He, indeed, has this day reaped the greatest possible reward for the virtuous tenor of his previous life; in the great unanimity of the senate in his favor, and also in your own most dignified and important opinion of him. And from this you, in truth, must perceive what great credit there is in conferring a kindness, when there is such glory to be got even by receiving one. And he, too, is fortunate whose safety is now the cause of scarcely less joy to all other men than it will be to himself when he is informed of it. And this honor has deservedly and most rightfully fallen to his lot. For who is superior to him either in nobleness of birth, or in honesty, or in zeal for virtuous studies, or in purity of life, or in any description whatever of excellence.

II. No one is blessed with such a stream of genius, no one is endowed with such vigor and richness of eloquence, either as a speaker or as a writer, as to be able, I will not say to extol, but even, O Caius Cæsar, plainly to relate all your achievements. Nevertheless, I assert, and with your leave I maintain,

that in all of them you never gained greater and truer glory
than you have acquired this day. I am accustomed often to
keep this idea before my eyes, and often to affirm in frequent
conversations, that all the exploits of our own generals, all
those of foreign nations and of most powerful states, all the
mighty deeds of the most illustrious monarchs, can be compared with yours neither in the magnitude of your wars, nor in
the number of your battles, nor in the variety of countries
which you have conquered, nor in the rapidity of your con-
quests, nor in the great difference of character with which your
wars have been marked; and that those countries the most remote from each other could not be traveled over more rapidly
by any one in a journey, than they have been visited by your, I
will not say journeys, but victories.

And if I were not to admit, that those actions are so great
that scarcely any man's mind or comprehension is capable of
doing justice to them, I should be very senseless. But there are
other actions greater than those. For some people are in the
habit of disparaging military glory, and of denying the whole
of it to the generals, and of giving the multitude a share of it
also, so that it may not be the peculiar property of the commanders. And, no doubt, in the affairs of war, the valor of the
troops, the advantages of situation, the assistance of allies,
fleets, and supplies, have great influence; and a most important
share in all such transactions, Fortune claims for herself, as of
her right; and whatever has been done successfully she considers almost entirely as her own work.

But in this glory, O Caius Cæsar, which you have just
earned, you have no partner. The whole of this, however great
it may be,—and surely it is as great as possible,—the whole of
it, I say, is your own. The centurion can claim for himself no
share of that praise, neither can the prefect, nor the battalion,
nor the squadron. Nay, even that very mistress of all human
affairs, Fortune herself, cannot thrust herself into any participation in that glory; she yields to you; she confesses that it is
all your own, your peculiar private desert. For rashness is
never united with wisdom, nor is chance ever admitted to regu-
late affairs conducted with prudence.

III. You have subdued nations, savage in their barbarism,
countless in their numbers, boundless, if we regard the extent

of country peopled by them, and rich in every kind of resource;
but still you were only conquering things, the nature and condition of which was such that they could be overcome by force.
For there is no strength so great that it cannot be weakened
and broken by arms and violence. But to subdue one's inclinations, to master one's angry feelings, to be moderate in the hour
of victory, to not merely raise from the ground a prostrate adversary, eminent for noble birth, for genius, and for virtue, but
even to increase his previous dignity,—they are actions of such
a nature, that the man who does them, I do not compare to the
most illustrious man, but I consider equal to God.

Therefore, O Caius Cæsar, those military glories of yours
will be celebrated not only in our own literature and language,
but in those of almost all nations; nor is there any age which
will ever be silent about your praises. But still, deeds of that
sort, somehow or other, even when they are read, appear to be
overwhelmed with the cries of the soldiers and the sound of the
trumpets. But when we hear or read of anything which has
been done with clemency, with humanity, with justice, with
moderation, and with wisdom, especially in a time of anger,
which is very adverse to prudence, and in the hour of victory,
which is naturally insolent and haughty, with what ardor are
we then inflamed, (even if the actions are not such as have
really been performed, but are only fabulous,) so as often to
love those whom we have never seen! But as for you, whom we
behold present among us, whose mind, and feelings, and countenance, we at this moment see to be such, that you wish to
preserve everything which the fortune of war has left to the
republic, oh with what praises must we extol you? with what
zeal must we follow you? with what affection must we devote
ourselves to you? The very walls, I declare, the very walls of
this senate-house appear to me eager to return you thanks; because, in a short time, you will have restored their ancient authority to this venerable abode of themselves and of their ancestors.

IV. In truth, O conscript fathers, when I just now, in common with you, beheld the tears of Caius Marcellus, a most
virtuous man, endowed with a never-to-be-forgotten affection
for his brother, the recollection of all the Marcelli presented
itself to my heart. For you, O Cæsar, have, by preserving

Marcus Marcellus, restored their dignity even to those Marcelli who are dead, and you have saved that most noble family,
now reduced to a small number, from perishing. You, therefore, justly prefer this day to all the splendid and innumerable
congratulations which at different times have been addressed
to you. For this exploit is your own alone; the other achievements which have been performed by you as general, were
great indeed, but still they were performed by the agency of
a great and numerous band of comrades. But in this exploit you
are the general, and you are your own sole comrade; and the
act itself is such that no lapse of time will ever put an end to
your monuments and trophies; for there is nothing which is
wrought by manual labor which time will not sometime or
other impair or destroy; but this justice and lenity of yours will
every day grow brighter and brighter, so that, in proportion as
time takes away from the effect of your deed, in the same degree it will add to your glory. And you had already surpassed
all other conquerors in civil wars, in equity, and clemency, but
this day you have surpassed even yourself. I fear that this
which I am saying cannot, when it is only heard, be understood
as fully as I myself think and feel it; you appear to have surpassed victory itself, since you have remitted in favor of the
conquered those things which victory had put in your power.
For though, by the conditions of the victory itself, we who
were conquered were all ruined, we still have been preserved
by the deliberate decision of your clemency. You therefore, deserve to be the only man who is never conquered, since you
conquered the conditions and the violent privileges of victory
itself.

V. And, O conscript fathers, remark how widely this decision of Caius Cæsar extends. For by it, all of us who, under
the compulsion of some miserable and fatal destiny of the
republic, were driven to take up arms as we did, though we
are still not free from the fault of having erred as men may, are
at all events released from all imputation of wickedness. For
when, at your entreaty, he preserved Marcus Marcellus to the
republic, he, at the same time, restored me to myself and to the
republic though no one entreated him in my favor, and he restored all the other most honorable men who were in the same
case to ourselves and to their country; whom you now behold

in numbers and dignity present in this very assembly. He has not brought his enemies into the senate-house; but he has decided that the war was undertaken by most of them rather out of ignorance, and because of some ungrounded and empty fear, than out of either any depraved desires or cruelty.

And in that war, I always thought it right to listen to all proposals that gave any hope of peace, and I always grieved, that not only peace, but that even the language of those citizens who asked for peace, should be rejected. For I never approved of either that or any civil war whatever; and my counsels were always allied to peace and peaceful measures, not to war and arms. I followed the man from my own private feelings, not because of my judgment of his public conduct; and the faithful recollection of the grateful disposition which I cherish had so much influence with me, that though I had not only no desire for victory, but no hope even of it, I rushed on, knowingly, and with my eyes open, as it were to a voluntary death. And, indeed, my sentiments in the matter were not at all concealed; for in this assembly, before any decisive steps were taken either way, I said many things in favor of peace, and even while the war was going on I retained the same opinions, even at the risk of my life. And from this fact, no one will form so unjust an opinion as to doubt what Cæsar's own inclination respecting the war was, when, the moment that it was in his power, he declared his opinion in favor of saving the advisers of peace, but showed his anger against the others. And, perhaps, that was not very strange at a time when the event of the war was still uncertain, and its fortune still undecided. But he who, when victorious, attaches himself to the advisers of peace, plainly declares that he would have preferred having no war at all even to conquering.

VI. And in this matter I myself am a witness in favor of Marcus Marcellus. For as our opinions have at all times agreed in time of peace, so did they then in respect of that war. How often have I seen him affected with the deepest grief at the insolence of certain men, and dreading also the ferocity of victory! On which account your liberality, O Caius Cæsar, ought to be more acceptable to us who have seen those things. For now we may compare, not the causes of the two parties together, but the use which each would have made of victory.

We have seen your victory terminated at once by the result of your battles; we have seen no sword unsheathed in the city. The citizens whom we have lost were stricken down by the force of Mars, not by evil feelings let loose by victory; so that no man can doubt that Caius Cæsar would even raise many from the dead if that were possible, since he does preserve all those of that army that he can.

But of the other party I will say no more than what we were all afraid of at the time, namely, that theirs would have been too angry a victory. For some of them were in the habit of indulging in threats not only against those of their enemies who were in arms, but even against those who remained quiet;[1] and they used to say that the matter to be considered was not what each man had thought, but where he had been. So that it appears to me that the immortal gods, even if they were inflicting punishment on the Roman people for some offense, when they stirred up so serious and melancholy a civil war, are at length appeased, or at all events satiated, and have now made all our hopes of safety depend on the clemency and wisdom of the conqueror.

Rejoice, then, in that admirable and virtuous disposition of yours; and enjoy not only your fortune and glory, but also your own natural good qualities, and amiable inclinations and manners; for those are the things which produce the greatest fruit and pleasure to a wise man. When you call to mind your other achievements, although you will often congratulate yourself on your valor, still you will often have reason to thank your good fortune also. But as often as you think of us whom you have chosen to live safely in the republic as well as yourself, you will be thinking at the same time of your own exceeding kindness, of your own incredible liberality, or your own unexampled wisdom; qualities which I will venture to call not only the greatest, but the only real blessings. For there is so

---

[1] Cicero was not present at the battle of Pharsalia, but remained at Dyrrachium, vexed at his advice being totally disregarded. Cato also remained at Dyrrachium. When Labienus brought them the news of Pompey's defeat, Cato offered Cicero the command, as the superior in dignity; and Plutarch relates, that on his refusal of it, young Pompey was so enraged, that he would have killed him on the spot if Cato had not prevented him. And this is what Middleton (who quotes the sentence in the text) thinks that Cicero is alluding to here.

much splendor in genuine glory, so much dignity in magnanimity and real practical wisdom, that these qualities appear to be given to a man by virtue, while all other advantages seem only lent to him by fortune.

Be not wearied then in the preservation of virtuous men; especially of those who have fallen, not from any evil desires, or depravity of disposition, but merely from an opinion of their duty,—a foolish and erroneous one perhaps, but certainly not a wicked one,—and because they were misled by imaginary claims which they fancied the republic had on them. For it is no fault of yours if some people were afraid of you; and, on the other hand, it is your greatest praise that they have now felt that they had no reason to fear you.

VII. But now I come to those severe complaints, and to those most terrible suspicions that you have given utterance to; of dangers which should be guarded against not more by you yourself than by all the citizens, and most especially by us who have been preserved by you. And although I trust that the suspicion is an ungrounded one, still I will not speak so as to make light of it. For caution for you is caution for ourselves. So that, if we must err on one side or the other, I would rather appear too fearful, than not sufficiently prudent. But still, who is there so frantic? Any one of your own friends? And yet who are more your friends than those to whom you have restored safety which they did not venture to hope for? Any one of that number who were with you? It is not credible that any man should be so insane as not to prefer the life of that man who was his general when he obtained the greatest advantages of all sorts, to his own. But if your friends have no thoughts of wickedness, need you take precautions lest your enemies may be entertaining such? Who are they. For all those men who were your enemies have either already lost their lives through their obstinacy, or else have preserved them through your mercy; so that either none of your enemies survive or those who do survive are your most devoted friends.

But still, as there are so many hiding places and so many dark corners in men's minds, let us increase your suspicions, for by so doing we shall at the same time increase your diligence. For who is there so ignorant of everything, so very now to the affairs of the republic, so entirely destitute of thought either for his own or for the general safety, as not to understand that his own safety is bound up with yours? that the lives of all men depend on your single existence? I myself, in truth, while I think of you day and night,—as I ought to do,—fear only the chances to which all men are liable, and the uncertain events of health and the frail tenure of our common nature, and I grieve that, while the republic ought to be immortal, it depends wholly on the life of one mortal man. But if to the chances of human life and the uncertain condition of man's health there were to be added also any conspiracy of wickedness and treachery, then what god should we think able to assist the republic, even if he were to desire to do so?

VIII. All things, O Caius Cæsar, which you now see lying stricken and prostrate—as it was inevitable that they should be —through the violence of war, must now be raised up again by you alone. The courts of justice must be re-established, confidence must be restored, licentiousness must be repressed, the increase of population must be encouraged, everything which has become lax and disorderly must be braced up and strengthened by strict laws. In so vast a civil war, when there was such ardor of feeling and of warlike preparation on both sides, it was impossible but that—whatever the ultimate result of the war might be—the republic which had been violently shaken by it should lose many ornaments of its dignity and many bulwarks of its security, and that each general should do many things while in arms, which he would have forbidden to have been done while clad in the garb of peace. And all those wounds of war thus inflicted now require your attention, and there is no one except you who is able to heal them. Therefore, I was concerned when I heard that celebrated and wise saying of yours, "I have lived long enough to satisfy either nature or glory." Sufficiently long, if you please, for nature, and I will add, if you like, for glory; but, which is of the greatest consequence of all, certainly not long enough for your country.

Give up then, I entreat you, that wisdom of learned men shown in their contempt of death; do not be wise at our expense. For it has often come to my ears that you are in the habit of using that expression much too frequently—that you have lived long enough for yourself. I dare say you have; but I could only be willing to hear you say so if you lived for yourself alone, or if you had been born for yourself alone. But as it is,—as your exploits have brought the safety of all the citizens and the entire republic to a dependence on you,—you are so far from having completed your greatest labors, that you have not even laid the foundations which you design to lay. And will you then limit your life, not by the welfare of the republic, but by the tranquillity of your own mind? What will you do, if that is not even sufficient for your glory, of which—wise man though you be—you will not deny that you are exceedingly desirous? "Is it then," you will say, "but small glory that we shall leave behind us?" It may, indeed, be sufficient for others, however many they may be, and insufficient for you alone. For whatever it is, however ample it may be, it certainly is insufficient, as long as there is anything greater still. And if, O Caius Cæsar, this was to be the result of your immortal achievements, that after conquering all your enemies, you were to leave the republic in the state in which it now is; then beware, I beg of you, lest your virtue should earn admiration rather than solid glory; since the glory which is illustrious and which is celebrated abroad, is the fame of many and great services done either to one's own friends, or to one's country, or to the whole race of mankind.

IX. This, then, is the part which remains to you; this is the cause which you have before you; this is what you must now labor at,—to settle the republic, and to enjoy it yourself, as the first of its citizens, in the greatest tranquillity and peacefulness. And then, if you please, when you have discharged the obligations which you owe to your country, and when you have satisfied nature herself with the devotion of your life, then you may say that you have lived long enough. For what is the meaning of this very word "long" when applied to what has an end? And when the end comes, then all past pleasure is to be accounted as nothing, because there is none to come after it. Although that spirit of yours has never been content with this narrow space which nature has afforded us to live in; but has always been inflamed with a desire of immortality. Nor is this to be considered your life which is contained in your body and in your breath. That,—that, I say, is your life, which will flourish in the memory of all ages; which posterity will cherish; which eternity itself will always preserve. This is what you must be subservient to; it is to this that you ought to display yourself; which indeed has long ago had many actions of yours to admire, and which now is expecting some which it may also praise.

Unquestionably, posterity will stand amazed when they hear and read of your military commands,—of the provinces which you have added to the empire,—of the Rhine, of the ocean, of the Nile, all made subject to us,—of your countless battles, of your incredible victories, of your innumerable monuments and triumphs. But unless this city is now securely settled by your counsels and by your institutions, your name will indeed be talked about very extensively, but your glory will have no secure abode, no sure home in which to repose. There will be also among those who shall be born hereafter, as there has been among us, great disputes, when some with their praises will extol your exploits to the skies, and others, perhaps, will miss something in them,—and that, too, the most important thing of all,—unless you extinguish the conflagration of civil war by the safety of the country, so that the one shall appear to have been the effect of destiny and the other the work of your own practical wisdom. Have regard, then, to those judges who will judge you many ages afterwards, and who will very likely judge you more honestly than we can. For their judgment will be unbiassed by affection or by ambition, and at the same time it will be untainted by hatred or by envy. And even if it will be incapable of affecting you at that time, (which is the false opinion held by some men,) at all events, it concerns you now to conduct yourself in such a manner that no oblivion shall ever be able to obscure your praises.

X. The inclinations of the citizens have been very diverse, and their opinions much distracted; for we showed our variance, not only by our counsels and desires, but by arms and warlike operations. And there was obscurity in the designs of, and contention between, the most illustrious generals: many doubted which was the best side; many, what was expedient for themselves; many, what was becoming; some even felt uncertain as to what it was in their power to do. The republic has at last come to the end of this miserable and fatal war; that man has been victorious who has not allowed his animosities to be inflamed by good fortune, but who has mitigated them by the goodness of his disposition; and who did not consider all those with whom he was displeased deserving on that account of exile or of death. Arms were laid aside by some, were wrested from the hands of others. He is an ungrateful and an unjust citizen, who, when released from the danger of arms, still retains, as it were, an armed spirit, so that that men is better who fell in battle, who spent his life in the cause. For that which seems obstinacy to some people may appear constancy in others. But now all dissension is crushed by the arms and extinguished by the justice of the conqueror; it only remains for all men for the future to be animated by one wish, all at least who have not only any wisdom at all, but who are at all in their senses. Unless you, O Caius Cæsar, continue safe, and also in the same sentiments as you have displayed on previous occasions, and on this day most eminently, we cannot be safe either. Wherefore we all—we who wish this constitution and these things around us to be safe—exhort and entreat you to take care of your own life, to consult your own safety; and we all promise to you, (that I may say also on behalf of others what I feel respecting myself,) since you think that there is still something concealed, against which it is necessary to guard,—we promise you, I say, not only our vigilance and our wariness also to assist in those precautions, but we promise to oppose our sides and our bodies as a shield against every danger which can threaten you.

XI. But let my speech end with the same sentiment as it began. We all, O Caius Cæsar, render you the greatest thanks, and we feel even deeper gratitude than we express; for all feel the same thing, as you might have perceived from the entreaties and tears of all. But because it is not necessary for all of them to stand up and say so, they wish it at all events that by me, who am forced in some degree to rise and speak, should be expressed both all that they feel, and all that is becoming, and all that I myself consider due to Marcus Marcellus, who is thus by you restored to this order, and to the Roman people, and to the republic. For I feel that all men are exulting, not in the safety of one individual alone, but in the general safety of all. And as it becomes the greatest possible affection, such as I was always well known by all men to have towards him, so that I scarcely yielded to Caius Marcellus, his most excellent and affectionate brother and certainly to no one except him,—that love for him which I displayed by my solicitude, by my anxiety, and my exertions, as long as there was a doubt of his safety, I certainly ought to display at this present time, now that I am relieved from my great care and distress and misery on his account.

Therefore, O Caius Cæsar, I thank you, as if,—though I have not only been preserved in every sort of manner, but also loaded with distinctions by you,—still, by this action of yours, a crowning kindness of the greatest importance was added to the already innumerable benefits which you have heaped upon me, which I did not before believe were capable of any augmentation.

IN DEFENSE OF TITUS ANNIUS MILO

THE ARGUMENT

Titus Annius Milo, often in the following speech called only Titus
Annius, stood for the consulship while Clodius was a candidate
for the prætorship, and daily quarrels took place in the streets
between their armed retainers and gladiators. Milo, who was dictator of Lanuvium, his native place, was forced to go thither to
appoint some priests, etc.; and Clodius, who had been to Aricia,
met him on his road. Milo was in his carriage with his wife, and
was accompanied by a numerous retinue, among whom were
some gladiators. Clodius was on horseback, with about thirty
armed men. The followers of each began to fight, and when the
tumult had become general, Clodius was slain, probably by Milo
himself. The disturbances at Rome became so formidable that
Pompey was created sole consul; and soon after he entered on his
office, A U. C. 702, Milo was brought to trial. This speech, however, though composed by Cicero, was not spoken, for he was
so much alarmed by the violence of Clodius's friends, that he did
not dare to use the plain language he had proposed. Milo was
convicted and banished to Marseilles.

I. ALTHOUGH I am afraid, O Judges, that it is a base thing for
one who is beginning to speak for a very brave man to be
alarmed, and though it is far from becoming, when Titus Annius Milo himself is more disturbed for the safety of the republic than for his own, that I should not be able to bring to the
cause a similar greatness of mind, yet this novel appearance of
a new[1] manner of trial alarms my eyes, which, wherever they
fall, seek for the former customs of the forum and the ancient
practise in trials. For your assembly is not surrounded by a cir-

[1] This was an extraordinary trial, held under a new law just passed by
Pompey; and it was presided over, not by the prætor, but by Lucius
Domitius Ahenobarbus, who was expressly appointed by the comitia
president of the judges on this occasion.

cle of bystanders as usual; we are not attended by our usual company.[2]

For those guards which you behold in front of all the temples, although they are placed there as a protection against violence, yet they bring no aid to the orator; so that even in the forum and in the court of justice itself, although we are protected with all salutary and necessary defenses, yet we cannot be entirely without fear. But if I thought this adverse to Milo, I should yield to the times, O judges, and among such a crowd of armed men, I should think there was no room for an orator. But the wisdom of Cnæus Pompeius, a most wise and just man, strengthens and encourages me; who would certainly neither think it suitable to his justice to deliver that man up to the weapons of the soldiery whom he had given over as an accused person to the decision of the judges, nor suitable to his wisdom to arm the rashness of an excited multitude with public authority.

So that those arms, those centurions, those cohorts, do not announce danger to us, but protection; nor do they expect us only to be calm, but even to be courageous; nor do they promise only assistance to my defense, but also silence. And the rest of the multitude, which consists of citizens, is wholly ours; nor is there any one individual among those whom you see from this place gazing upon us from all sides from which any part of the forum can be seen, and watching the result of this trial, who, while he favors the virtue of Milo, does not think that this day in reality his own interests, those of his children, his country, and his fortunes, are at stake.

II. There is one class adverse and hostile to us,—those whom the madness of Publius Clodius has fed on rapine, on conflagration, and on every sort of public disaster; and who were, even in the assembly held yesterday, exhorted [3] to teach you, by their clamor, what you were to decide. But such shouts, if any reached you, should rather warn you to retain him as a citizen who has always slighted that class of men, and their greatest

[2] Pompey was present at the trial, surrounded by his officers, and he had filled the forum and all its precincts with armed men, for the sake of keeping the peace.

[3] Munatius Plancus, the day before, had exhorted the people not to suffer Milo to escape.

clamor, in comparison with your safety. Wherefore, be of good courage, O judges, and lay aside your alarm, if indeed you feel any; for if ever you had to decide about good and brave men, and about citizens who had deserved well of their country, if ever an opportunity was given to chosen men of the most honorable ranks to show by their deeds and resolutions that disposition towards brave and good citizens which they had often declared by their looks and by their words, all that power you now have, when you are to determine whether we who have always been wholly devoted to your authority are to be miserable, and to mourn forever, or whether, having been long harassed by the most abandoned citizens, we shall at length be reprieved and set up again by you, your loyalty, your virtue, and your wisdom.

For what, O judges, is more full of labor than we both are, what can be either expressed or imagined more full of anxiety and uneasiness than we are, who being induced to devote ourselves to the republic by the hope of the most honorable rewards, yet cannot be free from the fear of the most cruel punishments? I have always thought indeed that Milo had to encounter the other storms and tempests in these billows of the assemblies because he always espoused the cause of the good against the bad; but in a court of justice, and in that council in which the most honorable men of all ranks are sitting as judges, I never imagined that Milo's enemies could have any hope of diminishing his glory by the aid of such men, much less of at all injuring his safety.

Although in this cause, O judges, we shall not employ the tribuneship of Titus Annius, and all the exploits which he has performed for the safety of the republic, as topics for our defense against this accusation, unless you see with your own eyes that a plot was laid against Milo by Clodius; and we shall not entreat you to pardon us this one offense in consideration of our many eminent services to the republic, nor shall we demand, if the death of Publius Clodius was your safety, that on that account you should attribute it rather to the virtue of Milo, than to the good fortune of the Roman people; but if his plots are made clearer than the day, then indeed I shall entreat, and shall demand of you, O judges, that, if we have lost everything else, this at least may be left us,—namely, the privilege of defending our lives from the audacity and weapons of our enemies with impunity.

III. But before I come to that part of my speech which especially belongs to this trial, it seems necessary to refute those things which have been often said, both in the senate by our enemies, and in the assembly of the people by wicked men, and lately, too, by our prosecutors; so that when every cause of alarm is removed you may be able distinctly to see the matter which is the subject of this trial. They say that that man ought no longer to see the light who confesses that another man has been slain by him. In what city, then, are these most foolish men using this argument? In this one, forsooth, where the first trial for a man's life that took place at all was that of Marcus Horatius, a most brave man, who even before the city was free was yet acquitted by the assembly of the Roman people, though he avowed that his sister had been slain by his hand.

Is there anyone who does not know, that when inquiry is made into the slaying of a man, it is usual either altogether to deny that the deed has been done, or else to defend it on the ground that it was rightly and lawfully done? unless, indeed, you think that Publius Africanus was out of his mind, who, when he was asked in a seditious spirit by Caius Carbo, a tribune of the people, what was his opinion of the death of Tiberius Gracchus, answered that he seemed to have been rightly slain. For neither could Servilius Ahala, that eminent man, nor Publius Nasica, nor Lucius Opimius, nor Caius Marius, nor indeed the senate itself during my consulship, have been accounted anything but wicked, if it was unlawful for wicked citizens to be put to death. And therefore, O judges, it was not without good reason, that even in legendary fables learned men have handed down the story, that he, who for the sake of avenging his father had killed his mother, when the opinions of men varied, was acquitted not only by the voices of the gods, but even by the very wisest goddess. And if the Twelve Tables have permitted that a nightly robber may be slain any way, but a robber by day if he defends himself, with a weapon, who is there who can think a man to be punished for slaying another, in whatever way he is slain, when he sees that sometimes a sword to kill a man with is put into our hands by the very laws themselves?

IV. But if there be any occasion on which it is proper to slay a man,—and there are many such,—surely that occasion is not only a just one, but even a necessary one, when violence is offered, and can only be repelled by violence. When a military tribune offered violence to a soldier in the army of Caius Marius, the kinsman of that commander was slain by the man whom he was insulting; for the virtuous youth chose to act, though with danger, rather than to suffer infamously; and his illustrious commander acquitted him of all guilt, and treated him well. But what death can be unjust when inflicted on a secret plotter and robber?

What is the meaning of our retinues, what of our swords? Surely it would never be permitted to us to have them if we might never use them. This, therefore, is a law, O judges, not written, but born with us,—which we have not learned, or received by tradition, or read, but which we have taken and sucked in and imbibed from nature herself; a law which we were not taught, but to which we were made,—which we were not trained in, but which is ingrained in us,—namely, that if our life be in danger from plots, or from open violence, or from the weapons of robbers or enemies, every means of securing our safety is honorable. For laws are silent when arms are raised, and do not expect themselves to be waited for, when he who waits will have to suffer an undeserved penalty before he can exact a merited punishment.

The law very wisely, and in a manner silently, gives a man a right to defend himself, and does not merely forbid a man to be slain, but forbids any one to have a weapon about him with the object of slaying a man; so that, as the object, and not the weapon itself, is made the subject of the inquiry, the man who had used a weapon with the object of defending himself would be decided not to have had his weapon about him with the object of killing a man. Let, then, this principle be remembered by you in this trial, O judges; for I do not doubt that I shall make good my defense before you, if you only remember—what you cannot forget—that a plotter against one may be lawfully slain.

V. The next point is one which is often asserted by the enemies of Milo, who say that the senate has decided that the slaughter by which Publius Clodius fell was contrary to the interests of the republic. But, in fact, the senate has approved, not merely by their votes, but even zealously. For how often has that cause been pleaded by us in the senate? with what great assent of the whole body? and that no silent nor concealed assent; for when in a very full senate were there ever four or five men found who did not espouse Milo's cause? Those lifeless assemblies of this nearly burned [4] tribune of the people show the fact; assemblies in which he daily used to try and bring my power into unpopularity, by saying that the senate did not pass its decrees according to what it thought itself, but as I chose.

And if, indeed, that ought to be called power, rather than a moderate influence in a righteous cause on account of great services done to the republic, or some popularity among the good on account of dutiful labors for its sake, let it be called so, as long as we employ it for the safety of the good in opposition to the madness of the wicked.

But this investigation, though it is not an unjust one, yet is not one which the senate thought ought to be ordered; for there were regular laws and forms of trial for murder, or for assault; nor did the death of Publius Clodius cause the senate such concern and sorrow that any new process of investigation need have been appointed; for when the senate had had the power of decreeing a trial in the matter of that impious pollution of which he was guilty taken from it, who can believe it thought it necessary to appoint a new form of trial about his death? Why then did the senate decide that this burning of the senate-house, this siege laid to the house of M. Lepidus, and this very homicide, had taken place contrary to the interest of the republic? Why, because no violence from one citizen to another can ever take place in a free state which is not contrary to the interests of the republic. For the defending of oneself against violence is never a thing to be wished for; but it is sometimes necessary, unless, indeed, one could say that that day on which Tiberius Gracchus was slain, or that

---

[4] After Clodius's death, Munatius Plancus, the tribune, exposed his body on the rostrum, and harangued the people against Milo; the populace carried the body into the senate-house, and made a pile on the seats to burn it, in doing which they burnt the senate-house and Plancus himself with difficulty escaped.

day when Caius was, or the day when the arms of Saturnius were put down, even if they ended as the welfare of the republic demanded, were yet no wound and injury to the republic.

VI. Therefore I myself voted, when it was notorious that a homicide had taken place on the Appian road, not that he who had defended himself had acted in a manner contrary to the interests of the republic; but as there was violence and treachery in the business, I reserved the charge for trial, I expressed my disapprobation of the business. And if the senate had not been hindered by that frantic tribune from executing its wishes, we should not now have this novel trial. For the senate voted that an extraordinary investigation should take place according to the ancient laws. A division took place, it does not signify on whose motion, for it is not necessary to mention the worthlessness of every one, and so the rest of the authority of the senate was destroyed by this corrupt intercession.

"Oh, but Cnæus Pompeius, by his bill, gave his decision both about the fact and about the cause. For he brought in a bill about the homicide which had taken place on the Appian road, in which Publius Clodius was slain." What then did he propose? That an inquiry should be made. What is to be inquired about? Whether it was committed? That is clear. By whom? That is notorious. He saw that a defense as to the law and right could be undertaken, even at the very moment of the confession of the act. But if he had not seen that he who confessed might yet be acquitted, when he saw that we did not confess the fact, he would never have ordered an investigation to take place, nor would he have given you at this trial the power[5] of acquitting as well as that of condemning. But it seems to me that Cnæus Pompeius not only delivered no decision at all unfavorable to Milo, but that he also pointed out what you ought to turn your attention to in deciding. For he who did not assign a punishment to the confession, but required a defense of it, he clearly thought that what was in-

[5] Literally, "this wholesome letter, as well as that melancholy one." The letter A was the "wholesome" letter, being the initial of *absolvo*, I acquit; the letter C the melancholy one, being the initial of *condemno*, I condemn.

quired into was the cause of the death, and not the mere fact
of the death. Now he himself shall tell us whether what he
did of his own accord was done out of regard for Publius
Clodius, or from a compliance with the times.

VII. A most noble man, a bulwark, and in those times,
indeed, almost a protector of the senate, the uncle of this our
judge, of that most fearless man Marcus Cato, Marcus Drusus,
a tribune of the people, was slain in his own house. The people had never any reference made to them in the matter of
his death, no investigation was voted by the senate. What great
grief was there, as we have heard from our forefathers in this
city, when that attack was made by night on Publius Africanus,
while sleeping in his own house! Who was there then who did
not groan, who did not burn with indignation, that men should
not have waited even for the natural and inevitable death of
that man whom, if possible, all would have wished to be
immortal?

Was there then any extraordinary investigation into the
death of Africanus[6] voted? Certainly none. Why so? Because
the crime of murder is not different when eminent men, or
when obscure ones are slain. Let there be a difference between
the dignity of the lives of the highest and lowest citizens. If
their death be wrought by wickedness, that must be avenged
by the same laws and punishments in either case; unless, indeed, he be more a parricide who murders a father of consular rank than he who murders one of low degree; or, as if the
death of Publius Clodius is to be more criminal because he was
slain among the monuments of his ancestors,—for this is constantly said by that party; as if, I suppose, that illustrious

---

[6] After the death of Tiberius Gracchus, Publius Æmilianus Africanus
Scipio, the conqueror of Carthage and Numantia, was known to be hostile to the agrarian law, and threw every obstacle in the way of it; his
enemies gave out that he intended to abrogate it by force. One morning
he was found dead in his bed without a wound. The cause and manner
of his death were unknown; some said it was natural; some, that he had
slain himself; some, that his wife Sempronia, the sister of Gracchus, had
strangled him. His slaves, it was said, declared that some strangers had
been introduced into the house at the back, who had strangled him,
and the triumvir Carbo is generally believed to have been the chief
agent in his murder, and is expressly mentioned as the murderer by
Cicero, Ep. ad Q. Fr. ii. 3.

Appius Cæcus made that road, not that the nation might have a road to use, but that his own posterity might have a place in which to rob with impunity.

Therefore in that same Appian road, when Publius Clodius had slain a most accomplished Roman knight, Marcus Papirius, that crime was not to be punished; for a nobleman among his own family monuments had slain a Roman knight. Now what tragedies does the name of that same Appian road awaken? which, though nothing was said about it formerly, when stained with the murder of an honorable and innocent man, is now incessantly mentioned ever since it has been dyed with the blood of a robber and a parricide. But why do I speak of these things? A slave of Publius Clodius was arrested in the temple of Castor, whom he had placed there to murder Cnæus Pompeius; the dagger was wrested from his hands and he confessed his design; after that Pompeius absented himself from the forum, absented himself from the senate, and from all public places; he defended himself within his own doors and walls, not by the power of the laws and tribunals.

Was any motion made? was any extraordinary investigation voted? But if any circumstance, if any man, if any occasion was ever important enough for such a step, certainly all these things were so in the greatest degree in that cause. The assassin had been stationed in the forum, and in the very vestibule of the senate. Death was being prepared for that man on whose life the safety of the senate depended. Moreover, at that crisis of the republic, when, if he alone had died, not only this state, but all the nations in the world would have been ruined,— unless, indeed, the crime was not to be punished because it was not accomplished, just as if the execution of crimes was chastised by the laws, and not the intentions of men,—certainly there was less cause to grieve, as the deed was not accomplished, but certainly not a whit the less cause to punish. How often, O judges, have I myself escaped from the weapons and from the bloody hands of Publius Clodius! But if my good fortune, or that of the republic, had not preserved me from them, who would have proposed any investigation into my death.

VIII. But it is foolish of us to dare to compare Drusus, Africanus, Pompeius, or ourselves, with Publius Clodius. All these things were endurable. The death of Publius Clodius no one can bear with equanimity. The senate is in mourning; the knights grieve; the whole state is broken down as if with age; the municipalities are in mourning; the colonies are bowed down; the very fields even regret so beneficent, so useful, so kind-hearted a citizen! That was not the cause, O judges, it was not indeed, why Pompeius thought an investigation ought to be proposed by him; but being a man wise and endowed with lofty and almost divine intellect, he saw many things,—that Clodius was his personal enemy, Milo his intimate friend; he feared that, if he were to rejoice in the common joy of all men, the belief in his reconciliation with Clodius would be weakened. He saw many other things, too, but this most especially,—that in whatever terms of severity he proposed the motion, still you would decide fearlessly. Therefore, he selected the very lights of the most eminent ranks of the state. He did not, indeed, as some are constantly saying, exclude my friends in selecting the tribunal; for neither did that most just man think of this, nor, when he was selecting good men, could he have managed to do so, even had he wished; for my influence would not be limited by my intimacies, which can never be very extensive, because one cannot associate habitually with many people; but, if we have any influence, we have it on this account, because the republic has associated us with the virtuous; and, when he was selecting the most excellent of them, and as he thought that it especially concerned his credit to do so, he was unable to avoid selecting men who were well-disposed towards me.

But as for his especially appointing you, O Lucius Domitius, to preside over this investigation, in that he was seeking nothing except justice, dignity, humanity and good faith. He passed a law that it must be a man of consular dignity, because, I suppose, he considered the duty of the men of the highest rank to resist both the fickleness of the multitude and the rashness of the profligate; and of the men of consular rank he selected you above all; for from your earliest youth you had given the most striking proofs how you despised the madness of the people.

IX. Wherefore, O judges, that we may at last come to the subject of action and the accusation, if it is neither the case

that all avowal of the deed is unprecedented, nor that anything has been determined about our cause by the senate
differently to what we could wish; and if the proposer of the
law himself, when there was no dispute as to the deed, yet
thought that there should be a discussion as to the law; and
if the judges had been chosen, and a man appointed to preside
over the investigation, to decide these matters justly and
wisely; it follows, O judges, that you have now nothing else
to inquire into but which plotted against the other; and that
you may the more easily discern this, attend carefully, I entreat you, while I briefly explain to you the matter as it occurred.

When Publius Clodius had determined to distress the republic by all sorts of wickedness during his prætorship, and saw
that the comitia were so delayed the year before, that he would
not be able to continue his prætorship many months, as he had
no regard to the degree of honor, as others have, but both
wished to avoid having Lucius Paullus, a citizen of singular
virtue, for his colleague, and also to have an entire year to
mangle the republic; on a sudden he abandoned his own year,
and transferred himself to the next year, not from any religious
scruple, but that he might have, as he said himself a full and
entire year to act as prætor, that is, to overthrow the republic.

It occurred to him that his prætorship would be crippled
and powerless, if Milo was consul; and, moreover, he saw that
he was being made consul with the greatest unanimity of the
Roman people. He betook himself to his competitors, but in
such a manner that he alone managed the whole election, even
against their will,—that he supported on his own shoulders, as
he used to say, the whole comitia,—he convoked the tribes,—
he interposed,—he erected a new Colline tribe by the enrol-
ment of the most worthless of the citizens. In proportion as
the one caused greater confusion, so did the other acquire
additional power every day. When the fellow, prepared for
every atrocity, saw that a most brave man, his greatest enemy,
was a most certain consul, and that that was declared, not only
by the conversation of the Roman people, but also by their
votes, he began to act openly, and to say without disguise that
Milo must be slain.

He had brought down from the Apennines rustic and barbarian slaves, whom you saw, with whom he had ravaged the public woods and Etruria. The matter was not concealed at all. In truth, he used, to say undisguisedly that the consulship could not be taken from Milo, but that life could. He often hinted as much in the senate; he said it plainly in the public assembly. Besides, when Favonius, a brave man, asked him what he hoped for by giving way to such madness while Milo was alive? he answered him, that in three, or at most in four days, he would be dead. And this saying of his Favonius immediately reported to Marcus Cato, who is here present.

X. In the meantime, as Clodius knew—and it was not hard to know it—that Milo was forced to take a yearly, legitimate, necessary journey on the twentieth of January to Lanuvium to appoint a priest,[7] because Milo was dictator of Lanuvium, on a sudden he himself left Rome the day before, in order (as was seen by the event) to lay an ambush for Milo in front of his farm; and he departed, so that he was not present at a turbulent assembly in which his madness was greatly missed, and which was held that very day, and from which he never would have been absent, if he had not desired to avail himself of the place and opportunity for a crime.

But Milo, as he had been that day in the senate till it was dismissed, came home, changed his shoes and his garments, waited a little, as men do, while his wife was getting ready, and then started at the time when Clodius might have returned, if, indeed, he had been coming to Rome that day. Clodius meets him unencumbered on horseback, with no carriage, with no baggage, with no Greek companions, as he was used to, without his wife, which was scarcely ever the case; while this plotter, who had taken, forsooth, that journey for the express purpose of murder, was driving with his wife in a carriage, in a heavy traveling cloak, with abundant baggage, and a delicate company of women, and maidservants, and boys. He meets Clodius in front of his farm, about the eleventh hour, or not far from it. Immediately a number of men attack him from the higher ground with missile weapons. The men who are in front kill his driver, and when he had jumped down from his chariot and flung aside his cloak, and while he was defending himself with vigorous courage, the men who were

[7] It was the priest of Juno Sospita, who was the patroness of Lanuvium.

with Clodius drew their swords, and some of them ran back towards his chariot in order to attack Milo from behind, and some, because, they thought that he was already slain, began to attack his servants who were behind him; and those of the servants who had presence of mind to defend themselves, and were faithful to their master, were some of them slain, and the others, when they saw a fierce battle taking place around the chariot, and as they were prevented from getting near their master so as to succor him, when they heard Clodius himself proclaim that Milo was slain, and they thought that it was really true, they, the servants of Milo, (I am not speaking for the purpose of shifting the guilt on to the shoulders of others, but I am saying what really occurred,) did, without their master either commanding it, or knowing it, or even being present to see it, what every one would have wished his servants to do in a similar case.

XI. These things were all done, O judges, just as I have related them. The man who laid the plot was defeated; violence was defeated by violence; or, I should rather say, audacity was crushed by valor. I say nothing about what the republic, nothing about what you, nothing about what all good men gained by the result. I do not desire it to be any advantage to me to hear that he was born with such a destiny that he was unable even to safe himself, without at the same time saving the republic and all of you. If he had not a right to do so, then I have nothing which I can urge in his defense. But if both reason has taught this lesson to learned men, and necessity to barbarians, and custom to all nations, and nature itself to the beasts, that they are at all times to repel all violence by whatever means they can from their persons, from their liberties, and from their lives, then you cannot decide this action to have been wrong, without deciding at the same time that all men who fall among thieves must perish, either by their weapons, or by your sentence.

And if he had thought that this was the law, it would have been preferable for Milo to offer his throat to Publius Clodius, —which was not attacked by him once only, nor for the first time on that day,—rather than now to be destroyed by you because he did not surrender himself then to be destroyed by him. But if there is no one of you who entertains such an opinion as that, then the question which arises for the consideration of the court is, not whether he was slain or not, which we admit, but whether he was slain legally or illegally, which is an inquiry which has often been instituted in many causes. It is quite plain that a plot was laid; and that is a thing which the senate has decided to be contrary to the laws of the republic. By whom it was laid is a question. And on this point an inquiry has been ordered to be instituted. So the senate has marked its disapproval of the fact, not of the man; and Pompeius has appointed this inquiry into the merits of the case, and not into the fact of its existence.

XII. Does then any other point arise for the decision of the court, except this one,—which laid a plot against the other? None whatever. The case comes before you in this way, that if Milo laid a plot against Clodius, then he is not to be let off with impunity. If Clodius laid it against Milo, then we are acquitted from all guilt.

How then are we to prove that Clodius laid a plot against Milo? It is quite sufficient in the case of such a wicked, of such an audacious monster as that, to prove that he had great reason to do so; that he had great hopes founded on Milo's death; that it would have been of the greatest service to him. Therefore, that maxim of Cassius, to see to whose advantage it was, may well have influence in respect of these persons. For although good men cannot be induced to commit crimes by any advantage whatever, wicked men often can by a very trifling one. And, if Milo were slain, Clodius gained this, not only that he should be prætor without having him for a consul, under whom he would not be able to commit any wickedness, but also that he should have those men for consuls while he was prætor, who, if they did not aid him, would at all events connive at all his proceedings to such an extent that he hoped he should be able to escape detection in all the frantic actions which he was contemplating; as they (so he argued to himself) would not, even if they were able to do so, be anxious to check his attempts when they considered that they were under such obligations to him; and on the other hand, if they did wish to do so, perhaps they would hardly be able to crush the audacity of that most wicked man when it got strength by its long continuance. Are you, O judges, the only persons ignorant of all this? Are you living in this city as ignorant of what passes as if you were visitors? Are your ears all abroad, do they keep aloof from all the ordinary topics of conversation of the city, as to what laws (if, indeed, they are to be called laws, and not rather firebrands to destroy the city, pestilences to annihilate the republic) that man was intending to impose upon all of us, to brand on our foreheads? Exhibit, I beg you, Sextus Clodius, produce, I beg, that copy of your laws which they say that you saved from your house, and from the middle of the armed band which threatened you by night, and bore aloft, like another palladium, in order, forsooth, to be able to carry that splendid present, that instrument for discharging the duties of the tribuneship, to some one, if you could obtain his election, who would discharge those duties according to your directions. And * * * [he was going to divide the freedmen among all the tribes, and by his new law to add all the slaves who were going to be emancipated, but who had not yet received their freedom, so that they might vote equally with the free citizens.][8]

Would he have dared to make mention of this law, which Sextus Clodius boasts was devised by him, while Milo was alive, not to say while he was consul? For of all of us——I cannot venture to say all that I was going to say. But do you consider what enormous faults the law itself must have had, when the mere mention of it, for the purpose of finding fault with it, is so offensive. And he looked at me with the expression of countenance which he was in the habit of putting on when he was threatening everybody with every sort of calamity. That light of the senate-house-moves me.[9]

XIII. What? do you suppose, O Sextus, that I am angry with you; I, whose greatest enemy you have punished with even much greater severity than my humanity could resolve to demand? You, cast the bloody carcass of Publius Clodius out of the house, you threw it out into the public street, you left it destitute of all images, of all funeral rights, of all funeral pomp, of all funeral panegyric, half consumed by a lot of

[8] The passage in brackets is a very doubtful supplement of Beier; which, however, Orellius prefers to any other.

[9] Cicero here supposes Sextus Clodius to look menacingly at him, in order to check him in his attack on this intended law.

miserable logs, to be torn to pieces by the dogs who nightly prowl about the streets. Wherefore, although in so doing you acted most impiously, still you were wreaking all your cruelty on my enemy; though I cannot praise you, I certainly ought not to be angry with you. * * *

[I have demonstrated now, O judges, of what great consequence it was to Clodius] that Milo should be slain. Now turn your attention to Milo. What advantage could it be to Milo that Clodius should be slain? What reason was there why Milo, I will not say should do such an action, but should even wish for his death? Oh, Clodius was an obstacle to Milo's hope of obtaining the consulship. But he was obtaining it in spite of him. Ay, I might rather say he was obtaining it all the more because Clodius was opposing him; nor in fact was I a more efficient support to him than Clodius was. The recollection, O judges, of the services which Milo had done to me and to the republic had weight with you. My entreaties and my tears, with which I perceived at that time that you were greatly moved, had weight with you; but still more weight had your own fear of the dangers which were impending. For who of the citizens was there who could turn his eyes to the unrestrained prætorship of Publius Clodius, without feeling the greatest dread of a revolution? and unrestrained you saw that it would be unless you had a consul who had both courage and power to restrain him; and as the whole Roman people saw that Milo alone was that man, who could hesitate by his vote to release himself from fear, and the republic from danger?

But now, now that Clodius is removed, Milo has got to labor by more ordinary practises to preserve his dignity. That preeminent glory, which was then attributed to him alone, and which was daily increasing in consequence of his efforts to repress the frenzy of Clodius, has been put an end to by the death of Clodius. You have gained your object of being no longer afraid of any one of the citizens; he has lost that incessant arena for his valor, that which procured him votes for the consulship, that ceaseless and ever-springing fountain of his glory. Therefore, Milo's canvass for the consulship, which could not be hindered from prospering while Clodius was alive, now, the moment that he is dead, is attempted to be checked.

So that the death of Clodius is not only no advantage, but is even a positive injury to Milo.

"Oh, but his hatred prevailed with him; he slew him in a passion; he slew him because he was his enemy; he acted as the avenger of his own injury; he was exacting atonement to appease his private indignation." But what will you say if these feelings, I do not say existed in a greater degree in Clodius than in Milo, but if they existed in the greatest possible degree in the former, and not at all in the latter? What will you require beyond that? For why should Milo have hated Clodius, the material and ground-work of his glory, except as far as that hatred becoming a citizen goes, with which we hate all worthless men? There was plenty of reason for Clodius to hate Milo, first, as the defender of my safety; secondly, as the repressor of his frenzy, the defeater of his arms; and lastly, also, as his prosecutor. For Clodius was liable to the prosecution of Milo, according to the provisions of the Plotian law, as long as he lived. And with what feelings do you suppose that that tyrant bore that? how great do you suppose was his hatred towards him? and, indeed, how reasonable a hatred was it for a wicked man to entertain.

XIV. It remains for me now to urge his natural disposition and his habits of life in the defense of the one, and the very same things as an accusation against the other. Clodius, I suppose, had never done anything by violence; Milo had done everything by violence. What then shall I say, O judges? When, amid the grief of all of you, I departed from the city, was I afraid of the result of a trial? was I not afraid of slaves, and arms and violence? What, I pray you, was the first ground of my restoration, except that I had been unjustly driven out? Clodius, I suppose, had commenced a formal prosecution against me; he had named a sum as damages; he had commenced an action for high treason; and, I suppose too, I had cause to fear your decision in a cause which was an unjust one, which was my own private cause, not one which was a most righteous one, and which was, in reality, your cause, and not mine? No—I was unwilling that my fellow-citizens, who had been saved by my prudence and by my own personal danger, should be exposed to the arms of slaves and needy citizens and convicted malefactors. For I saw—I saw, I say, this very Quintus Hortensius, the light and ornament of the republic, almost slain by the hand of slaves, while he was standing by me. In which crowd Caius Vibienus, a senator, a most excellent man, who was with Hortensius, was so maltreated that he lost his life.

When, then, was it that that assassin's dagger of his, which he had received from Catiline, rested? It was aimed at us; I would not allow you all to be exposed to it for my sake. It was prepared in treachery for Pompeius. It stained with blood, through the murder of Papirius, the very Appian road, the monument of his name; this, this same dagger, after a long interval was again turned against me; lately, as you know, it nearly murdered me close to the palace of Ancus.

What is there of Milo's conduct like all this? when all the violence that he has ever displayed has amounted to this, that he wished to prevent Publius Clodius (as he could not be brought to trial) from oppressing the city by violence. And if he wished to put him to death, what great, what repeated, and what splendid opportunities he had of doing so! Might he not have avenged himself without violating the law when he was defending his own house and his household gods from his attacks? might he not have done so when that illustrious citizen and most gallant man, Publius Sextius, his own colleague, was wounded? might he not have done so when that most excellent man, Quintus Fabricius, while carrying a bill for my restoration, was driven away, and when a most cruel slaughter was taking place in the forum? might he not have done so when the house of Lucius Cæcilius, that most upright and fearless prætor, was attacked? might he not have done so on the day on which the law concerning me was passed, and when that vast concourse of people from all parts of Italy, whom a regard for my safety had roused up, would have gladly recognized and adopted as its own the glory of that action? so that, even if Milo had performed it, the whole state would claim the praise of it as belonging to itself?

XV. And what a time was it? A most illustrious and fearless consul, Publius Lentulus, an enemy to Clodius the avenger of his wickedness, the bulwark of the senate, the defender of your inclinations, the patron of that general unanimity, the restorer of my safety; seven prætors, eight tribunes of the people, adversaries of him, defenders of me; Cnæus Pompeius, the prime mover of and chief agent in my return his open enemy; whose opinion respecting my return, delivered in the most dignified and most complimentary language, the whole senate adopted; he who exhorted the whole Roman people, and, when he passed a decree concerning me at Capua, gave himself the signal to all Italy, which was eager for it, and which was imploring his good faith, to join together for the purpose of restoring me to Rome; in short, universal hatred on the part of all the citizens, was excited against him, while their minds were inflamed with as earnest a regret for me; so that if any one had slain him at that time, people's thoughts would have been, not how to procure impunity for such a man, but how to reward him sufficiently.

Nevertheless, Milo restrained himself, and twice summoned Publius Clodius before the court, but never once invited him to a trial of strength in scenes of violence. What do I say? while Milo was a private individual, and on his trial before the people, on the accusation of Publius Clodius, when an attack was made on Cnæus Pompeius, while speaking in defense of Milo, was there not then not only an admirable opportunity of, but even a reasonable pretext for slaying him? And lately, when Marcus Antonius had inspired all virtuous men with the very greatest hope of safety, and when he, being a most noble young man, had with the greatest gallantry espoused the cause of the republic, and had that beast almost in his toils in spite of his avoiding the snares of the law; what an opportunity, what a time and place was there, O ye immortal gods! And when Clodius had fled and hidden himself in the darkness of the stairs, there was a fine opportunity for Milo to slay him without incurring the slightest odium himself, and to load Antonius at the same time with the greatest glory! What? How repeatedly had he a similar chance in the comitia! when he had broken into the voting booth, and contrived to have swords drawn and stones thrown, and then on a sudden, terrified at the look of Milo, fled towards the Tiber, and you and all virtuous men prayed to heaven that Milo might take it into his head to give full scope to his valor.

XVI. If then he did not choose to slay him, when he might have done so with the gratitude of every one, is it likely that

he should have chosen to do so when some people were sure
to complain of it? If he did not venture to do it when he might
have done so lawfully, when he had both place and time in
his favor, when he might have done so with impunity, can we
believe that he did not hesitate to slay him unjustly at a time
and place which supplied him with no excuse for the deed,
when it was at the hazard of his life? especially, O judges,
when the day of contest for the greatest distinction of the
state, and the day of the comitia, was at hand. At which time,
(for I know what a nervous thing ambition is, how vehement
and how anxious is the desire for the consulship,) we are
afraid of everything, not only of those things which can be
openly found fault with, but even of whatever can be secretly
thought; we shudder at every rumor, at every idle and empty
story; we look anxiously at every one's countenance, at every
one's eye. For there is nothing so soft, so tender, so frail, so
flexible, as the inclinations and feelings of our fellow-citizens
towards us; for they are not only angry at any impropriety
in the conduct of candidates, but they often even take a dis-
gust at our virtuous actions.

Did Milo then, keeping in view this long hoped-for and
wished-for day of the Campus Martius, propose to himself to
come to those venerable auspices of the centuries with bloody
hands, owing and confessing a wickedness and a crime? How
perfectly incredible is such conduct in such a man! At the
same time, how undoubted is it in the case of Clodius, who
thought that he should be a king as soon as Milo was slain.
What shall I say more? This is the very mainspring of audacity, O judges, for who is there who does not know that the
greatest temptation of all to do wrong is the hope of impunity?
Now, in which of the two did this exist? In Milo? who is even
now on his trial for an action which I contend was an illustrious one, but which was at all events a necessary one; or in
Clodius? who had shown such contempt for courts of justice
and punishment, that he took no pleasure in anything which
was not either impious, from its disregard of the prohibition
of nature, or illegal, from its violation of law.

But what am I arguing about? why do I keep on disputing
at greater length? I appeal to you, O Quintus Petillius, a most
virtuous and fearless citizen; I call you to witness, O Marcus

Cato; whom some heavenly interposition has given me for judges. You have heard from Marcus Favonius, and you heard it too while Clodius was alive, that he, Clodius, had said to him that Milo would die within three days,—and on the third day the deed which he had mentioned was put in execution. When he did not hesitate to reveal what he was thinking of, can you have any doubt what he did?

XVII. How then was it, that he was so correct in the day? I told you that just now. There was no great difficulty in knowing the regular days of sacrifice for the dictator of Lanuvium. He saw that it was necessary for Milo to go to Lanuvium on the very day in which he did go,—therefore, he anticipated him. But on what day? Why, on the day on which, as I have said before, there was a most furious assembly of the people, stirred up by the tribune of the people whom he had in his pay —a day, and an assembly, and an uproar which he would never have missed if he had not been hastening to some premeditated crime. Therefore, he had not only no reason for going on a journey, but he had even a reason for stopping at home. Milo had no possibility of stopping at home, and he had not only a reason, but a positive necessity for going on a journey. What more? Suppose, while he knew that Milo must go on the road on that day, so, on the other hand, Milo could not even suspect that Clodius would? For, first of all, I ask, how could Milo know it? a question which you cannot ask respecting Clodius. For even if he had not asked any one beyond his own intimate friend Titus Patina, he could have ascertained from him that on that particular day a priest must absolutely be appointed at Lanuvium by Milo as the dictator there. But there were plenty more people from whom he could easily learn that; for instance, all the people of Lanuvium. Of whom did Milo make any inquiry about the return of Clodius? Grant that he did make inquiry; see what large allowances I am making you: grant even that he bribed his slave, as my good friend Quintus Arrius said.—Read the evidence of your own witnesses.

Caius Cassinius Schola, a man of Interamna, gave his evidence,—a most intimate friend of Publius Clodius, and more, a companion of his at the very time; according to whose testimony, Publius Clodius was at Interamna and at Rome at the very same time. Well, he said, that Publius Clodius had intended to remain that day at his Alban villa; but that on a sudden news was brought to him, that Cyrus his architect was dead; and, therefore, that he determined to proceed to Rome immediately. Caius Clodius, who was also a companion of Publius Clodius, said the same.

XVIII. Take notice, O judges, what the real effect of this evidence must be. First of all, Milo is certainly acquitted of having set out with the express intention of waylaying Clodius on his road; this must be, since there was apparently no chance whatever of his meeting him. In the next place, (for I see no reason why I should not do something for myself at the same time,) you know, O judges, that there have been men found to say, while urging on this bill against Milo, that the murder was committed by the hand indeed of Milo, but by the plan of some one of more importance than he. Those abject and profligate men, forsooth, pointed me out as a robber and assassin. Now they lie convicted by their own witnesses, who say that Clodius would not have returned to Rome that day if he had not heard the news about Cyrus. I breathed again; I was delivered; I am not any longer afraid of being supposed to have contemplated an action which I could not possibly have suspected.

Now I will examine the other point. For this expression occurs in their speech: "Therefore, Clodius never even thought of the plot against Milo, since he intended to remain in his Alban villa." Yes, he meant to remain there, if he did not rather intend to go out and commit a murder. For I see that the messenger who is said to have brought him news of Cyrus's death did not announce that to him, but told him that Milo was at hand. For why should he bring any news about Cyrus, whom Clodius had left at Rome on his deathbed? I was with him; I signed his will as a witness together with Clodius; and he had openly made his will, and had left him and me his heirs. When he had left him the day before, at the third hour, at the very point of death, was news sent express to him the next day, at the tenth hour, that he was at last dead?

XIX. Well, be it so; what reason had he for hastening to Rome? for starting at nightfall? Why should the fact of his being his heir cause him to make so much haste? In the first place, there was no reason why there should be need of any haste;

secondly, even if there was, still what was there which he could obtain that night, but which he would lose if he arrived at Rome early the next morning? And as an arrival in the city by night was rather to be avoided by him than to be desired, so it was just suited for Milo to lie in ambush and wait for him, as he was a plotter of that sort, if he knew that he was likely to come to the city by night. He would have slain him by night, in a place calculated for an ambush and full of robbers; no one would have refused to believe him if he denied it, when now all men wish to save him even when he confesses it. The brunt of the blame would have fallen on the place itself, so well suited to receive and conceal robbers, while neither the voiceless solitude would have informed against, nor the dark night discovered Milo; secondly, the numbers of men who had been insulted by Clodius, or plundered by him, or stripped of all their property by him, many, too, who were in constant fear of such misfortunes, would have fallen under suspicion; in short, the whole of Etruria would have been impeached in people's opinion.

And certainly on that day Clodius returning from Aricia did turn aside to his Alban villa. But although Milo knew that he was at Aricia, still he ought to have suspected that he, even if he was desirous to return to Rome that day, would turn aside to his own villa, the grounds of which skirted the road. Why, then, did he not meet him before, and prevent his going to his villa? nor wait in that place where he would certainly arrive by night?

I see that all things up to this point are plain and consistent. That it was even desirable for Milo that Clodius should live; that for Clodius the death of Milo was the most advantageous thing possible, with reference to those objects on which he had set his heart; that he bore him the most bitter hatred, but that Milo had no such feelings towards him; that the one lived in a perpetual round of violence, that the other's habits were limited to repelling it; that Milo had been threatened by him with death; and that his death had been openly predicted by him; that no such expression had ever been heard from Milo; that the day of Milo's journey was well known to Clodius, but that Clodius's return was unknown to Milo; that the journey of the one was inevitable, and that of the other was even inconvenient to himself; that the one had openly declared that on that day he should set out from Rome, that the other had concealed the fact of his intending to return on that day; that the one had in no respect whatever changed his intention, that the other had invented a false pretense for changing his mind; that the one, if he were plotting, would naturally wish night to come on when he was near the city, while an arrival at the city by night was to be feared by the other, even if he had no apprehension of danger from this man.

XX. Let us now consider this, which is the main point of all; for which of the two the identical spot where they did meet was the best suited for planting an ambush. But is that, O judges, a matter about which one can possibly doubt or think seriously for a moment? In front of Clodius's farm,—that farm on which, on account of those absurd erections and excavations for foundations of his, there were pretty well a thousand vigorous men employed,—on that high and raised ground belonging to his adversary, did Milo think that he should get the better in the contest, and had he with that view selected that spot above all others? Or was he rather waited for in that place by a man who had conceived the idea of attacking, because of the hopes that that particular spot suggested to him? The facts, O judges, speak for themselves; facts, which are always of the greatest weight in a cause. If you were not hearing of this transaction, but were looking at a picture of it, still it would be quite visible which of the two was the plotter, which was thinking no evil, when one of the two was driving in a chariot wrapped up in a mantle, with his wife sitting by his side. It is hard to say which was the greatest hindrance to him, his dress, or his carriage, or his wife. How could a man be less ready for battle than when he was entangled in a mantle as in a net, hampered with a carriage, and fettered as it were by his wife clinging to him? Look on the other hand, at Clodius, first setting out from his villa; all on a sudden: why? It was evening. Why was he forced to set out at such a time? Going slowly. What was the object of that, especially at that time of night. He turns aside to the villa of Pompeius. To see Pompeius? He knew that he was near Alsium. To see the villa? He had been in it a thousand times. What, then, was his object? Delay; he wanted to waste the time. He did not choose to leave the spot till Milo arrived.

XXI. Come now, compare the journey of this unencumbered bandit with all the hindrances which beset Milo. Before this time he always used to travel with his wife; now he was without her. He invariably went in a carriage; now he was on horseback. His train were a lot of Greeklings wherever he was going; even when he was hastening to the camp in Etruria;[10] but this time there were no triflers in his retinue. Milo, who was never in the habit of doing so, did by chance have with him some musical slaves belonging to his wife, and troops of maid servants. The other man, who was always carrying with him prostitutes, worn-out debauchees both men and women, this time had no one with him except such a band that you might have thought every one of them picked men. Why, then, was he defeated? Because the traveler is not always murdered by the robber; sometimes the robber is killed by the traveler; because, although Clodius in a state of perfect preparation was attacking men wholly unprepared, still it was the case of a woman falling upon men. And, indeed, Milo was never so utterly unprepared for his violence, as not to be nearly sufficiently prepared. He was always aware how greatly it concerned the interest of Publius Clodius that he should be slain, how greatly he hated him, and how great was his daring. Wherefore, he never exposed his life to danger without some sort of protection and guard, knowing that it was threatened, and that a large price, as it were, was set upon it.

Add to this consideration all the chances; add the always uncertain result of a battle, and the common fortune of Mars, who often overthrows the man who is already exulting and stripping his enemy, and strikes him to the ground by some mean agent; add the blundering conduct of a leader who had dined and drank, and who was yawning and drowsy; who, when he had left his enemy cut off in the rear, never thought of his companions on the outskirts of his train; and then when he fell among them inflamed with anger, and despairing of saving the life of their master he fell on that punishment which the faithful slaves inflicted on him as a retribution for their master's death. Why, then, has Milo emancipated them? He

---

[10] That is, to Manlius's camp in Etruria at the time of Catiline's conspiracy in which, in all probability, Clodius was implicated.

was afraid, I suppose, lest they should give information against him; lest they should be unable to bear pain; lest they should be compelled by tortures to confess that Publius Clodius was slain in the Appian road by the slaves of Milo.

What need is there of any torturer? What do you want to know? whether he was slain? He was slain. Whether he was slain lawfully or unlawfully? That is beyond the province of the torturer. For the rack can only inquire into the fact; it is the bench of judges that must decide on the law.

XXII. Let us then here confine our attention to what must be investigated in this trial. All that you can want to find out by tortures we admit. But if you prefer asking why he emancipated his slaves, rather than why he gave them inadequate rewards, you are but a bungling hand at finding fault with an enemy. For Marcus Cato, who says everything with great wisdom, and consistency, and courage, said the same thing; and he said, too, in a very turbulent assembly of the people, which, however, was pacified by his authority, that those slaves were worthy not only of liberty, but even of every sort of reward possible, who had defended the life of their master. For what reward can be sufficiently great for such well-affected, such virtuous, such faithful slaves, owing to whom it is that he is still alive? Although even that is not putting it so strongly as to say, that it is owing to those very men that he did not glut the eyes and mind of his most cruel enemy with his blood and wounds. And if he had not emancipated them, then those preservers of their master, those avengers of wickedness, those defenders of their master from death, must have even been surrendered to torture. But in all these misfortunes the most comfortable reflection which Milo has is, that, even if anything should happen to himself, still he has given them the reward which they deserved.

But now the examinations which have just been conducted in the hall of liberty, are said to press against Milo. Who are the slaves who have been examined? Do you ask? The slaves of Publius Clodius. Who demanded that they should be examined? Appius. Who produced them? Appius. Where were they brought from? From the house of Appius. O ye good gods, what can be done with more animosity? There is no law which authorizes slaves to be examined as witnesses against their master, except on accusations of impiety, as was the case in the prosecution instituted against Clodius. Clodius has been raised nearly to the gods, more nearly than even when he penetrated into their sanctuary, when an investigation into the circumstances of his death is carried on like one into a profanation of sacred ceremonies. But still, our ancestors did not think it right that slaves should be examined as witnesses against their masters, not because the truth could not be discovered, but because it seemed a scandalous thing to do, and more oppressive to the masters than even death itself. Well, then, when the slaves of the prosecutor are examined as witnesses against the defendant, can the truth be found out?

Come, however, what was the examination; and how was it conducted? Holloa, you Rufio, (that name will do as well as another,) take care you tell the truth. Did Clodius lay a plot against Milo? "He did." He is sure to be crucified for saying so. "Certainly not." He has hopes of obtaining his liberty. What can be more certain than this mode of examination? The men are suddenly carried off to be examined; they are separated from all the rest, and put into cells that no one may be able to speak to them. Then, when they have been kept a hundred days in the power of the prosecutor, they are produced as witnesses, by the prosecutor himself. What can be imagined more upright than this sort of examination? What can be more free from all suspicion of corruption?

XXIII. And if you do not yet see with sufficient clearness, (though the transaction is evident of itself by so many and such irresistible arguments and proofs,) that Milo was returning to Rome with a pure and guiltless intention, with no taint of wickedness, under no apprehension, without any consciousness of crime to disquiet him; recollect, I implore you, in the name of the immortal gods, how rapid his speed while returning was; how he entered the forum while the senate-house was all on fire with eagerness; how great was the magnanimity which he displayed; how he looked, and what he said. Nor did he trust himself to the people only, but also to the senate; nor to the senate only, but also to the public guards and their arms; nor to them only, but also to the power of that man to whom the senate had already entrusted [11] the whole republic, all the youth of Italy, and all the arms of the Roman people. And surely he never would have put himself in his power, if he had not been confident in the justice of his cause; especially as he was one who heard everything, and feared great danger, and suspected many things, and even believed some. The power of conscience is very great, O judges, and is of great weight on both sides: so that they fear nothing who have done no wrong, and they, on the other hand, who have done wrong think that punishment is always hanging over them.

Nor, indeed, is it without good reason that Milo's cause has always been approved of by the senate. For these wisest of men took into their consideration the whole circumstances of the case; Milo's presence of mind, and vigor in defending himself. Have you forgotten, O judges, when the news of Clodius's death was still recent, the opinions and the language which was held, not only by Milo's enemies, but also by other ignorant people? They said that he would not return to Rome at all. For if he had committed the deed in a passionate and excited mood, so that he had slain his enemy while under the influence of strong hatred, they thought that he would consider the death of Publius Clodius an event of such importance, that he would bear being deprived of his country with equanimity, as he had sated his hatred in the blood of his enemy; or, if he had deliberately intended to deliver his country by the slaughter of Clodius, then they thought that he, as a brave man,

[11] The disturbances on the death of Clodius arose to such a height, that the senate at last passed a resolution that Marcus Lepidus the Interrex, assisted by the tribunes of the people and Pompeius, should take care that the republic received no injury. And at last the senate appointed Pompeius consul without a colleague, who immediately published several new laws, and among them the one under which this trial was conducted, (see note con c. 1,) and he now limited the duration of trials, allowing only three days for the examination of witnesses, and on the fourth day the accuser was only allowed two hours to enforce the accusation, and the defendant three hours to speak in his defense. Cœlius endeavored to arrest these laws by his veto as tribune, declaring that they were framed solely with a view to crush Milo, whom Pompeius certainly desired to get rid of; to effect which he even descended to the artifice of pretending to believe that Milo had laid a plot to assassinate him.

would not hesitate, after having brought safety to his country at his own risk, to submit with equanimity to the laws, to carry off with himself everlasting renown, and to leave those things to us to enjoy which he had preserved for us himself.

Many also spoke of Catiline and the monsters of his train. "We shall have another Catiline breaking out. He will occupy some strong place; he will make war on his country." Wretched sometimes is the fate of those citizens who have faithfully served the republic! when men not only forget the illustrious exploits which they have performed, but even suspect them of the most nefarious designs! Therefore, all those things were false, which would certainly have turned out true if Milo had committed any action which he could not defend with honor and with truth.

XXIV. What shall I say of the charges which were afterwards heaped upon him? which would have crushed any one who was conscious of even trifling offenses. How nobly did he support them? O ye immortal gods, do I say support them? Say rather, how did he despise them, and treat them as nothing! Charges which no guilty man, were he ever so high minded, and, indeed, no innocent man, unless he were also a most fearless man, could possibly have disregarded. I was said that a vast collection of shields, swords, bridles, lances, and javelins had been seized. They said that there was no street, no alley in the whole city, in which there was not a house hired for Milo; that arms had been carried down the Tiber to his villa at Oriculum; that his house on the Capitoline Hill was full of shields; that every place was full of fire brands prepared for the burning of the city. These things were not only reported, but were almost believed, and were not rejected till they had been thoroughly investigated. I praised, indeed, the incredible diligence of Cnæus Pompeius; but still I will say what I really think, O judges.

Those men are compelled to listen to too many statements; indeed, they cannot do otherwise, who have the whole republic entrusted to them. It was necessary even to listen to that eating-house keeper Licinius, if that was his name, a fellow out of the Circus Maximus, who said that Milo's slaves had got drunk in his house,—that they had confessed to him that they were engaged in a conspiracy to assassinate Cnæus Pompeius, and that he himself was afterwards stabbed by one of them to prevent him from giving information. He went to Pompeius's villa to tell him this. I am sent for among the first. By the advice of his friends, Pompeius reports the affair to the senate. It was impossible for me to be otherwise than frightened almost to death at the bare suspicion of such danger to one who was the protector both of me and of my country; but still I wondered that an eating-house keeper should be at once believed,—that the confession of the slaves should be listened to, and that a wound in the side, which looked like the prick of a needle, should be admitted to be a wound inflicted by a gladiator. But, as I take the fact to have been, Pompeius was rather taking precautions than feeling any actual alarm, guarding not only against those things which it was reasonable to fear, but also against everything which could possibly disquiet you.

The house of Caius Cæsar, that most illustrious and gallant man, was beseiged, as was reported, during many hours of the night. No one in that frequented part of the city had either seen or heard of any such thing. Still such a report was spread about. I could not possibly suspect Cnæus Pompeius, a man of the most admirable valor, of being timid, and I thought no diligence could be over-strained in a man who had undertaken the management and protection of the whole of the republic. In a very full meeting of the senate, lately held in the Capitol, a senator was found to say that Milo had a weapon about him. He threw back his garments in that most sacred temple, that, since the life of so good a citizen and so good a man could not procure him credit, the facts themselves might speak for him, while he held his peace.

XXV. Every word was ascertained to be a false and treacherous invention. And if people are even now afraid of Milo, we are not now under apprehension because of the charge respecting Clodius, but we are shuddering at your suspicions,—at yours, I say, O Cnæus Pompeius (for I address you yourself, and I speak loudly so that you may be able to hear me). If you are afraid of Milo,—if you believe that he either now cherishes wicked designs against your life, or that he ever has entertained such; if the levying of troops throughout Italy, as some of your recruiting-sergeants pretend,—if these arms,—if these cohorts in the Capitol,—if these watchmen, these sentinels,—if

this picked body of youths, which is the guard of your person
and your house, is all armed against an attack on the part of
Milo; and if all these measures have been arranged, and prepared, and aimed against him alone,—then certainly he must
be a man of great power, of incredible courage; surely it must
be more than the power and resources of one single man which
are attributed to him, if the most eminent of our generals is
invested with a command, and all Italy is armed against this
one man. But who is there who does not understand that all the
diseased and feeble parts of the republic were entrusted to you,
O Pompeius, that you might heal and strengthen them with
your arms? And if an opportunity had been afforded to Milo,
he would, doubtless, have proved to you yourself that no man
was ever more dear to another than you are to him; that he had
never shunned any danger which might be of service in pro-
moting your dignity; that he had often contended against that
most foul pest on behalf of your glory; that his conduct in his
tribuneship had been entirely regulated by your counsels for
the protection of my safety, which was an object very dear to
you; that he afterwards had been defended by you when in
danger of his life,[12] and had been assisted by you when he was
a candidate for the prætorship; and that he had always believed that the two firmest friends whom he had were you and
I,—you, as shown by the kindness of your behavior to him, and
I, secured to him by the services which he himself had done
me. And if he could not convince you of this,—if that suspicion
had sunk so deep in your mind that it could not possibly be
eradicated; if, in short, Italy was never to have any rest from
those levies, nor the city from arms, till Milo was ruined,—then
no doubt he, without hesitation, would have departed from his
country, a man born to make such sacrifices and accustomed to
make them; but still he would have cited you, O Magnus, as a
witness in his favor, as he now does.

XXVI. See, now, how various and changeable is the course

[12] When Clodius was ædile, he instituted a prosecution against Milo
for violence. Pompeius, Crassus and Cicero appeared for him; and
though Clodius's mob raised a great uproar, and endeavored to prevent
Pompeius from being heard, he made a long speech, lasting three hours,
in his defense. The trial was adjourned from February till May, and
does not appear to have ever been brought to a regular termination.

of human life,—how fickle and full of revolutions is fortune; what instances of perfidy are seen in friends, how they dissemble and suit their behavior to the occasion; when dangers beset one, how one's nearest connections fly off, and what cowardice they show. The time will come, ay, will most certainly come,—that day will surely dawn some time or other, when you, though your affairs are all, as I trust they will be, in a really sound condition, though they may, perhaps, wear an altered appearance in consequence of some commotion of the times, such as we are all liable to, (and how constantly such things happen we may know from experience,)—when you, I say, may be in need of the good-will of one who is most deeply attached to you, and the good faith of a man of the greatest weight and dignity, and the magnanimity of the very bravest man that ever lived in the world. Although, who would believe that Cnæus Pompeius, a man most thoroughly versed in public law, in the usages of our ancestors, and in all the affairs of the republic, after the senate has entrusted to him the charge of taking care "that the republic suffered no injury," by which one line the consuls have always been sufficiently armed, even though no warlike weapons were given to them,—that he, I say, after having had an army and a levy of troops given to him, would wait for a legal decision to repress the designs of that man who was seeking by violence to abolish the courts of justice themselves?

It was sufficiently decided by Pompeius, quite sufficiently, that all those charges were falsely brought against Milo; when he passed a law by which, as I conceive, he was bound to be acquitted by you,—at all events, as all men allow, might legally be acquitted. But when he sits in that place, surrounded by all those bands of public guards, he declares plainly enough that he is not striking terror into you, (for what could be less worthy of him than to condemn a man whom he himself might punish if guilty, both by his own authority and in strict accordance with the precedents of our ancestors?) but that he keeps them about him for the sake of protection; that you may be aware that it is allowed to you to decide with freedom according to your own opinions, in contradiction to that assembly of the people which was held yesterday.

XXVII. Nor, O judges, am I at all moved by the accusation

respecting Clodius. Nor am I so insane, and so ignorant of, and inexperienced in, your feelings, as not to be aware what your opinions are about the death of Clodius, concerning which, if I were unwilling to do away with the accusation in the manner in which I have done away with it, still I assert that it would have been lawful for Milo to proclaim openly, with a false but glorious boast, "I have slain, I have slain, not Spurius Mælius, who fell under the suspicion of aiming at kingly power by lowering the price of corn, and by squandering his own family estate, because by that conduct he was thought to be paying too much court to the common people; not Tiberius Gracchus, who, out of seditious spirit, abrogated the magistracy of his own colleague; whose slayers have filled the whole world with the renown of their name; but him" (for he would venture to name him when he had delivered his country at his own risk) "who was detected in the most infamous adultery in the most sacred shrine, by most noble women; him, by the execution of whom the senate has repeatedly resolved that solemn religious observances required to be propitiated; him whom Lucius Lucullus, when he was examined on the point, declared on his oath that he had detected in committing unhallowed incest with his own sister; him, who by means of armed bands of slaves drove from his country that citizen whom the senate, whom the Roman people, whom all nations had declared to be the savior of the city and of the lives of all the citizens; him, who gave kingdoms, took them away, and distributed the whole world to whomsoever he pleased; him who, after having committed numberless murders in the forum, drove a citizen of the most extraordinary virtue and glory to his own house by violence and by arms; him, to whom nothing was ever too impious to be done, whether it was a deed of atrocity or of lust; him, who burned the temple of the nymphs, in order to extinguish the public record of the census which was committed to the public registers; lastly, him who acknowledged no law, no civil rights, no boundaries to any man's possessions,—who sought to obtain other people's estates, not by actions at law and false accusations, not by unjust claims and false oaths, but by camps, by an army, by regular standards and all the pomp of war,— who, by means of arms and soldiers, endeavored to drive from their possessions, not only the Etrurians, for he thoroughly despised them, but even this Publius Varius, that most gallant man and most virtuous citizen, one of our judges,—who went into many other people's villas and grounds with architects and surveyors, who limited his hopes of acquiring possessions by Janiculum and the Alps; him who, when he was unable to prevail on an estimable and gallant Roman knight, Marcus Paconius, to sell him his villa on the Preliam Lake, suddenly conveyed timber, and lime, and mortar, and tools in barques to the island, and while the owner of the island was looking at him from the opposite bank, did not hesitate to build a house on another man's land; who said to Titus Furfanius—O ye immortal gods, what a man! (for why should I mention that insignificant woman, Scantia, or that youth Aponius, both of whom he threatened with death if they did not abandon to him the possession of their villas?) but he dared to say to Furfanius, that if he did not give him as much money as he demanded, he would carry a dead body into his house, and so raise a storm of unpopularity against him; who turned his brother Appius, a man connected with me by the most faithful friendship, while he was absent, out of the possession of his farm; who determined to run a wall across the vestibule of his sister's house in such a manner, and to draw the line of foundation in such a direction, as not only to deprive his sister of her vestibule, but of all access to her house, and of her own threshold."

XXVIII. Although all these things appeared such as might be endured,—although he attacked with equal fury the republic, and private individuals, and men who were at a distance, and men who were near, people who had no connection with him, and his own relations; yet somehow or other the incredible endurance of the state had by long use grown hardened and callous. But as for the things which were at hand, and were impending over you, in what manner was it possible for you either to avert them or to bear them? If he had once obtained real power,—I say nothing of our allies, of foreign nations, and kings, and tetrarchs; for you would have prayed that he might turn himself against them rather than against your possessions, your houses, and your money: money do I say? your children rather,—I solemnly swear he would never have restrained himself from your children and from your wives. Do you think that these things are inventions of mine? They are

evident; they are notorious to every one; they are proved. Is it
an invention of mine that he was about to enlist an army of
slaves in the city, by whose instrumentality he might take possession of the whole republic, and of the private fortune of
every one?

Wherefore, if Titus Annius, holding in his hand a bloody
sword, had cried out, "Come hither, I beg of you, and listen to
me, O citizens: I have slain Publius Clodius; with this sword
and with this right hand I have turned aside from your necks
the frenzied attacks of that man whom we were unable to
restrain by any laws, or by any judicial proceedings whatever;
by my single efforts has it been brought to pass that right,
and equity, and laws, and liberty, and modesty, and chastity
remain in this city;" would there in truth have been any reason
to fear in what manner the city would receive this announce-
ment? For now, as it is, who is there who does not approve of
what has been done? who does not praise it? who does not both
say and feel that of all men to whom recollection can reach
back, Titus Annius has done the republic the greatest service;
that of all men he has diffused the greatest joy among the
Roman people, and over the whole of Italy, and throughout
all nations? I cannot form a conception of what would have
been the old-fashioned joy of the Roman people. Already our
age has seen many, and those most illustrious victories, won by
consummate generals; but not one of them has brought with it
a joy that either lasted so long or that was so excessive while it
did last.

Commit this fact to memory, O judges. I trust that you and
your children will see many happy days in the republic. On
every such occasion these will always be your feelings,—that
if Publius Clodius had been alive, you never would have seen
one of them. We have been led now to conceive the greatest,
and, as I feel sure, the best-founded hopes, that this very day,
this most admirable man being made our consul, when the
licentiousness of men is checked, their evil passions put down,
the laws and courts of justice reestablished on a firm footing,
will be a salutary day for the republic. Is there, then, any one
so insane as to think that he could have obtained all this while
Publius Clodius was alive? What? why, what power of perpetual possession could you have had even in those things

which you possess as your private property and in the strictest sense your own, while that frenzied man held the reins of government?

XXIX. I have no fear, O judges, lest it should seem that, because I am inflamed with hatred against him, on account of my own personal enmity to the man, I am vomiting forth these charges against him with more zeal than truth. In truth, though it is natural that that should be an especial stimulus to me, yet he was so completely the common enemy of all men, that my own hatred only bore about its fair proportion to the general detestation with which he was regarded. It cannot be expressed, O judges, it cannot even be imagined, how much wickedness, how much mischief there was in that man.

Moreover, attend to me with this idea, O judges. This investigation relates to the death of Publius Clodius. Imagine in your minds,—for our thoughts are free, and contemplate whatever they choose in such a manner that we do discern those things which we think we see;—place, therefore, before your mind's eye the image of this my condition; if I am able to induce you to acquit Milo, but still only on condition of Publius Clodius being restored to life. What fear is that that you show by your countenances? How would he affect you if alive, when even now that he is dead he has so agitated you by the bare thought of him? What? if Cnæus Pompeius himself, who is a man of such virtue and such good fortune that he has at all times been able to do things which no one except him ever could have done,—if even he, I say, had been able, in the same manner as he has ordered an investigation into the death of Publius Clodius to take place, so also to raise him from the dead, which do you think he would have preferred to do? Even if out of friendship he had been willing to raise him from the shades below, out of regard for the republic he would not have done it. You, then, are sitting now as avengers of the death of that man, whom you would not restore to life if you thought it possible that his life could be restored by you. And this investigation is appointed to be made into to death of a man who would never have seen such a law passed, if the law which ordered the inquiry had been able to restore him to life. Ought, then, the slayer of this man, if any such slayer there be, to have any reason, while confessing the deed, to fear punishment at the hand of those men whom he delivered by the deed?

Grecian nations give the honors of the gods to those men who have slain tyrants. What have I not seen at Athens? what in the other cities of Greece? What divine honors have I not seen paid to such men? What odes, what songs have I not heard in their praise? They are almost consecrated to immortality in the memories and worship of men. And will you not only abstain from conferring any honors on the savior of so great a people, and the avenger of such enormous wickedness, but will you even allow him to be borne off for punishment? He would confess,—I say, if he had done it, he would confess with a high and willing spirit that he had done it for the sake of the general liberty; a thing which would certainly deserve not only to be confessed by him, but even to be boasted of.

XXX. In truth, if he does not deny an action from which he seeks no advantage beyond being pardoned for having done it, would he hesitate to avow an action for which he would be entitled to claim rewards? Unless indeed he thinks it more pleasing to you to look upon him as having been the defender of his own life, rather than of you; especially as from that confession, if you were to choose to be grateful, he would reap the very highest honors. If his action were not approved of by you, (although, how is it possible that any one should not approve of what secured his own safety?)—but still, if the virtue of a most gallant man had happened to be at all unpleasing to his fellow-citizens, then with a lofty and firm mind he would depart from an ungrateful city. For what could be more ungrateful than for all other men to be rejoicing, and for him alone to be mourning, to whom it was owing that the rest were rejoicing? Although we have all at all times been of this disposition with respect to crushing traitors to our country,—that since the glory would be ours, we should consider the danger and the unpopularity ours also. For what praise should I have deserved to have given to me, when I showed so much courage in my consulship on behalf of you and of your children, if I had supposed that I could venture on the exploits which I was attempting without very great struggles and dangers to myself? What woman is there who would not dare to slay a wicked and mischievous citizen, if she was not afraid of the danger of the attempt? But the man who, though unpopularity, and death, and punishment are before his eyes, still ventures to defend the republic with no less alacrity than if no such evils threatened him, he deserves to be considered really a man.

It behooves a grateful people to reward those citizens who have deserved well of the republic; it is the part of a brave man, not to be so moved even by execution itself, as to repent of having acted bravely. Wherefore, Titus Annius may well make the same confession which Ahala made, which Nasica, which Opimius, which Marius, which we ourselves have made: and then, if the republic were grateful, he would rejoice; if ungrateful, then though under the pressure of heavy misfortune, he would still be supported by his own conscience.

But, O judges, the fortune of the Roman people, and your felicity, and the immortal gods, all think that they are entitled to your gratitude for this service which has been thus done to you. Nor, indeed, can any one think otherwise except it be a man who thinks that there is no such thing at all as any divine power or authority—a man who is neither moved by the vastness of your empire, nor by that sun above us, nor by the motions of heaven and of the stars, nor by the vicissitudes and regular order of things, nor (and that is the greatest thing of all) by the wisdom of our ancestors; who both themselves cultivated with the most holy reverence the sacred rites and religious ceremonies and auspices, and also handed them down to us their posterity to be so cultivated by us.

XXXI. There is, there is indeed, such a heavenly power. It is not the truth, that in these bodies and in this feebleness of ours there is something which is vigorous and endued with feeling, and nothing which is so in this vast and beautiful movement of nature. Unless perhaps some people think that there is no such thing in existence because it is not apparent, nor visible: just as if we were able to see our own mind,—that by which we are wise, by which we have foresight, by which we do and say these very things which we are doing and saying; or as if we could plainly feel what sort of thing it is, or where it is. That divine power, that very same divine power which has often brought incredible prosperity and power to this city, has extinguished and destroyed this mischief; by first

of all inspiring it with the idea of venturing to irritate by violence and to attack with the sword the bravest of men, and so
leading it on to be defeated by the man whom if it had only
been able to defeat it would have enjoyed endless license and
impunity. That result was brought about, O judges, not by human wisdom, nor even by any moderate degree of care on the
part of the immortal gods. In truth, those very holy places
themselves which beheld that monster fall, appear to have
been moved themselves, and to have asserted their rights over
him.

I implore you, I call you to witness,—you, I say, O ye Alban
hills and groves, and you, O ye altars of the Albans, now over-
thrown, but nevertheless partners of and equals in honor with
the sacred rites of the Roman people,—ye, whom that man
with headlong insanity, having cut down and destroyed the
most holy groves, had overwhelmed with his insane masses of
buildings; it was your power then that prevailed, it was the
divinity of your altars, the religious reverence due to you, and
which he had profaned by every sort of wickedness, that prevailed; and you, too, O sacred Jupiter of Latium, whose lakes
and groves and boundaries he had constantly polluted with
every sort of abominable wickedness and debauchery, you at
last, from your high and holy mountain, opened your eyes for
the purpose of punishing him; it is to you, to all of you, that
those punishments, late indeed, but still just and well deserved,
have been made an atonement for his wickedness.

Unless, perchance, we are to say that it was by accident that
it happened that it was before the very shrine of the Good
Goddess which is in the farm of Titus Sextus Gallius, a most
honorable and accomplished young man,—before the Good
Goddess herself, I say, that when he had begun the battle, he
received that first wound under which he gave up that foul
soul of his; so that he did not seem to have been acquitted in
that iniquitous trial, but only to have been reserved for this
conspicuous punishment.

XXXII. Nor, indeed, did that same anger of the gods abstain from inflicting the very same insanity on his satellites, so
that without the images of his ancestors, without any funeral
song or funeral games, without any obsequies, any lamentation, or any panegyric,—without, in short, any funeral at all,

smeared over with gore and mud, and deprived even of the
honors which are paid to every one on that last day, and which
even enemies are wont to allow to a man, he was cast out in
the street half burnt. It was not right, I suppose, for the effigies
of most illustrious men to confer any honor on that most foul
parricide; nor was there any place in which it was more seemly
that his corpse should be ill-treated than that where his life had
been condemned.

I swear to you, the fortune of the Roman people appeared
to me hard and cruel, while it for so many years beheld and endured that man triumphing over the republic. He had polluted
the holiest religious observances with his debauchery; he had
broken the most authoritative decrees of the senate; he had
openly bought himself from the judges with money; he had
harassed the senate in his tribuneship; he had rescinded acts
which had been passed for the sake of the safety of the republic, by the consent of all orders of the state; he had driven
me from my country; he had plundered my property; he had
burnt my house; he had ill-treated my children and my wife;
he had declared a wicked war against Cnæus Pompeius; he
had made slaughter of magistrates and private individuals; he
had burnt the house of my brother; he had laid waste Etruria;
he had driven numbers of men from their homes and their pro-
fessions. He kept pursuing and oppressing men; the whole
state, all Italy, all the provinces, all foreign kingdoms could not
contain his frenzy. Laws were already being drawn up in his
house which were to hand us over to the power of our slaves.
There was nothing belonging to any one, which he had taken
a fancy to, which he did not think would become his in the
course of this year. No one was an obstacle to his expectations
except Milo; the very man who was most able to be an obstacle
to them he thought when he returned again would be reconciled and, as it were, bound to him. The power of Cæsar, he
said, was all his own. The inclinations of all good men he had
treated with contempt, while accomplishing my ruin. Milo
alone weighed on his mind.

XXXIII. On this the immortal gods, as I have said before,
put into the head of that abandoned and frantic man the idea
of laying an ambush for Milo. That pest was not to perish any
other way; the republic would never have chastened him by

her laws. The senate, I suppose, would have been able to restrain him when prætor. Why, it had not been able to do anything when it tried to restrain him while a private individual.
Would the consuls have been vigorous in bridling the prætor?
In the first place, if Milo had been slain, he would have had his
own consuls. Secondly, what consul would have behaved fearlessly against him as prætor, who remembered that he, when
tribune, had offered the most cruel injuries to the virtue of the
consuls? He would have oppressed everything; he would have
taken possession and held possession of everything. By a new
law, the draft of which was found in his house, with the rest
of the Clodian laws, he would have made all our slaves his own
freedmen. Lastly, if the immortal gods had not inspired him
with such ideas that he, an effeminate creature, attempted to
slay a most gallant man, you would have no republic at all this
day. Would that man when prætor, much more when consul,
provided only that these temples and these walls could have
stood so long if he had been alive, and could have remained
till his consulship; would he, I say, if alive, have done no harm,
when even after he was dead he burned the senate-house, one
of his satellites, Sextus Clodius, being the ringleader in the
tumult? What more miserable, more grievous, more bitter sight
have we ever seen than that? that that temple of sanctity, of
honor, of wisdom, of the public council, the head of the city,
the altar of the allies, the harbor of all nations, the abode
granted by the universal Roman people to one of the orders of
the state, should be burnt, profaned, and destroyed? [13] and that
that should be done, not by an ignorant mob, although that
would have been a miserable thing, but by one single person?
who, if he dared so much in his character of burner of a dead

[13] When Clodius was killed, his slaves fled, and left his dead body in
the road; and it was brought to Rome the next day by Sextus Tedius, a
senator, who was passing by and saw it; and then it was exposed to the
view of the populace of the city. The next day the mob, headed by Sextus
Clodius, carried the body naked, so as to show his wounds, into the
forum, and placed it on the rostra; and then the tribunes harangued the
people on the subject, and wrought them up to such a pitch of excite-
ment, that, snatching up the body, they carried it into the senate-house,
and tearing up the benches and tables, dressed up a funeral pile on the
spot, and, together with the body, burnt the senate-house itself, with the
Basilica Porcia which joined it.

man, what would he not have done as standard-bearer of a living one? He selected the senate-house, of all the places in the city, to throw him down in, in order that when dead he might burn what he had overturned while alive.

And are there men, then, who complain of what took place in the Appian road, and say nothing of what happened in the senate-house? and who think that the forum could have been defended from him when alive, whose very corpse the senate-house was unable to resist? Arouse the man himself; resuscitate him, if you can, from the shades below. Will you be able to check his violence when alive, when you were hardly able to support his fury while he lies unburied? unless, indeed, you did support the sight of those men who ran with firebrands to the senate-house, with scythes of the temple of Castor, and who ranged over the whole forum sword in hand. You saw the Roman people slaughtered, you saw the assembly disturbed by the drawn swords, while Marcus Cælius, a tribune of the people, was listened to in silence, a man of the greatest courage in the affairs of state, of the greatest firmness in any cause which he undertook, wholly devoted to the service of the virtuous part of the citizens, and to the authority of the senate, and in this—shall I say unpopularity, or misfortune of Milo's? behaving with singular, and god-like, and incredible good faith.

XXXIV. But I have said enough about the cause; and, perhaps, too much that was foreign to the cause. What remains, except for me to pray and entreat you, O judges, to show that mercy to a most gallant man, which he himself does not implore; but which I, even against his will, implore and demand in his behalf? Do not, if amid the tears of all of us you have seen no tears shed by Milo,—if you see his countenance always the same, his voice and language steady and unaltered,—do not, on that account, be the less inclined to spare him. I know not whether he does not deserve to be assisted all the more on that account. In truth, if in the battles of gladiators, and in the case of men of the very lowest class and condition and fortune, we are accustomed to dislike those who are timid and suppliant, and who pray to be allowed to live, and if we wish to save those who are brave and courageous, and who offer themselves cheerfully to death; and if we feel more pity for those

men who do not ask our pity, than for those who entreat it;
how much more ought we to nourish those feelings in the case
of our bravest citizens? As for me, O judges, I am dispirited
and almost killed by those expressions of Milo, which I hear
continually, and at the utterance of which I am daily present:
"May my fellow-citizens fare well," says he; "may they fare
well. May they be safe, and prosperous and happy; may this
illustrious city, and my country, which I love so well, long endure, however it may treat me; may my fellow-citizens (since
I may not enjoy it with them) enjoy the republic in tranquility
without me, but still in consequence of my conduct. I will submit, and depart; if it cannot be allowed me to enjoy a virtuous
republic, at least I shall be at a distance from a bad one; and
the first well regulated and free city that I arrive at, in that will
I rest. Oh how vain," says he, "are the labors which I have
undertaken! Oh how fallacious have been my hopes! Oh how
empty all my thoughts! When as tribune of the people, when
the republic was oppressed, I had devoted myself to the senate,
which, when I came into office, was utterly extinct; and to the
Roman knights, whose power was enfeebled, and to the virtuous part of the citizens, who had given up all their authority
under the arms of Clodius; could I ever have thought that I
should fail to find protection from the citizens? When I had
restored you" (for he very frequently converses with me and
addresses me) "to your country, could I ever suppose that I
myself should have no place in my country? Where now is the
senate which we followed? where are those Roman knights,
those knights," says he, "so devoted to you? where is the zeal
of the municipal towns? where is the voice of Italy? what,
above all, has become of that voice of yours, O Marcus Tullius,
which has been an assistance to many; what has become of
your voice and defensive eloquence? am I the only person
whom it is unable to help, I who have so often exposed myself
to death for your sake?"

XXXV. Nor does he say these things to me, O judges, weeping, as I now repeat them; but with the same unmoved countenance that you behold. For he says, he never did all the
things which he had done for citizens who are ungrateful; ungrateful, he says, they are not. That they are timid, and thinking too much of every danger, he does not deny. He says, that

he treated the common people, and that multitude of the lower class which, while they had Publius Clodius for their leader, threatened the safety of all of you, in such a way, in order to render all your lives more secure; that he not only subdued it by his virtue, but won it over at the expense of three estates which he inherited. Nor has he any apprehension that, while he was conciliating the common people by his liberality, he was not also securing your attachment by his singular services to the republic. He says, that the good-will of the senate towards him has been repeatedly experienced by him in the times that have lately gone by; and that he shall carry with him, and ever retain in his recollection, the way in which you and all your order flocked to meet him, the zeal you showed in his behalf, and the kindness of your language to him, whatever may be the destiny which fortune allots to him. He remembers, also, that the voice of the crier, proclaiming his triumph, was the only thing wanting to him; but that he was declared consul by the unanimous vote of the people, and that was the great object of his ambition. And now if all these things are to go against him, it will be only the suspicion of guilt, not the reality of any crime which has injured him. He adds this, which is unquestionably true; that brave and wise men are not in the habit of setting their hearts so much on the rewards for virtuous conduct, as on the fact of their conduct being so; that he has never acted throughout his life in any but the most honorable manner, since there can be nothing better for a man to do than to deliver his country from dangers; that those men are happy for whom such conduct procures honor among their fellow-citizens, but yet, that those men are not miserable who have exceeded their fellow-citizens in good deeds. Moreover, that of all the rewards of virtue, if one is to make an estimate of the different rewards, the most honorable of all is glory; that this is the only reward which can make amends for the shortness of life, by the recollection of posterity; which can cause us while absent to be present, when dead to be still alive; that this is the thing by the steps of which men appear to mount even to heaven.

"Concerning me," says he, "the Roman people and all nations will be continually talking. The remotest ages will never be silent about me. Even at this very time when the firebrands of envy are being hurled against me by my enemies, still I am celebrated in every company of men, who express their thanks to me, who congratulate themselves on my conduct, who make me the sole topic of their conversation. I say nothing of the days of festival, and sacrifice, and joyful celebration in Etruria. This is the hundredth, or I rather think the hundred and first day since the death of Publius Clodius; a day on which, wherever the boundaries of the Roman empire extend, there did not only the report of, but the joy caused by that occurrence penetrate. Wherefore," said he, "I am not anxious as to where this body of mine may be; since the glory of my name already is and always will be in every country upon earth."

XXXVI. This is what you have constantly said to me, O Milo, when these men who hear me now have been absent; but this is what I say to you when they are present to listen. I cannot, indeed, praise you sufficiently for being of such a spirit as you are; but the more godlike that virtue of yours is, the greater is the pain which I feel at being separated from you. Nor, indeed, if you are taken from me, will the complaints, which are all that is left to me, do anything to comfort me, or to prevent my being angry with those men from whom I had received so severe a blow. For it is not my enemies who will tear you from me, but those who are my greatest friends. It is not men who have at times deserved ill at my hands, but those who have always deserved exceedingly well. You never, O judges, will inflict such grief upon me, (although, what grief can be so great as this?) but you will never inflict this particular grief upon me, of forcing me to forget how greatly you have always regarded me. And if you, yourselves, have forgotten it, or if any part of my conduct has offended you, why do you not make me atone for that offense rather than Milo? For I shall have lived gloriously enough if I die before seeing any such great misfortune happen to him.

At present one consolation supports me, that no exertion that affection, or that zeal, or that gratitude could possibly make, has been wanting on my part to promote your interests, O Titus Annius. For your sake I have courted the enmity of powerful citizens; I have repeatedly exposed my person and my life to the weapons of your enemies; I have thrown myself as a suppliant at the feet of many for your sake; I have con-

sidered my fortunes and those of my children as united with
yours in the time of your necessities. Lastly, on this very day,
if any violence is prepared against you, or any struggle, or any
danger of death, I claim my share in that. What remains now?
What is there that I can say, or that I can do in return for
your services to me, except considering whatever fortune is
yours mine also? I do not object, I do not refuse so to consider
it. And I entreat you, O judges, either to add to the kindnesses
which you have already conferred on me by granting me this
man's safety, or else to take notice that they will all perish in
his fall.

XXXVII. These tears of mine have no effect on Milo. He is
of an incredible strength of mind. He thinks that any place
where there is no room for virtue is a place of banishment; and
death he considers the end appointed by nature, and not a
punishment. Let him continue to cherish these ideas in which
he was born. What will you think yourselves, O judges? What
will be your feelings? Will you preserve the recollection of
Milo, and drive away the man himself? And will you allow any
place in the whole earth to be more worthy to receive this virtue of his than this place which produced him? You, you, I
appeal to you, O you brave men, who have shed much of your
blood for the sake of the republic. I appeal to you, O centurions, and to you, O soldiers, in this time of danger to a brave
man and an invincible citizen. While you are not only looking
on, but armed, and standing as guards around this court of justice, shall this mighty virtue be driven from the city, be banished, be cast out?

Oh, miserable man that I am! Oh, unhappy man that I am!
Were you, O Milo, able through the instrumentality of these
men to recall me to my country, and cannot I through the
agency of the very same men even retain you in yours? What
answer shall I make to my children, who consider you a second
father? What answer shall I make to you, O my brother Quintus, you who are now absent, you who were my companion in
that cruel time? Shall I reply, that I was unable to preserve the
safety of Milo by the instrumentality of those very men by
whose means he had preserved mine? And what is the cause
in which I shall have failed to do so? One which is sanctioned
by all the nations of the earth. From whom must I say that I

failed to procure it? From those very men who of all others
have gained the greatest tranquillity by the death of Publius
Clodius. And who will it be who has entreated in vain? I. What
great wickedness is it that I planned, what enormous crime did
I commit, O judges, when I traced out, and laid open, and revealed, and forever crushed those beginnings and signs of the
general destruction that was intended? For what is the spring
from which all the distresses of myself and my friends arise.
Why did you wish me to return to my country? Was it in order
that I might look on while those men were being driven out,
by whose efforts I had been restored? Do not, I entreat you,
suffer my return to be more miserable than even my departure
was. For how can I think that I have been restored if I am
torn from those men by whom I was restored?

XXXVIII. Would that the immortal gods had granted, (I
must entreat your permission to say it, O my country, for I fear
lest it should be a wicked wish as far as you are concerned,
though it may be a pious one for Milo,)—would that they had
granted that Publius Clodius should not only be alive, but
should even be prætor, consul, dictator, rather than I should
see this sight! O ye immortal gods, before I should see this
brave man, this man who deserves to be saved by you, O
judges, in this plight! "Say not so, say not so," says Milo.
"Rather let him have suffered the penalty which he deserved,
and let us, if so it must be, suffer what we have not deserved."

Shall this man, born for his country, die in any other land
except his country? or, as it may perchance turn out, for his
country? Will you preserve the monuments of this man's courage, and yet allow no sepulchre containing his body to exist
in Italy? Will any one by his vote banish this man from this
city, when all other cities will gladly invite him to them if he
is driven out from among you? O happy will that land be
which shall receive him! Ungrateful will this land be if it
banishes him; miserable if it loses him.

However, I must make an end. Nor, indeed, can I speak any
longer for weeping; and this man forbids me to defend him by
tears. I pray and entreat you, O judges, when you are giving
your votes, to dare to decide as you think just. And believe me
that man[14] will be sure greatly to approve of your virtue, and

[14] Cnæus Pompeius.

justice, and good faith; who, in selecting the judges, selected all the best, and wisest, and most fearless men whom he could find.[15]

[15] Milo, as has been said before, was convicted by a majority of thirty-eight to thirteen, though Cato voted openly for his acquittal. He went into exile to Marseilles. Some years afterwards, A. U. C. 706, Cœlius, when prætor, recalled him from banishment, and endeavored to raise some public commotion in favor of Pompey, between whom and Cæsar (who was in his second consulship) the civil war was just breaking out. But he and Cœlius were both killed by the soldiers with whom they were tampering.

THE FOURTH BOOK OF THE SECOND PLEADING IN THE PROSECUTION OF VERRES

About the Statues

THE ARGUMENT

The subject of this oration is the manner in which Verres had plundered not only private individuals, but even some temples, of valuable statues, and other works of art. Among the instances given some of the most prominent are the plunder of Heius, a Messanian; of Philarchus, of Centuripa; of several other private citizens; of Antiochus, the king; and of the temples of Diana, Mercury, and Ceres. A French translator in commenting on this oration says, with reference to the slighting way in which Cicero speaks of the works of art thus stolen,—"The Romans struggled for some time against the seductive power of the arts of Greece, to which for many ages they were strangers. At first they really did despise them, afterwards they affected to despise them; but at last they were forced to bow the head beneath the brilliant yoke of luxury; and Greece, industrious, learned, and polite, subdued by the admiration which it extorted, the ignorant, unlettered, and rude barbarians who had conquered her by force. Faithful to the ancient maxims of the republic, Cicero in this oration speaks only with a sort of disdain of the arts and works of the most famous artists. He even pretends sometimes not to be too well acquainted with the names of the most celebrated statuaries; he often repeats, and with a kind of affectation, that he knows very little of painting or sculpture; and rather prides himself, as one may say, on his ignorance. He seems to regard a taste for art as unworthy of the Romans, and the finest *chefs d'œuvre* as children's toys, fit to amuse the trifling and frivolous minds of the Greeks, whose name he usually expresses by a contemptuous diminutive, (Græculi,) but little calculated to fix the attention, or attract the esteem or wishes of a Roman mind.

*   *   *   *   *   *   *

In general there runs through these orations a tone more calculated to render Verres ridiculous, than to make one feel how much there was in all his attempts which was odious and horrible. The orator even permitted himself some pleasantries, for which his taste has been, perhaps too severely, called in question. Cicero had no dislike to puns, and has played a good deal on the name of Verres, which means a boar. He was too eager to acquire the reputation of a wit. It is true that the person of Verres was sufficiently inviting as a subject for ridicule. He was one of those gross men overloaded with fat, in whom the bulk of body appears to stifle all delicacy of moral feeling. As he had tried to carry off a statue of Hercules which his people could with difficulty move upon its pedestal, Cicero calls this the thirteenth of the labors of Hercules. And playing continually on the name of Verres, he compares him to the boar of Erymanthus. At another time he calls him the dragnet of Sicily, because the name Verres has some resemblance to the word *everriculum*, which signifies a dragnet."

Hortensius endeavored to defend Verres from the charge of having stolen these statues, etc. of which he admits that he had become the possessor, by contending that he had bought them. But it was contrary to the laws for a magistrate to purchase any such articles in his province; and Cicero shows also that the prices alleged to have been given are so wholly disproportionate to their value, that it is ridiculous to assert that the things had been purchased and not taken by force.

I. I COME now to what Verres himself calls his passion; what his friends call his disease, his madness; what the Sicilians call his rapine; what I am to call it, I know not. I will state the whole affair to you, and do you consider it according to its own importance and not by the importance of its name. First of all, O judges, suffer me to make you acquainted with the description of this conduct of his; and then, perhaps, you will not be very much puzzled to know by what name to call it. I say that in all Sicily, in all that wealthy and ancient province, that in that number of towns and families of such exceeding riches, there was no silver vessel, no Corinthian or Delian plate, no jewel or pearl, nothing made of gold or ivory, no statue of marble or brass or ivory, no picture whether painted or embroidered, that he did not seek out, that he did not inspect, that, if he liked it, he did not take away. I seem to be making a very extensive charge; listen now to the manner in which I make it. For I am not embracing everything in one charge for

the sake of making an impression, or of exaggerating his guilt.
When I say that he left nothing whatever of the sort in the
whole province, know that I am speaking according to the
strict meaning of the words, and not in the spirit of an accuser.
I will speak even more plainly; I will say that he has left nothing in any one's house, nothing even in the towns, nothing in
public places, not even in the temples, nothing in the possession of any Sicilian, nothing in the possession of any Roman
citizen; that he has left nothing, in short, which either came
before his eyes or was suggested to his mind, whether private
property or public, or profane or sacred, in all Sicily.

Where then shall I begin rather than with that city which
was above all others in your affection, and which was your
chosen place of enjoyment? or with what class of men rather
than with your flatterers? For by that means it will be the more
easily seen how you behaved among those men who hate you,
who accuse you, who will not let you rest, when you are proved
to have plundered among the Mamertines, who are your
friends in the most infamous manner.

II. Caius Heius is a Mamertine—all men will easily grant me
this who have ever been to Messana; the most accomplished
man in every point of view in all that city. His house is the
very best in all Messana,—most thoroughly known, most constantly open, most especially hospitable to all our fellow-citizens. That house before the arrival of Verres was so splendidly
adorned, as to be an ornament even to the city. For Messana
itself, which is admirable on account of its situation, its fortifi-
cations, and its harbor, is very empty and bare of those things
in which Verres delights. There was in the house of Heius a
private chapel of great sacredness, handed down to him from
his ancestors, very ancient; in which he had four very beautiful
statues, made with the greatest skill, and of very high character; calculated not only to delight Verres, that clever and accomplished man, but even any one of us whom he calls the
mob:—one, a statue of Cupid, in marble, a work of Praxiteles;
for in truth, while I have been inquiring into that man's conduct, I have learned the names of the workmen; it was the
same workman, as I imagine, who made that celebrated Cupid
of the same figure as this which is at Thespiæ, on account of
which people go to see Thespiæ, for there is now other reason

for going to see it; and therefore that great man Lucius Mum-mius, when he carried away from that town the statues of the Muses which are now before the temple of Good Fortune, and the other statues which were not consecrated, did not touch this marble Cupid, because it had been consecrated.

III. But to return to that private chapel; there was this statue, which I am speaking of, of Cupid, made of marble. On the other side there was a Hercules, beautifully made of brass; that was said to be the work of Myron, as I believe, and it un-doubtedly was so. Also before those gods there were little al-tars, which might indicate to any one the holiness of the chapel. There were besides two brazen statues, of no very great size, but of marvelous beauty, in the dress and robes of virgins, which with uplifted hands were supporting some sa-cred vessels which were placed on their heads, after the fash-ion of the Athenian virgins. They were called the Canephoræ, but their maker was . . . . (who? who has he? thank you, you are quite right,) they called him Polycletus. Whenever any one of our citizens went to Messana, he used to go and see these statues. They were open every day for people to go to see them. The house was not more an ornament to its master, than it was to the city.

Caius Claudius, whose ædileship we know to have been a most splendid affair, used his statue of Cupid, as long as he kept the forum decorated in honor of the immortal gods and the Roman people. And as he was connected by ties of hos-pitality with the Heii, and was the patron of the Mamertine people,—as he availed himself of their kindness to lend him this, so he was careful to restore it. There have lately been noble men of the same kind, O judges;—why do I say lately? Ay, we have seen some very lately, a very little while ago in-deed, who have adorned the forum and the public buildings, not with the spoils of the provinces, but with ornaments be-longing to their friends,—with splendid things lent by their own connections, not with the produce of the thefts of guilty men,—and who afterwards have restored the statues and decorations, each to its proper owner; men who have not taken things away out of the cities of our allies for the sake of a four-day festival, under pretense of the shows to be exhibited in their ædileship, and after that carried them off to their own homes, and their own villas. All these statues which I have mentioned, O judges, Verres took away from Heius, out of his private chapel. He left, I say, not one of those things, nor anything else, except one old wooden figure,—Good Fortune, as I believe; that, forsooth, he did not choose to have in his house!

IV. Oh! for the good faith of gods and men! What is the meaning of all this? What a cause is this! What impudence is this! The statues which I am speaking of, before they were taken away by you, no commander ever came to Messana without seeing. So many prætors, so many consuls as there have been in Sicily, in time of peace, and in time of war; so many men of every sort as there have been—I do not speak of upright, innocent, conscientious men, but so many covetous, so many audacious, so many infamous men as there have been, not one of them all was violent enough, or seemed to himself powerful enough or noble enough, to venture to ask for, or to take away, or even to touch anything in that chapel. Shall Verres take away everything which is most beautiful everywhere? Shall it not be allowed to any one besides to have anything? Shall that one house of his contain so many wealthy houses? Was it for this reason that none of his predecessors ever touched these things, that he might be able to carry them off? Was this the reason why Caius Claudius Pulcher restored them, that Caius Verres might be able to steal them? But that Cupid had no wish for the house of a pimp and the establishment of a harlot; he was quite content to stay in that chapel where he was hereditary; he knew that he had been left to Heius by his ancestors, with the rest of the sacred things which he inherited; he did not require the heir of a prostitute. But why am I borne on so impetuously? I shall in a moment be refuted by one word. "I bought it," says he. O ye immortal gods, what a splendid defense! we sent a broker into the province with military command and with the forces, to buy up all the statues, all the paintings, all the silver plate and gold plate, and ivory, and jewels, and to leave nothing to any body. For this defense seems to me to be got ready for everything; that he bought them. In the first place, if I should grant to you that which you wish, namely, that you bought them, since against all this class of accusations you are going to use this defense alone, I ask what sort of tribunals you thought that there would be at Rome, if you thought that any one would grant you this that you in your prætorship and in your command [1] bought up so many and such valuable things,—everything, in short, which was of any value in the whole province.

V. Remark the care of our ancestors, who as yet suspected no such conduct as this, but yet provided against the things which might happen in affairs of small importance. They thought that no one who had gone as governor[2] or as lieutenant into a province would be so insane as to buy silver, for that was given him out of the public funds; or raiment, for that was afforded him by the laws; they thought he might buy a slave, a thing which we all use, and which is not provided by the laws. They made a law, therefore, "that no one should buy a slave except in the room of a slave who was dead." If any slave had died at Rome? No, if any one had died in the place where his master was. For they did not mean you to furnish your house in the province, but to be of use to the province in its necessities. What was the reason why they so carefully kept us from making purchases in the provinces? This was it, O judges, because they thought it a robbery, not a purchase, when the seller was not allowed to sell on his own terms. And they were aware that, in the provinces, if he who was there with the command and power[2] of a governor wished to pur-

[1] The Latin word is *imperium*. "Imperium (as opposed to Potestas) is the power which was conferred by the state upon an individual who was appointed to command an army. . . . The imperium was as necessary for the governor of a province, as for a general who merely commanded the armies of the republic; as without it he could not exercise military authority. . . . It was conferred by a special law, and was limited, if not by the terms in which it was conferred, at least by usage. It could not be held or exercised within the city."

Smith, Dict. Ant. p. 508, v. *Imperium*.

[2] The Latin word in each case is *potestas*. "According to Paulus, potestas, as applied to a magistrate, is equivalent to imperium. . . . But potestas is applied to magistrates who had not the imperium, as, for instance, to quæstors and tribunes of the people; and potestas and imperium are often opposed in Cicero. Thus it seems that potestas, like many other Roman terms, had both a wider signification and a narrower one; in its wider signification it might mean all the power that was delegated to any person by the state, whatever might be the extent of that power; in its narrower signification, it was on the one hand equivalent to imperium and on the other, it expressed the power of these functionaries who had not the imperium." Smith, Dict. Ant. p. 721, v. *Potestas*.

chase what was in any one's possession, and was allowed to do so, it would come to pass that he would get whatever he chose, whether it was to be sold or not, at whatever price he pleased. Some one will say, "Do not deal with Verres in that manner; do not try and examine his actions by the standard of old-fashioned conscientiousness; allow him to have bought them without being punished for it, provided he bought them in a fair way, not through any arbitrary exercise of power, nor from any one against his will, or by violence." I will so deal with him. If Heius had anything for sale, if he sold it for the price at which he valued it, I give up inquiring why you bought it.

VI. What then are we to do? Are we to use arguments in a case of this sort? We must ask, I suppose, whether Heius was in debt, whether he had an auction,—if he had, whether he was in such difficulties about money matters, whether he was oppressed by such want, by such necessity, as to strip his private chapel, to sell his paternal gods. But I see that the man had no auction; that he never sold anything except the produce of his land; that he not only had no debts, but that he had always abundance of ready money. Even if all these things were contrary to what I say they were, still I say that he would not have sold things which had been so many years in the household and chapel of his ancestors. "What will you say if he was persuaded by the greatness of the sum given him for them?" It is not probable that a man, rich as he was, honorable as he was, should have preferred money to his own religious feelings and to the memorials of his ancestors. "That may be, yet men are sometimes led away from their habits and principles by large sums of money." Let us see, then, how great a sum this was which could turn Heius, a man of exceeding riches, by no means covetous, away from decency, from affection, and from religion. You ordered him, I suppose, to enter in his account books, "All these statues of Praxiteles, of Myron, of Polycletus, were sold to Verres for six thousand five hundred sesterces." Read the extracts from his accounts—

[*The accounts of Heius are read.*]

I am delighted that the illustrious names of these workmen, whom those men extol to the skies, have fallen so low in the estimation of Verres—the Cupid of Praxiteles for sixteen hundred sesterces. From that forsooth has come the proverb, "I had rather buy it than ask for it."

VII. Some one will say, "What! do you value those things at a very high price?" But I am not valuing them according to any calculation of my own, or any need which I have for them; but I think that the matter ought to be looked at by you in this light,—what is the value of these things in the opinion of those men who are judges of these things; at what price they are accustomed to be sold; at what price these very things could be sold, if they were sold openly and freely; lastly, at what price Verres himself values them. For he would never have been so foolish, if he had thought that Cupid worth only four hundred denarii, as to allow himself to be made a subject for the common conversation and general reproach of men. Who then of you all is ignorant at how great a price these things are valued? Have we not seen at an auction a brazen statue of no great size sold for a hundred and twenty thousand sesterces? What if I were to choose to name men who have bought similar things for no less a price, or even for a higher one? Can I not do so? In truth, the only limit to the valuation of such things is the desire which any one has for them, for it is difficult to set bounds to the price unless you first set bounds to the wish. I see then that Heius was neither led by his inclination, nor by any temporary difficulties, nor by the greatness of the sum given, to sell these statues; and that you, under the pretense of purchase which you put forward, in reality seized and took away these things by force, through fear, by your power and authority, from that man, whom, along with the rest of our allies in that country, the Roman people had entrusted not only to your power, but also to your upright exercise of it. What can there be, judges, so desirable for me in making this charge, as that Heius should say this same thing? Nothing certainly; but let us not wish for what is difficult to be obtained. Heius is a Mamertine. The state of the Mamertines alone, by a common resolution, praises that man in the name of the city. To all the rest of the Sicilians he is an object of hatred; by the Mamertines alone is he liked. But of that deputation which has been sent to utter his praises, Heius is the chief man; in truth, he is the chief man of his city, and

too much occupied in discharging the public duties imposed
upon him to speak of his private injuries. Though I was aware
of and had given weight to these considerations, still, O judges,
I trusted myself to Heius. I produced him at the first pleading;
and indeed I did it without any danger, for what answer could
Heius give even if he turned out a dishonest man, and unlike
himself? Could he say that these statues were at his house, and
not with Verres? How could he say anything of that sort? If
he were the basest of men, and were inclined to lie most
shamelessly, he would say this; that he had had them for sale,
and that he had sold them at the price he wanted for them.
The man the most noble in all his city, who was especially
anxious that you should have a high opinion of his conscientiousness and of his worth, says first, that he spoke in Verres's
praise by the public authority of his city, because that commission had been given to him; secondly, that he had not had
these things for sale and that, if he had been allowed to do
what he wished, he could never have been induced by any
terms to sell those things which were in his private chapel,
having been left to him and handed down to him from his
ancestors.

VIII. Why are you sitting there, O Verres? What are you
waiting for? Why do you say that you are hemmed in and
overwhelmed by the cities of Centuripa, of Catina, of Halesa,
of Tyndaris, of Enna, of Agyrium, and by all the other cities
of Sicily? Your second country, as you used to call it, Messana
herself attacks you; your own Messana I say; the assistant in
your crimes, the witness of your lusts, the receiver of your
booty and your thefts. For the most honorable man of that
city is present, a deputy sent from his home on account of this
very trial, the chief actor in the panegyric on you; who praises
you by the public order of his city, for so he has been charged
and commanded to do. Although you recollect, O judges, what
he answered when he was asked about the ship; that it had
been built by public labor, at the public expense, and that a
Mamertine senator had been appointed by the public authority to superintend its building. Heius in his private capacity flees to you for aid, O judges; he avails himself of this
law, the common fortress of our allies, by which this tribunal
is established. Although there is a law for recovering money

which has been unjustly extorted, he says that he does not seek to recover any money; which, though it has been taken from him, he does not so much care about; but he says he does demand back from you the sacred images belonging to his ancestors, he does demand back from you his hereditary household gods. Have you any shame, O Verres? have you any religion? have you any fear? You have lived in Heius's house at Messana; you saw him almost daily performing sacred rites in his private chapel before those gods. He is not influenced by money; he does not even ask to have those things restored which were merely ornaments. Keep the Canephoræ; restore the images of the gods. And because he said this, because after a given time he, an ally and friend of the Roman people, addressed his complaints to you in a moderate tone, because he was very attentive to religious obligation not only while demanding back his paternal gods, but also in giving his evidence on oath; know that one of the deputies has been sent back to Messana, that very man who superintended the building of that ship at the public expense, to demand from the senate that Heius should be condemned to an ignominious punishment.

IX. O most insane of men, what did you think? that you should obtain what you requested? Did you not know how greatly he was esteemed by his fellow-citizens; how great his influence was considered? But suppose you had obtained your request; suppose that the Mamertines had passed any severe vote against Heius, what do you think would have been the authority of their panegyric, if they had decreed punishment to the man who it was notorious had given true evidence? Although, what sort of praise is that, when he who utters it, being questioned, is compelled to give answers injurious to him whom he is praising? What! are not those who are praising you, my witnesses? Heius is an ecomiast of yours; he has done you the most serious injury. I will bring forward the rest; they will gladly be silent about all that they are allowed to suppress; they will say what they cannot help saying, unwillingly. Can they deny that a transport of the largest size was built for that man at Messana? Let them deny it if they can. Can they deny that a Mamertine senator was appointed by the public authority to superintend the building of that ship? I wish they would deny it. There are other points also which I prefer reserving unmentioned at present, in order to give as little time as possible to them for planning and arranging their perjury. Let this praise, then, be placed to your account; let these men come to your relief with their authority, who neither ought to help you if they were able, nor could do so if they wished; on whom in their private capacity you have inflicted many injuries, and put many affronts, while in their city you have dishonored many families for ever by your adulteries and crimes. "But you have been of public service to their city." Not without great injury to the republic and to the province of Sicily. They were bound to supply and they used to supply sixty thousand modii of wheat to the Roman people for payment; that was remitted by you of your own sole authority. The republic was injured because by your means its right of dominion over one city was disparaged; the Sicilians were injured, because this quantity was not deducted from the total amount of the corn to be provided by the island, but was only transferred to the cities of Centuripa and Halesa, whose inhabitants were exempt from that tax; and on them a greater burden was imposed than they were able to bear. It was your duty to require them to furnish a ship, in compliance with the treaty. You remitted it for three years. During all those years you never demanded one soldier. You acted as pirates are accustomed to act, who, though they are the common enemies of all men, still select some friends, whom they not only spare, but even enrich with their booty; and especially such as have a town in a convenient situation, where they often, and sometimes even necessarily, put in with their vessels.

X. The town of Phaselis, which Publius Servilius took, had not been in former times a city of Cilicians and pirates. The Lycians, a Greek tribe, inhabited it; but because it was in such a situation as it was, and because it projected into the sea, so that pirates from Cilicia often necessarily touched at it when departing on an expedition, and were also often borne thither on their retreats, the pirates connected that city with themselves; at first by commercial intercourse, and afterwards by a regular alliance. The city of the Mamertines was not formerly of bad character; it was even a city hostile to dishonest men, and detained the luggage of Caius Cato, the one who was consul. But then what sort of a man was he? a most eminent and most influential man; who, however, though he had been consul, was convicted. So Caius Cato, the grandson of two most illustrious men, Lucius Paullus and Marcus Cato, and the son of the sister of Publius Africanus, who, even when convicted, at a time when severe judgments were in the habit of being passed, found the damages to which he was liable only estimated at eighteen thousand sesterces; with this man, I say, the Mamertines were angry, who have often expended a greater sum than the damages in the action against Cato were laid at, in one banquet for Timarchides. But this city was the Phaselis for that robber and pirate of Sicily. Hither everything was brought from all quarters; with them it was left; whatever required to be concealed, they kept separate and stored away. By their agency he contrived everything which he wished put on board ship privily, and exported secretly; and in their harbor he contrived to have a vessel of the largest size built, for him to send to Italy loaded with plunder. In return for these services, he gave them immunity from all expense, all labor, all military service in short, from everything. For three years they were the only people, not only in Sicily, but, according to my opinion, in the whole world at such a time, who enjoyed excuse, relief, freedom, and immunity from every sort of expense, and trouble, and office. Hence arose that Verrean festival; hence it was that he ventured to order Sextus Cominius to be tragged before him at a banquet, at whom he attempted to throw a goblet, whom he ordered to be seized by the throat, and to be hurried from the banquet and thrown into a dark prison; hence came that cross, on which, in the sight of many men, he suspended a Roman citizen; that cross which he never ventured to erect anywhere except among that people, whom he had made sharers in all his crimes and robberies.

XI. Do you, O Mamertines! dare to come to praise any one? By what authority? by that which you ought to have with the Senatorial order? by that which you ought to have with the Roman people? Is there any city, not only in our provinces, but in the most distant nations, either so powerful, or so free, or so savage and uncivilized? is there any king, who would not invite a Senator of the Roman people to his house and to

his home? An honor which is paid not only to the man, but
in the first place to the Roman people, by whose indulgence
we have risen to this order, and secondly to the authority of
this order; and unless that is respected among our allies, where
will be the name and dignity of the empire among foreign
nations? The Mamertines did not give me any public invita-
tion—when I say me, that is a trifle; but when they did not
invite a Senator of the Roman people, they withheld an honor
due not to the man but to his order. For to Tullius himself, the
most splendid and magnificent house of Cnæus Pompeius
Basilicus was opened; with whom he would have lodged even
if he had been invited by you. There was also the most honorable house of the Percennii, who are now also called Pompeius; where Lucius my brother lodged and was received by
them with the greatest eagerness. A Senator of the Roman
people, as far as depended on you as a body, lay in your town,
and passed the night in the public streets. No other city ever
did such a thing. "Yes," say you, "for you were instituting a
prosecution against our friend." Will you put your own inter-
pretation on what private business I have of my own, by
diminishing the honor due to the Senate? But I will make my
complaint of this conduct, if ever the time comes that there
is any discussion concerning you among that body, which, up
to this time, has been affronted by no one but you. With what
face have you presented yourself before the eyes of the Roman
people? when you have not yet pulled down that cross, which
is even now stained with the blood of a Roman citizen, which
is fixed up in your city by the harbor, and have not thrown it
into the sea and purified all that place, before you came to
Rome, and before this tribunal. On the territory of the Mamertines, connected with us by treaty, at peace with us, is that
monument of your cruelty raised. Is not your city the only one
where, when any one arrives at it from Italy, he sees the cross
of a Roman citizen before he sees any friend of the Roman people? which you are in the habit of displaying to the people of
Rhegium, whose city you envy, and to your inhabitants, Roman
citizens as they are, to make them think less of themselves, and
be less inclined to despise you, when they see the privileges
of our citizenship extinguished by such a punishment.

XII. But you say you bought these things? What? did you forget to purchase of the same Heius that Attalic[3] tapestry, celebrated over the whole of Sicily? You might have bought them in the same way as you did the statues. For what did you do? Did you wish to spare the account-books? This escaped the notice of that stupid man; he thought that what he stole from the wardrobe would be less notorious than what he had stolen from the private chapel. But how did he get it? I cannot relate it more plainly than Heius himself related it before you. When I asked, whether any other part of his property had come to Verres, he answered that he had sent him orders to send the tapestry to Agrigentum to him. I asked whether he had sent it. He replied as he must, that is, that he had been obedient to the prætor; that he had sent it.—I asked whether it had arrived at Agrigentum; he said it had arrived.—I asked in what condition it had returned; he said it had not returned yet.—There was a laugh and a murmur from all the people. Did it never occur to you in this instance to order him to make an entry in his books, that he had sold you this tapestry too, for six thousand five hundred sesterces? Did you fear that your debts would increase, if these things were to cost you six thousand five hundred sesterces, which you could easily sell for two hundred thousand? It was worth that, believe me. You would have been able to defend yourself if you had given that sum for it. No one would then have asked how much it was worth. If you could only prove that you had bought it, you could easily make your cause and your conduct appear reasonable to any one. But as it is, you have no way of getting out of your difficulty about the tapestry. What shall I say next? Did you take away by force some splendid harness, which is said to have belonged to King Hiero, from Philarchus of Centuripa, a wealthy and high-born man, or did you buy it of him? When I was in Sicily, this is what I heard from the Centuripans and from everybody else, for the case was very notorious; people said that you had taken away this harness from Philarchus of Centuripa, and other very beautiful harness from Aristus of Panormus, and a third set from Cratippus of Tyndarus. Indeed,

[3] Attalus, king of Pergamus, had been the inventor of weaving gold thread into tapestry work, and therefore tapestry with gold threads interwoven in it was called by his name.

if Philarchus had sold it to you, you would not, after the prosecution was instituted against you, have promised to restore it. But because you saw that many people knew of it, you thought that if you restored it to him, you would only have so much the less, but the original transaction would be proved against you nevertheless; and so you did not restore it. Philarchus said in his evidence, that when he became acquainted with this disease of yours, as your friends call it, he wished to conceal from you the knowledge of the existence of this harness; that when he was summoned by you, he said that he had not got any; and indeed, that he had removed them to another person's house, that they might not be found; but that your instinct was so great, that you saw them by the assistance of the very man in whose custody they were deposited; that then he could not deny that you had found him out, and so that the harness was taken from him against his will, and without any payment.

XIII. Now, O judges, it is worth your while to know how he was accustomed to find and trace out all these things. There are two brothers, citizens of Cibyra, Tlepolemus and Hiero, one of whom, I believe was accustomed to model in wax, the other was a painter. I fancy these men, as they had become suspected by their fellow-citizens of having plundered the temple of Apollo at Cibyra, fearing a trial and the punishment of the law, had fled from their homes. As they had known that Verres was a great connoisseur of such works as theirs, at the time that he, as you learned from the witnesses, came to Cibyra with fictitious bills of exchange, they, when flying from their homes as exiles, came to him when he was in Asia. He has kept them with him ever since that time; and in the robberies he committed, and in the booty he acquired during his lieutenancy, he greatly availed himself of their assistance and their advice. These are the men who were meant when Quintus Tadius made an entry in his books that he had given things by Verres's order to some Greek painters. They were already well known to, and had been thoroughly tried by him, when he took them with him into Sicily. And when they arrived there, they scented out and tracked everything in so marvelous a manner, (you might have thought they were bloodhounds,) that, wherever anything was they found it out by some means or other. Some things they found out by threatening, some by promising; this by means of slaves, that through freemen; one thing by a friend, another by an enemy. Whatever pleased them was sure to be lost. They whose plate was demanded had nothing else to hope, than that Tlepolemus and Hiero might not approve of it.

XIV. I will relate to you this fact, O judges, most truly. I recollect that Pamphilus of Lilybæum, a connection of mine by ties of hospitality, and a personal friend of mine, a man of the highest birth, told me, that when that man had taken from him, by his absolute power, an ewer made by the hand of Doethus, of exquisite workmanship and great weight, he went home very sad in truth, and greatly agitated, because a vessel of that sort, which had been left to him by his father and his forefathers, and which he was accustomed to use on days of festival, and on the arrival of ancient friends, had been taken from him. While I was sitting at home, said he, in great indignation, up comes one of the slaves of Venus; he orders me immediately to bring to the prætor some embossed goblets. I was greatly vexed, said he; I had two; I order them both to be taken out of the closet, lest any worse thing should happen, and to be brought after me to the prætor's house. When I got there the prætor was asleep; the Cibyratic brothers were walking about, and when they saw me, they said, Pamphilus, where are the cups? I show them with great grief;—they praise them. —I begin to complain that I shall have nothing left of any value at all, if my cups too were taken away. Then they, when they see me vexed, say, What are you willing to give us to prevent these from being taken from you? To make my story short, I said that I would give six hundred sesterces. Meantime the prætor summons us; he asks for the cups. Then they began to say to the prætor, that they had thought from what they had heard, that Pamphilus's cups were of some value, but that they were miserable things, quite unworthy of Verres's having them among his plate. He said, he thought so too. So Pamphilus saved his exquisite goblets. And indeed, before I heard this, though I knew that it was a very trifling sort of accomplishment to understand things of that sort, yet I used to wonder that he had any knowledge of them at all, as I knew that in nothing whatever had he any qualities like a man.

XV. But when I heard this, I then for the first time under-stood that that was the use of these two Cibyratic brothers; that in his robberies he used his own hands, but their eyes. But he was so covetous of that splendid reputation of being thought to be a judge of such matters, that lately, (just observe the man's madness,) after his case was adjourned, when he was already as good as condemned, and civilly dead, at the time of the games of the circus, when early in the morning the couches were spread in preparation for a banquet at the house of Lucius Sisenna, a man of the first consideration, and when the plate was all set out, and when, as was suited to the dig-nity of Lucius Sisenna, the house was full of honorable men, he came to the plate, and began in a leisurely way to examine and consider every separate piece. Some marvelled at the folly of the man, who, while his trial was actually going on, was increasing the suspicion of that covetousness of which he was accused; others marveled at his insensibility, that any such things could come into his head, when the time for judgment in his cause was so near at hand, and when so many witnesses had spoken against him. But Sisenna's servants, who, I sup-pose, had heard the evidence which had been given against him, never took their eyes off him, and never departed out of reach of the plate. It is the part of a sagacious judge, from small circumstances to form his opinion of every man's covet-ousness or incontinence. And will any one believe that this man when prætor, was able to keep either his covetousness or his hands from the plate of the Sicilians, when, though a defendant, and a defendant within two days of judgment, a man in reality, and in the opinion of all men as good as al-ready condemned, he could not in a large assembly restrain himself from handling and examining the plate of Lucius Sisenna?

XVI. But that my discourse may return to Lilybæum, from which I have made this digression, there is a man named Diocles, the son-in-law of Pamphilus, of that Pamphilus from whom the ewer was taken away, whose surname is Popillius. From this man he took away every article on his sideboard

where his plate was set out. He may say, if he pleases, that he
had bought them. In fact, in this case, by reason of the magnitude of the robbery, an entry of it, I imagine, has been made
in the account-books. He ordered Timarchides to value the
plate. How did he do it? At as low a price as any one ever
valued any thing presented to an actor. Although I have been
for some time acting foolishly in saying so much about your
purchases, and in asking whether you bought the things, and
how, and at what price you bought them, when I can settle
all that by one word. Produce me a written list of what plate
you acquired in the province of Sicily, from whom, and at
what price you bought each article. What will you do? Though
I ought not to ask you for these accounts, for I ought to have
your account-books and to produce them. But you say that
you never kept any accounts of your expenses in these years.
Make me out at least this one which I am asking for, the
account of the plate, and I will not mind the rest at present.
"I have no writings of the sort; I cannot produce any accounts."
What then is to be done? What do you think that these judges
can do? Your house was full of most beautiful statues already,
before your prætorship; many were placed in your villas, many
were deposited with your friends; many were given and presented to other people; yet you have no accounts speaking of
any single one having been bought. All the plate in Sicily has
been taken away. There is nothing left to any one that can
be called his own. A scandalous defense is invented, that the
prætor bought all that plate; and yet that cannot be proved by
any accounts. If you do produce any accounts, still there is
no entry in them how you have acquired what you have got.
But of these years during which you say that you bought the
greatest number of things, you produce no accounts at all.
Must you not inevitably be condemned, both by the accounts
which you do, and by those which you do not produce?

XVII. You also took away at Lilybæum whatever silver
vessels you chose from Marcus Cælius, a Roman knight, a
most excellent young man. You did not hesitate to take away
the whole furniture of Caius Cacurius, a most active and accomplished man, and of the greatest influence in his city. You
took away, with the knowledge of everybody, a very large and
very beautiful table of citron-wood from Quintus Lutatius

Diodorus, who, owing to the kind exertion of his interest by Quintus Catulus, was made a Roman citizen by Lucius Sylla. I do not object to you that you stripped and plundered a most worthy imitator of yours in his whole character, Apollonius, the son of Nico, a citizen of Drepanum, who is now called Aulus Clodius, of all his exquisitely wrought silver plate;—I say nothing of that. For he does not think that any injury has been done to him, because you came to his assistance when he was a ruined man, with the rope round his neck, and shared with him the property belonging to their father, of which he had plundered his wards at Drepanum. I am even very glad if you took anything from him, and I say that nothing was ever better done by you. But it certainly was not right that the statue of Apollo should have been taken away from Lyso of Lilybæum, a most eminent man, with whom you had been staying as a guest. But you will say that you bought it—I know that—for six hundred sesterces. So I suppose: I know it, I say; I will produce the accounts; and yet that ought not to have been done. Will you say that the drinking vessels with emblems of Lilybæum on them were bought from Heius, the minor to whom Marcellus is guardian, whom you had plundered of a large sum of money, or will you confess that they were taken by force?

But why do I enumerate all his ordinary iniquities in affairs of this sort, which appear to consist only in robberies committed by him, and in losses borne by those whom he plundered? Listen, if you please, O judges, to an action of such a sort as will prove to you clearly his extraordinary madness and frenzy, rather than any ordinary covetousness.

XVIII. There is a man of Melita, called Diodorus, who has already given evidence before you. He has been now living at Lilybæum many years; a man of great nobility at home, and of great credit and popularity with the people among whom he has settled, on account of his virtue. It is reported to Verres of this man that he has some exceedingly fine specimens of chased work; and among them two goblets called Thericlean,[4] made by the hand of Mentor with the most exqui-

---

[4] "Thericles was a potter in the time of Aristophanes, who made earthenware vessels of a peculiar black clay. In subsequent time, any goblets made in imitation of his, whether of wood, silver, or glass, were called Thericlean."—Grævius.

site skill. And when Verres heard of this, he was inflamed
with such a desire, not only of beholding, but also of appro-
priating them, that he summoned Diodorus, and demanded
them. He replied, as was natural for a man who took great
pride in them, that he had not got them at Lilybæum; that he
had left them at Melita, in the house of a relation of his. On
this he immediately sends men on whom he can rely to Melita;
he writes to certain inhabitants of Melita to search out those
vessels for him; he desires Diodorus to give them letters to
that relation of his—the time appeared to him endless till he
could see those pieces of plate. Diodorus, a prudent and careful man, who wished to keep his own property, writes to his
relation to make answer to those men who came from Verres,
that he had sent the cups to Lilybæum a few days before. In
the meantime he himself leaves the place. He preferred leaving his home, to staying in it and losing that exquisitely
wrought silver work. But when Verres heard of this, he was
so agitated that he seemed to every one to be raving, and to be
beyond all question mad. Because he could not steal the plate
himself, he said that he had been robbed by Diodorus of some
exquisitely wrought vessels; he poured out threats against the
absent Diodorus; he used to roar out before people; sometimes he could not restrain his tears. We have heard in the
mythology of Eriphyla being so covetous that when she had
seen a necklace, made, I suppose, of gold and jewels, she was
so excited by its beauty, that she betrayed her husband for
the sake of it. His covetousness was similar; but in one respect
more violent and more senseless, because she was desiring a
thing which she had seen, while his wishes were excited not
only by his eyes, but even by his ears.

XIX. He orders Diodorus to be sought for over the whole
province. He had by this time struck his camp, packed up his
baggage, and left Sicily. Verres, in order by some means or
other to bring the man back to the province, devises this plan,
if it is to be called a plan, and not rather a piece of madness.
He sets up one of the men he calls his hounds, to say that
he wishes to institute a prosecution against Diodorus of Melita
for a capital offense. At first all men wondered at such a thing
being imputed to Diodorus, a most quiet man, and as far removed as any man from all suspicion, not only of crime, but

of even the slightest irregularity. But it soon became evident, that all this was done for the sake of his silver. Verres does not hesitate to order the prosecution to be instituted; and that, I imagine, was the first instance of his allowing an accusation to be made against an absent man. The matter was notorious over all Sicily, that men were prosecuted for capital offenses because the prætor coveted their chased silver plate; and that prosecutions were instituted against them not only when they were present, but even in their absence. Diodorus goes to Rome, and putting on mourning, calls on all his patrons and friends; relates the affair to every one. Earnest letters are written to Verres by his father, and by his friends, warning him to take care what he did, and what steps he took respecting Diodorus; that the matter was notorious and very unpopular; that he must be out of his senses; that this one charge would ruin him if he did not take care. At that time he considered his father, if not in the light of a parent, at least in that of a man. He had not yet sufficiently prepared himself for a trial; it was his first year in the province; he was not, as he was by the time of the affair of Sthenius, loaded with money. And so his frenzy was checked a little, not by shame, but by fear and alarm. He does not dare to condemn Diodorus; he takes his name out of the list of defendants while he is absent. In the meantime Diodorus, for nearly three years, as long as that man was prætor, was banished from the province and from his home. Every one else, not only Sicilians, but Roman citizens too, settled this in their minds, that, since he had carried his covetousness to such an extent, there was nothing which any one could expect to preserve or retain in his own possession if it was admired ever so little by Verres.

XX. But after they understood that that brave man, Quintus Arrius, whom the province was eagerly looking for, was not his successor, they then settled that they could keep nothing so carefully shut up or hidden away, as not to be most open and visible to his covetousness. After that, he took away from an honorable and highly esteemed Roman knight, named Cnæus Calidius, whose son he knew to be a senator of the Roman people and a judge, some beautiful silver horses which had belonged to Quintus Maximus. I did not mean to say this, O judges, for he bought those, he did not steal them; I wish

I had not mentioned them. Now he will boast, and have a fine ride on these horses. "I bought them, I have paid the money for them." I have no doubt account-books also will be produced. It is well worth while. Give me then the account-books. You are at liberty to get rid of this charge respecting Calidius, as long as I can get a sight of these accounts; still, if you had bought them, what ground had Calidius for complaining at Rome, that, though he had been living so many years in Sicily as a trader, you were the only person who had so despised and so insulted him, as to plunder him in common with all the rest of the Sicilians? what ground had he for declaring that he would demand his plate back again from you, if he had sold it to you of his own free will? Moreover, how could you avoid restoring it to Cnæus Calidius; especially when he was such an intimate friend of Lucius Sisenna, your defender, and as you had restored their property to the other friends of Sisenna? Lastly, I do not suppose you will deny that by the intervention of Potamo, a friend of yours, you restored his plate to Lucius Cordius, an honorable man, but not more highly esteemed than Cnæus Calidius; and it was he who made the cause of the rest more difficult to plead before you; for though you had promised many men to restore them their property, yet, after Cordius had stated in his evidence that you had restored him his, you desisted from making any more restorations, because you saw that you lost your plunder, and yet could not escape the evidence against you. Under all others prætors Cnæus Calidius, a Roman knight, was allowed to have plate finely wrought; he was permitted to be able from his own stores to adorn and furnish a banquet handsomely, when he had invited a magistrate or any superior officer. Many men in power and authority have been with Cnæus Calidius at his house; no one was ever found so mad as to take from him that admirable and splendid plate; no one was found bold enough to ask for it; no one impudent enough to beg him to sell it. For it is an arrogant thing, an intolerable thing, O judges, for a prætor to say to an honorable, and rich, and well-appointed man in his province, "Sell me those chased goblets." For it is saying, "You do not deserve to have things which are so beautifully made; they are better suited to a man of my stamp." Are you, O Verres, more worthy

than Calidius? whom (not to compare your way of life with
his, for they are not to be compared, but) I will compare you
with in respect of this very dignity owing to which you make
yourself out his superior. You gave eighty thousand sesterces
to canvassing agents to procure your election as prætor; you
gave three hundred thousand to an accuser not to press hardly
upon you: do you, on that account, look down upon and despise the equestrian order? Is it on that account that it seemed
to you a scandalous thing that Calidius should have anything
that you admired rather than that you should?

XXI. He has been long boasting of this transaction with
Calidius, and telling every one that he bought the things. Did
you also buy that censer of Lucius Papirius, a man of the
highest reputation, wealth, and honor, and a Roman knight?
who stated in his evidence that, when you had begged for it
to look at, you returned it with the emblems torn off; so that
you may understand that it is all taste in that man, not avarice;
that it is the fine work that he covets, not the silver. Nor was
this abstinence exercised only in the case of Papirius; he prac-
ticed exactly the same conduct with respect to every censer in
Sicily; and it is quite incredible how many beautifully wrought
censers there were. I imagine that, when Sicily was at the
height of its power and opulence, there were extensive work-
shops in that island; for before that man went thither as prætor
there was no house tolerably rich, in which there were not
these things, even if there was no other silver plate besides;
namely, a large dish with figures and images of the gods embossed on it, a goblet which the women used for sacred pur-
poses, and a censer. And all these were antique, and executed
with the most admirable skill, so that one may suspect everything else in Sicily was on a similar scale of magnificence; but
that though fortune had deprived them of much, those things
were still preserved among them which were retained for pur-
poses of religion. I said just now, O judges, that there were
many censers, in almost every house in fact; I assert also, that
now there is not even one left. What is the meaning of this?
what monster, what prodigy did we send into the province?
Does it not appear to you that he desired, when he returned
to Rome, to satisfy not the covetousness of one man, not his
own eyes only, but the insane passion of every covetous man;

for as soon as he ever came into any city, immediately those
Cibyratic hounds of his were slipped, to search and find out
everything. If they found any large vessel, any considerable
work, they brought it to him with joy; if they could hunt out
any smaller vessel of the same sort, they looked on those as a
sort of lesser game, whether they were dishes, cups, censers,
or anything else. What weepings of women, what lamenta-
tions do you suppose took place over these things? things
which may perhaps seem insignificant to you, but which excite great and bitter indignation, especially among women,
who grieve when those things are torn from their hands which
they have been accustomed to use in religious ceremonies,
which they have received from their ancestors, and which have
always been in their family.

XXII. Do not now wait while I follow up this charge from
door to door, and show you that he stole a goblet from
Æschylus the Tyndaritan; a dish from another citizen of Tyndaris named Thraso; a censer from Nymphodorus of Agrigentum. When I produce my witnesses from Sicily he may
select whom he pleases for me to examine about dishes, goblets, and censers. Not only no town, no single house that is
tolerably well off will be found to have been free from the
injurious treatment of this man; who, even if he had come
to a banquet, if he saw any finely wrought plate, could not,
O judges, keep his hands from it. There is a man named Cnæus
Pompeius Philo, who was a native of Tyndaris; he gave Verres
a supper at his villa in the country near Tyndaris; he did
what Sicilians did not dare to do, but what, because he was a
citizen of Rome, he thought he could do with impunity, he
put before him a dish on which were some exceedingly beautiful figures. Verres, the moment he saw it, determined to rob his
host's table of that memorial of the Penates and of the gods
of hospitality. But yet, in accordance with what I have said
before of his great moderation, he restored the rest of the
silver after he had torn off the figures; so free was he from
all avarice! What want you more? Did he not do the same
thing to Eupolemus of Calacta, a noble man, connected with,
and an intimate friend of the Luculli; a man who is now serving in the army under Lucius Lucullus? He was supping with
him; the rest of the silver which he had set before him had

no ornament on it, lest he himself should also be left without any ornament; but there were also two goblets, of no large size, but with figures on them. He, as if he had been a professional diner-out, who was not to go away without a present, on the spot, in the sight of all the other guests tore off the figures. I do not attempt to enumerate all his exploits of this sort; it is neither necessary nor possible. I only produce to you tokens and samples of each description of his varied and universal rascality. Nor did he behave in these affairs as if he would some day or other be called to account for them, but altogether as if he was either never likely to be prosecuted, or else as if the more he stole, the less would be his danger when he was brought before the court; inasmuch as he did these things which I am speaking of not secretly, not by the instrumentality of friends or agents, but openly, from his high position, by his own power and authority.

XXIII. When he had come to Catina, a wealthy, honorable, influential city, he ordered Dionysiarchus, the proagorus, that is to say, the chief magistrate, to be summoned before him; he openly orders him to take care that all the silver plate which was in anybody's house at Catina, was collected together and brought to him. Did you not hear Philarchus of Centuripa, a man of the highest position as to noble birth, and virtue, and riches, say the same thing on his oath; namely, that Verres had charged and commanded him to collect together, and order to be conveyed to him, all the silver plate at Centuripa, by far the largest and wealthiest city in all Sicily? In the same manner at Agyrium, all the Corinthian vessels there were there, in accordance with his command, were transported to Syracuse by the agency of Apollodorus, whom you have heard as a witness. But the most extraordinary conduct of all was this; when that painstaking and industrious prætor had arrived at Haluntium, he would not himself go up into the town, because the ascent was steep and difficult; but he ordered Archagathus of Haluntium, one of the noblest men, not merely in his own city, but in all Sicily, to be summoned before him, and gave him a charge to take care that all the chased silver that there was at Haluntium, and every specimen of Corinthian work too, should be at once taken down from the town to the sea-side. Archagathus went up into the town. That noble man, as one who wished to be loved and esteemed by his fellow-citizens, was very indignant at having such an office imposed upon him, and did not know what to do. He announces the commands he has received. He orders every one to produce what they had. There was great consternation, for the tyrant himself had not gone away to any distance; lying on a litter by the sea-side below the town, he was waiting for Archagathus and the silver plate. What a gathering of people do you suppose took place in the town? what an uproar? what weeping of women? they who saw it would have said that the Trojan horse had been introduced, and that the city was taken. Vessels were brought out without their cases; others were wrenched out of the hands of women; many people's doors were broken open, and their locks forced. For what else can you suppose? Even if ever, at a time of war and tumult, arms are demanded of private citizens, still men give them unwillingly, though they know that they are giving them for the common safety. Do not suppose then that any one produced his carved plate out of his house for another man to steal, without the greatest distress. Everything is brought down to the shore. The Cibyratic brothers are summoned; they condemn some articles; whatever they approve of has its figures in relief or its embossed emblems torn off. And so the Haluntines, having had all their ornaments wrenched off, returned home with the plain silver.

XXIV. Was there ever, O judges, a drag-net of such a sort as this in that province? People have sometimes during their year of office diverted some part of the public property to their own use, in the most secret manner; sometimes they even secretly plundered some private citizen of something; and still they were condemned. And if you ask me, though I am detracting somewhat from my own credit by saying so, I think those were the real accusers, who traced the robberies of such men as this by scent, or by some lightly imprinted footsteps; for what is it that we are doing in respect of Verres, who has wallowed in the mud till we can find him out by the traces of his whole body? It is a great undertaking to say anything against a man, who while he was passing by a place, having his litter put down to rest for a little time, plundered a whole city, house by house without condescending to any pretenses.

openly, by his own authority, and by an absolute command?
But still, that he might be able to say that he had bought
them, he orders Archagathus to give those men, to whom the
plate had belonged some little money, just for form's sake.
Archagathus found a few who would accept the money, and
those he paid. And still Verres never paid Archagathus that
money. Archagathus intended to claim it at Rome; but Cnæus
Lentulus Marcellinus dissuaded him, as you heard him state
himself. Read the evidence of Archagathus, and of Lentulus,—
and that you may not imagine that the man wished to heap
up such a mass of figures without any reason, just see at what
rate he valued you, and the opinion of the Roman people, and
the laws, and the courts of justice, and the Sicilian witnesses
and traders. After he had collected such a vast number of
figures that he had not left one single figure to anybody, he
established an immense shop in the palace at Syracuse; he
openly orders all the manufacturers, and carvers, and gold-
smiths to be summoned—and he himself had many in his own
employ; he collects a great multitude of men; he kept them
employed uninterruptedly for eight months, though all that
time no vessels were made of anything but gold. In that time
he had so skilfully wrought the figures which he had torn off
the goblets and censers, into golden goblets, or had so in-
geniously joined them into golden cups, that you would say
that they had been made for that very purpose; and he, the
prætor, who says that it was owing to his vigilance that peace
was maintained in Sicily, was accustomed to sit in his tunic
and dark cloak the greater part of the day in this workshop.

XXV. I would not venture, O judges, to mention these
things, if I were not afraid that you might perhaps say that
you had heard more about that man from others in common
conversation, than you had heard from me in this trial; for
who is there who has not heard of this workshop, of the golden
vessels, of Verres's tunic and dark cloak? Name any respectable man you please out of the whole body of settlers at Syracuse, I will produce him; there will not be one person who
will not say that he has either seen this or heard of it. Alas
for the age! alas for the degeneracy of our manners! I will not
mention anything of any great antiquity; there are many of
you, O judges, who knew Lucius Piso, the father of this Lucius

Piso, who was prætor. When he was prætor in Spain, in which province he was slain, somehow or other, while he was practicing his exercises in arms, the golden ring which he had was broken and crushed. As he wanted to get himself another ring, he ordered a goldsmith to be summoned into the forum before his throne of office, at Corduba, and openly weighed him out the gold. He ordered the man to set up his bench in the forum, and to make him a ring in the presence of every one. Perhaps in truth some may say that he was too exact, and to this extent anyone who chooses may blame him, but no further. Still such conduct was allowable for him, for he was the son of Lucius Piso, of that man who first made the law about extortion and embezzlement. It is quite ridiculous for me to speak of Verres now, when I have just been speaking of Piso the Thrifty; still, see what a difference there is between the men: that man while he was making some sideboards full of golden vessels, did not care what his reputation was, not only in Sicily, but also at Rome in the court of justice; the other wished all Spain to know to half an ounce how much gold it took to make a prætor's ring. Forsooth, as the one proved his right to his name, so did the other to his surname.

XXVI. It is utterly impossible for me either to retain in my memory, or to embrace in my speech, all his exploits. I wish just to touch briefly on the different kinds of deeds done by him, just as here the ring of Piso reminded me of what had otherwise entirely escaped my recollection. From how many honorable men do you imagine that that man tore the golden rings from off their fingers? He never hesitated to do so whenever he was pleased with either the jewels or the fashion of the ring belonging to anyone. I am going to mention an incredible fact, but still one so notorious that I do not think that he himself will deny it. When a letter had been brought to Valentius his interpreter from Agrigentum, by chance Verres himself noticed the impression on the seal; he was pleased with it, he asked where the letter came from; he was told, from Agrigentum. He sent letters to the men with whom he was accustomed to communicate, ordering that ring to be brought to him as soon as possible. And accordingly, in compliance with his letter, it was torn off the finger of a master of a family, a certain Lucius Titius, a Roman citizen. But that covetousness of his is quite beyond belief. For as he wished to provide three hundred couches beautifully covered, with all other decorations for a banquet, for the different rooms which he has, not only at Rome, but in his different villas, he collected such a number, that there was no wealthy house in all Sicily where he did not set up an embroiderer's shop.

There is a woman, a citizen of Segesta, very rich, and nobly born, by name Lamia. She, having her house full of spinning jennies, for three years was making him robes and coverlets, all dyed with purple; Attalus, a rich man at Netum; Lyso at Lilybæum; Critolaus at Enna; at Syracuse Æschrio, Cleomenes, and Theomnastus; at Elorum Archonides and Megistus. My voice will fail me before the names of the men whom he employed in this way will; he himself supplied the purple— his friends supplied only the work, I dare say; for I have no wish to accuse him in every particular, as if it were not enough for me, with a view to accuse him, that he should have had so much to give, that he should have wished to carry away so many things; and, besides all that, this thing which he admits, namely, that he should have employed the work of his friends in affairs of this sort. But now do you suppose that brazen vouches and brazen candelabra were made at Syracuse for anyone but for him the whole of that three years? He bought them, I suppose; but I am informing you so fully, O judges, of what that man did in his province as prætor, that he may not by chance appear to anyone to have been careless, and not to have provided and adorned himself sufficiently when he had absolute power.

XXVII. I come now, not to a theft, not to avarice, not to covetousness, but to an action of that sort that every kind of wickedness seems to be contained in it, and to be in it; by which the immortal gods were insulted, the reputation and authority of the name of the Roman people was impaired, hospitality was betrayed and plundered, all the kings who were most friendly to us, and the nations which are under their rule and dominion, were alienated from us by his wickedness. For you know that the kings of Syria, the boyish sons of King Antiochus, have lately been at Rome. And they came not on account of the kingdom of Syria; for that they had obtained possession of without dispute, as they had received it from their father and their ancestors; but they thought that the kingdom of Egypt belonged to them and to Selene their mother. When they, being hindered by the critical state of the republic at that time, were not able to obtain the discussion of the subject as they wished before the senate, they departed for Syria, their paternal kingdom. One of them—the one whose name is Antiochus—wished to make his journey through Sicily. And so, while Verres was prætor, he came to Syracuse. On this Verres thought that an inheritance had come to him, because a man whom he had heard, and on other accounts suspected had many splendid things with him, had come into his kingdom and into his power. He sends him presents—liberal enough —for all domestic uses; as much wine and oil as he thought fit; and as much wheat as he could want, out of his tenths. After that he invites the king himself to supper. He decorates a couch abundantly and magnificently. He sets out the numerous and beautiful silver vessels, in which he was so rich; for he had not yet made all those golden ones. He takes care that the banquet shall be splendidly appointed and provided in every particular. Why need I make a long story of it? The king departed thinking that Verres was superbly provided with everything, and that he himself had been magnificently treated. After that, he himself invites the prætor to supper. He displays all his treasures; much silver, also not a few goblets of gold, which as is the custom of kings, and especially in Syria, were studded all over with most splendid jewels. There was also a vessel for wine, a ladle hollowed out of one single large precious stone, with a golden handle, concerning which, I think, you heard Quintus Minutius speak, a sufficiently capable judge, and sufficiently credible witness. Verres took each separate piece of plate into his hands, praised it—admired it. The king was delighted that that banquet was tolerably pleasant and agreeable to a prætor of the Roman people. After the banquet was over, Verres thought of nothing else, as the facts themselves showed, than how he might plunder and strip the king of everything before he departed from the province. He sends to ask for the most exquisite of the vessels which he had seen at Antiochus's lodgings. He said that he wished to show them to his engravers. The king, who did not know the man, most willingly sent them, without any suspicion of his intention. He sends also to borrow the jeweled ladle. He said that he wished to examine it more attentively; that also is sent to him.

XXVIII. Now, O judges, mark what followed; things which you have already heard, and which the Roman people will not hear now for the first time, and which have been reported abroad among foreign nations to the furthest corners of the earth. The kings, whom I have spoken of, had brought to Rome a candelabrum of the finest jewels, made with most extraordinary skill, in order to place it in the Capitol; but as they found that temple not yet finished, they could not place it there. Nor were they willing to display it and produce it in common, in order that it might seem more splendid when it was placed at its proper time in the shrine of the great and good Jupiter; and brighter, also, as its beauty would come fresh and untarnished before the eyes of men. They determined, therefore, to take it back with them into Syria, with the intention, when they should hear that the image of the great and good Jupiter was dedicated, of sending ambassadors who should bring that exquisite and most beautiful present, with other offerings, to the Capitol. The matter, I know not how, got to his ears. For the king had wished it kept entirely concealed; not because he feared or suspected anything, but because he did not wish many to feast their eyes on it before the Roman people. He begs the king, and entreats him most earnestly to send it to him; he says that he longs to look at it himself, and that he will not allow anyone else to see it. Antiochus, being both of a childlike and royal disposition, suspected nothing of that man's dishonesty, and orders his servants to take it as secretly as possible, and well wrapped up, to the prætor's house. And when they brought it there, and placed it on a table, having taken off the coverings, Verres began to exclaim that it was a thing worthy of the kingdom of Syria, worthy of being a royal present, worthy of the Capitol. In truth, it was of such splendor as a thing must be which is made of the most brilliant and beautiful jewels; of such variety of pattern that the skill of the workmanship seemed to vie with the richness of the materials; and of such a size that it might easily be seen that it had been made not for the furniture of men, but for the decoration of a most noble temple. And when he appeared to

have examined it sufficiently, the servants begin to take it up
to carry it back again. He says that he wishes to examine it
over and over again; that he is not half satiated with the sight
of it; he orders them to depart and to leave the candelabrum.
So they then return to Antiochus empty-handed.

XXIX. The king at first feared nothing, suspected nothing.
One day passed—two days—many days. It was not brought
back. Then the king sends to Verres to beg him to return it,
if he will be so good. He bids the slaves come again. The king
begins to think it strange. He sends a second time. It is not
returned. He himself calls on the man; he begs him to restore
it to him. Think of the face and marvelous impudence of the
man. That thing which he knew, and which he had heard
from the king himself was to be placed in the Capitol, which
he knew was being kept for the great and good Jupiter, and
for the Roman people, that he began to ask and entreat
earnestly to have given to him. When the king said that he was
prevented from complying by the reverence due to Jupiter
Capitolinus, and by his regard for the opinion of men, because
many nations were witnesses to the fact of the candelabrum
having been made for a present to the god, the fellow began
to threaten him most violently. When he sees that he is no
more influenced by threats than he had been by prayers, on
a sudden he orders him to leave his province before night. He
says, that he has found out that pirates from his kingdom were
coming against Sicily. The king, in the most frequented place
in Syracuse, in the forum,—in the forum at Syracuse, I say,
(that no man may suppose I am bringing forward a charge
about which there is any obscurity, or imagining anything
which rests on mere suspicion,) weeping, and calling gods
and men to witness, began to cry out that Caius Verres had
taken from him a candelabrum made of jewels, which he was
about to send to the Capitol, and which he wished to be in
that most splendid temple as a memorial to the Roman people
of his alliance with and friendship for them. He said that he
did not care about the other works made of gold and jewels
belonging to him which were in Verres's hands, but that it
was a miserable and scandalous thing for this to be taken
from him. And that, although it had long ago been consecrated

in the minds and intentions of himself and his brother, still that he then, before that assembled body of Roman citizens, offered, and gave, and dedicated, and consecrated it to the great and good Jupiter, and that he invoked Jupiter himself as a witness of his intention and of his piety.

XXX. What voice, what lungs, what power of mine can adequately express the indignation due to this atrocity? The King Antiochus, who had lived for two years at Rome in the sight of all of us, with an almost royal retinue and establishment,—though he had been the friend and ally of the Roman people; though his father, and his grandfather, and his ancestors, most ancient and honorable sovereigns, had been our firmest friends; though he himself is monarch of a most opulent and extensive kingdom, is turned headlong out of a province of the Roman people. How do you suppose that foreign nations will take this? How do you suppose the news of this exploit of yours will be received in the dominions of other kings, and in the most distant countries of the world, when they hear that a king has been insulted by a prætor of the Roman people in his province? that a guest of the Roman people has been plundered? a friend and ally of the Roman people insultingly driven out? Know that your name and that of the Roman people will be an object of hatred and detestation to foreign nations. If this unheard-of insolence of Verres is to pass unpunished, all men will think, especially as the reputation of our men for avarice and covetousness has been very extensively spread, that this is not his crime only, but that of those who have approved of it. Many kings, many free cities, many opulent and powerful private men, cherish intentions of ornamenting the Capitol in such a way as the dignity of the temple and the reputation of our empire requires. And if they understand that you show a proper indignation at this kingly present being intercepted, they will then think that their zeal and their presents will be acceptable to you and to the Roman people. But if they hear that you have been indifferent to the complaint of so great a king, in so remarkable a case, in one of such bitter injustice, they will not be so crazy as to spend their time, and labor, and expense on things which they do not think will be acceptable to you.

XXXI. And in this place I appeal to you, O Quintus Catulus;[5] for I am speaking of your most honorable and most splendid monument. You ought to take upon yourself not only the severity of a judge with respect to this crime, but something like the vehemence of an enemy and an accuser. For, through the kindness of the senate and people of Rome, your honor is connected with that temple. Your name is consecrated at the same time as that temple in the everlasting recollection of men. It is by you that this case is to be encountered; by you, that this labor is to be undergone, in order that the Capitol, as it has been restored more magnificently, may also be adorned more splendidly than it was originally; that then that fire may seem to have been sent from heaven, not to destroy the temple of the great and good Jupiter, but to demand one for him more noble and more magnificent. You have heard Quintus Minucius Rufus say, that King Antiochus stayed at his house while at Syracuse; that he knew that this candelabrum had been taken to Verres's house; that he knew that it had not been returned. You heard, and you shall hear from the whole body of Roman settlers at Syracuse, that they will state to you that in their hearing it was dedicated and consecrated to the good and great Jupiter by King Antiochus. If you were not a judge, and this affair were reported to you, it would be your especial duty to follow it up; to reclaim the candelabrum, and to prosecute this cause. So that I do not doubt what ought to be your feelings as judge in this prosecution, when before anyone else as judge you ought to be a much more vehement advocate and accuser than I am.

XXXII. And to you, O judges, what can appear more scandalous or more intolerable than this? Shall Verres have at his own house a candelabrum, made of jewels and gold, belonging to the great and good Jupiter? Shall that ornament be set out in his house at banquets which will be one scene of adultery and debauchery with the brilliancy of which the temple of the great and good Jupiter ought to glow and to be lighted up? Shall the decorations of the Capitol be placed in the house of that most infamous debauchee with the other ornaments

[5] The Capitol had been burnt in the civil war between Marius and Sylla; and it was now being restored under the superintendence of Quintus Catulus, to whom that office had been entrusted by the senate.

which he has inherited from Chelidon? What do you suppose
will ever be considered sacred or holy by him, when he does
not now think himself liable to punishment for such enormous
wickedness? who dares to come into this court of justice, where
he cannot, like all others who are arraigned, pray to the great
and good Jupiter, and entreat help from him? from whom even
the immortal gods are reclaiming their property, before that
tribunal which was appointed for the benefit of men, that they
might recover what had been extorted unjustly from them?
Do we marvel that Minerva at Athens, Apollo at Delos, Juno
at Samos, Diana at Perga, and that many other gods besides
all over Asia and Greece, were plundered by him, when he
could not keep his hands off the Capitol? That temple which
private men are decorating and are intending to decorate out
of their own riches, that Caius Verres would not suffer to be
decorated by a king; and, accordingly, after he had once conceived this nefarious wickedness, he considered nothing in all
Sicily afterwards sacred or hallowed; and he behaved himself
in his province for three years in such a manner that war was
thought to have been declared by him, not only against men,
but also against the immortal gods.

XXXIII. Segesta is a very ancient town in Sicily, O judges,
which its inhabitants assert was founded by Æneas when he
was flying from Troy and coming to this country. And accordingly the Segestans think that they are connected with the
Roman people, not only by a perpetual alliance and friendship,
but even by some relationship. This town, as the state of the
Segestans was at war with the Carthaginians on its own account and of its own accord, was formerly stormed and destroyed by the Carthaginians; and everything which could be
any ornament to the city was transported from thence to
Carthage. There was among the Segestans a statue of Diana,
of brass, not only invested with the most sacred character, but
also wrought with the most exquisite skill and beauty. When
transferred to Carthage, it only changed its situation and its
worshippers; it retained its former sanctity. For on account of
its eminent beauty it seemed, even to their enemies, worthy
of being most religiously worshipped. Some ages afterwards,
Publius Scipio took Carthage, in the third Punic war; after
which victory, (remark the virtue and carefulness of the man,

so that you may both rejoice at your national examples of most eminent virtue, and may also judge the incredible audacity of Verres, worthy of the greater hatred by contrasting it with that virtue,) he summoned all the Sicilians, because he knew that during a long period of time Sicily had repeatedly been ravaged by the Carthaginians, and bids them seek for all they had lost, and promises them to take the greatest pains to ensure the restoration to the different cities of everything which had belonged to them. Then those things which had formerly been removed from Himera, and which I have mentioned before, were restored to the people of Thermæ; some things were restored to the Gelans, some to the Agrigentines; among which was that noble bull, which that most cruel of all tyrants, Phalaris, is said to have had, into which he was accustomed to put men for punishment, and to put fire under. And when Scipio restored that bull to the Agrigentines, he is reported to have said, that he thought it reasonable for them to consider whether it was more advantageous to the Sicilians to be subject to their own princes, or to be under the dominion of the Roman people, when they had the same thing as a monument of the cruelty of their domestic masters, and of our liberality.

XXXIV. At that time the same Diana of which I am speaking is restored with the greatest care to the Segestans. It is taken back to Segesta; it is replaced in its ancient situation, to the greatest joy and delight of all the citizens. It was placed at Segesta on a very lofty pedestal, on which was cut in large letters the name of Publius Africanus; and a statement was also engraved that "he had restored it after having taken Carthage." It was worshipped by the citizens; it was visited by all strangers; when I was quæstor it was the very first thing they showed me. It was a very large and tall statue with a flowing robe, but in spite of its large size it gave the idea of the age and dress of a virgin; her arrows hung from her shoulder, in her left hand she carried her bow, her right hand held a burning torch. When that enemy of all sacred things, that violator of all religious scruples saw it, he began to burn with covetousness and insanity, as if he himself had been struck with that torch. He commands the magistrates to take the statue down and give it to him; and declares to them that nothing can be more agreeable to him. But they said that it was impossible for them to do so; that they were prevented from doing so, not only by the most extreme religious reverence, but also by the greatest respect for their own laws and courts of justice. Then he began to entreat this favor of them, then to threaten them, then to try and excite their hopes, then to arouse their fears. They opposed to this demands the name of Africanus; they said that it was the gift of the Roman people; that they themselves had no right over a thing which a most illustrious general, having taken a city of the enemy, had chosen to stand there as a monument of the victory of the Roman people. As he did not relax in his demand, but urged it every day with daily increasing earnestness, the matter was brought before their senate. His demand raises a violent outcry on all sides. And so at that time, and at his first arrival at Segesta, it is refused. Afterwards, whatever burdens could be imposed on any city in respect of exacting sailors and rowers, or in levying corn, he imposed on the Segestans beyond all other cities and a good deal more than they could bear. Besides that, he used to summon their magistrates before him; he used to send for all the most noble and most virtuous of the citizens, to hurry them about with him to all the courts of justice in the province, to threaten every one of them separately to be the ruin of him, and to announce to them all in a body that he would utterly destroy their city. Therefore, at last, the Segestans, subdued by much ill-treatment and by great fear, resolved to obey the command of the prætor. With great grief and lamentation on the part of the whole city, with many tears and wailings on the part of all the men and women, a contract is advertised for taking down the statue of Diana.

XXXV. See now with what religious reverence it is regarded. Know, O judges, that among all the Segestans none was found, whether free man or slave, whether citizen or foreigner, to dare to touch that statue. Know that some barbarian workmen were brought from Lilybæum; they at length, ignorant of the whole business, and of the religious character of the image, agreed to take it down for a sum of money, and took it down. And when it was being taken out of the city, how great the concourse of women! how great was the weeping of the old men! some of whom even recollected that day when that same Diana being brought back to Segesta from Carthage, had announced to them, by its return, the victory of the Roman people. How different from that time did this day seem! then the general of the Roman people, a most illustrious man, was bringing back to the Segestans the gods of their fathers, recovered from an enemy's city; now a most base and profligate prætor of the same Roman people, was taking away, with the most nefarious wickedness, those very same gods from a city of his allies. What is more notorious throughout all Sicily than that all the matrons and virgins of Segesta came together when Diana was being taken out of their city? that they anointed her with precious unguents? that they crowned her with chaplets and flowers? that they attended her to the borders of their territory with frankincense and burning perfumes? If at the time you, by reason of your covetousness and audacity, did not, while in command, fear these religious feelings of the population, do you not fear them now, at a time of such peril to yourself and to your children? What man, against the will of the immortal gods, or what god, when you so trample on all the religious reverence due to them, do you think will come to your assistance? Has that Diana inspired you, while in quiet and at leisure, with no religious awe;—she, who though she had seen two cities, in which she was placed, stormed and burnt, was yet twice preserved from the flames and weapons of two wars; she who, though she changed her situation owing to the victory of the Carthaginians, yet did not lose her holy character; and who, by the valor of Publius Africanus, afterwards recovered her old worship, together with her old situation? And when this crime had been executed, as the pedestal was empty, and the name of Publius Africanus carved on it, the affair appeared scandalous and intolerable to every one, that not only was religion trampled on, but also that Caius Verres had taken away the glory of the exploits, the memorial of the virtues, the monument of the victory of Publius Africanus, that most gallant of men. But when he was told afterwards of the pedestal and the inscription, he thought that men would forget the whole affair, if he took away the pedestal too, which was severing as a sort of signpost to point out his crime. And so, by his command, the Segestans contracted to take away the pedestal too; and the terms of that contract were read to you

from the public register of the Segestans, at the former pleading.

XXXVI. Now, O Publius Scipio, I appeal to you; to you, I
say, a most virtuous and accomplished youth; from you I request and demand that assistance which is due to your family
and to your name. Why do you take the part of that man who
has embezzled the credit and honor of your family? Why do
you wish him to be defended? Why am I undertaking what is
properly your business? Why am I supporting a burden which
ought to fall on you?—Marcus Tullius is reclaiming the monuments of Publius Africanus; Publius Scipio is defending the
man who took them away. Though it is a principle handed
down to us from our ancestors, for every one to defend the
monuments of his ancestors, in such a way as not even to allow
them to be decorated by one of another name, will you take the
part of that man who is not charged merely with having in
some degree spoilt the view of the monuments of Publius
Scipio, but who has entirely removed and destroyed them?
Who then, in the name of the immortal gods, will defend the
memory of Publius Scipio now that he is dead? who will defend the memorials and evidences of his valor, if you desert
and abandon them; and not only allow them to be plundered
and taken away, but even defend their plunderer and de-
stroyer? The Segestans are present, your clients, the allies and
friends of the Roman people. They inform you that Publius
Africanus, when he had destroyed Carthage, restored the
image of Diana to their ancestors; and that was set up among
the Segestans and dedicated in the name of that general;—
that Verres has had it taken down and carried away, and as far
as that is concerned, has utterly effaced and extinguished the
name of Publius Scipio. They entreat and pray you to restore
the object of their worship to them, its proper credit and glory
to your own family, so enabling them by your assistance to
recover from the house of a robber, what they recovered from
the city of their enemies by the beneficence of Publius Africanus.

XXXVII. What can you reply to them with honor, or what
can they do but implore the aid of you and your good faith?
They are present, they do implore it. You, O Publius, can pro-

tect the honor of your family renown, you can, you have every advantage which either fortune or nature ever gives to men. I do not wish to anticipate you in gathering the fruit that belongs to you; I am not covetous of the glory which ought to belong to another. It does not correspond to the modesty of my disposition, while Publius Scipio, a most promising young man, is alive and well, to put myself forward as the defender and advocate of the memorials of Publius Scipio. Wherefore, if you will undertake the advocacy of your family renown, it will behove me not only to be silent about your monuments, but even to be glad that the fortune of Publius Africanus, though dead, is such, that his honor is defended by those who are of the same family as himself, and that it requires no adventitious assistance. But if your friendship with that man is an obstacle to you,—if you think that this thing which I demand of you is not so intimately connected with your duty,—then I, as your *locum tenens,* will succeed to your office, I will undertake that business which I have thought not to belong to me. Let that proud aristocracy give up complaining that the Roman people willingly gives, and at all times has given, honors to new and diligent men. It is a foolish complaint that virtue should be of the greatest influence in that city which by its virtue governs all nations. Let the image of Publius Africanus be in the houses of other men; let heroes now dead be adorned with virtue and glory. He was such a man, he deserved so well of the Roman people, that he deserves to be recommended to the affection, not of one single family, but of the whole state. And so it partly does belong to me also to defend his honors with all my power, because I belong to that city which he rendered great, and illustrious, and renowned; and especially, because I practise, to the utmost of my power, those virtues in which he was pre-eminent,—equity, industry, temperance, the protection of the unhappy, and hatred of the dishonest; a relationship in pursuits and habits which is almost as important as that of which you boast, the relationship of name and family.

XXXVIII. I reclaim from you, O Verres, the monument of Publius Africanus; I abandon the cause of the Sicilians, which I undertook; let there be no trial of you for extortion at present; never mind the injuries of the Segestans; let the pedestal of Publius Africanus be restored; let the name of that invincible

commander be engraved on it anew; let that most beautiful
statue, which was recovered when Carthage was taken, be replaced. It is not I, the defender of the Sicilians,—it is not I, your
prosecutor,—they are not the Segestans who demand this of
you; but he who has taken on himself the defence and the
preservation of the renown and glory of Publius Africanus. I
am not afraid of not being able to give a good account of my
performance of this duty to Publius Servilius the judge; who,
as he has performed great exploits, and raised very many
monuments of his good deeds, and has a natural anxiety about
them, will be glad, forsooth, to leave them an object of care and
protection not only to his own posterity, but to all brave men
and good citizens; and not as a mark for the plunder of rogues.
I am not afraid of its displeasing you, O Quintus Catulus, to
whom the most superb and splendid monument in the whole
world belongs, that there should be as many guardians or such
monuments as possible, or that all good men should think it
was a part of their duty to defend the glory of another. And indeed I am so far moved by the other robberies and atrocities of
that fellow, as to think them worthy of great reproof; but that
might be sufficient for them. But in this instance I am roused to
such indignation, that nothing appears to me possible to be
more scandalous or more intolerable. Shall Verres adorn his
house, full of adultery, full of debauchery, full of infamy, with
the monuments of Africanus? Shall Verres place the memorial
of that most temperate and religious man, the image of the
ever virgin Diana, in that house in which the iniquities of harlots and pimps are incessantly being practised?

XXXIX. But is this the only monument of Africanus which
you have violated? What! did you take away from the people
of Tyndaris an image of Mercury most beautifully made, and
placed there by the beneficence of the same Scipio? And how?
O ye immortal gods! How audaciously, how infamously, how
shamelessly did you do so! You have lately, O judges, heard
the deputies from Tyndaris, most honorable men, and the chief
men of that city, say that the Mercury, which in their sacred
anniversaries was worshipped among them with the extremest
religious reverence, which Publius Africanus, after he had
taken Carthage, had given to the Tyndaritans, not only as a
monument of his victory, but as a memorial and evidence of

their loyalty to and alliance with the Roman people, had been
taken away by the violence, and wickedness, and arbitrary
power of this man; who, when he first came to their city, in a
moment, as if it were not only a becoming, but an indispensable thing to be done,—as if the senate had ordered it and
the Roman people had sanctioned it,—in a moment, I say, ordered them to take the statue down and to transport it to
Messana. And as this appeared a scandalous thing to those who
were present and who heard it, it was not persevered in by him
during the first period of his visit; but when he departed, he
ordered Sopater, their chief magistrate, whose statement you
have heard, to take it down. When he refused, he threatened
him violently; and then he left the city. The magistrate refers
the matter to the senate; there is a violent outcry on all sides.
To make my story short, some time afterwards he comes to that
city again. Immediately he asks about the statue. He is answered that the senate will not allow it to be removed; that
capital punishment is threatened to anyone who should touch
it without the orders of the senate: the impiety of removing is
also urged. Then says he, "What do you mean by talking to me
of impiety? or about punishment? or about the senate? I will
not leave you alive; you shall be scourged to death if the statue
is not given up." Sopater with tears reports the matter to the
senate a second time, and relates to them the covetousness and
the threats of Verres. The senate gives Sopater no answer, but
breaks up in agitation and perplexity. Sopater, being summoned by the prætor's messenger, informs him of the state of
the case, and says that it is absolutely impossible.

XL. And all these things (for I do not think that I ought to
omit any particular of his impudence) were done openly in the
middle of the assembly, while Verres was sitting on his chair of
office, in a lofty situation. It was the depth of winter; the
weather, as you heard Sopater himself state, was bitterly cold;
heavy rain was falling; when that fellow orders the lictors to
throw Sopater headlong down from the portico on which he
himself was sitting, and to strip him naked. The command was
scarcely out of his mouth, before you might have seen him
stripped and surrounded by the lictors. All thought that the unhappy and innocent man was going to be scourged. They were
mistaken. Do you think that Verres would scourge without any

reason an ally and friend of the Roman people? He is not so
wicked. All vices are not to be found in that man; he was never
cruel. He treated the man with great gentleness and clemency.
In the middle of the forum there are some statues of the Marcelli, as there are in most of the other towns of Sicily; out of
these he selected the statue of Caius Marcellus, whose services
to that city and to the whole province were most recent and
most important. On that statue he orders Sopater, a man of
noble birth in his city, and at that very time invested with the
chief magistracy, to be placed astride and bound to it. What
torture he suffered when he was bound naked in the open air,
in the rain and in the cold, must be manifest to every body. Nor
did he put an end to this insult and barbarity, till the people
and the whole multitude, moved by the atrocity of his conduct
and by pity for his victim, compelled the senate by their outcries to promise him that statue of Mercury. They cried out
that the immortal gods themselves would avenge the act, and
that in the meantime it was not fit that an innocent man should
be murdered. Then the senate comes to him in a body, and
promises him the statue. And so Sopater is taken down scarcely
alive from the statue of Marcellus, to which he had almost become frozen. I cannot adequately accuse that man if I were to
wish to do so; it requires not only genius, but an extraordinary
amount of skill.

XLI. This appears to be a single crime, this of the Tyndaritan Mercury, and it is brought forward by me as a single one;
but there are many crimes contained in it—only I do not know
how to separate and distinguish them. It is a case of money extorted, for he took away from the allies a statue worth a large
sum of money. It is a case of embezzlement, because he did not
hesitate to appropriate a public statue belonging to the Roman
people, taken from the spoils of the enemy, placed where it
was in the name of our general. It is a case of treason, because
he dared to overturn and to carry away monuments of our empire, of our glory, and of our exploits. It is a case of impiety,
because he violated the most solemn principles of religion. It
is a case of inhumanity, because he invented a new and extraordinary description of punishment for an innocent man, an ally
and friend of our nation. But what the other crime is, that I
am unable to say; I know not by what name to call the crime

which he committed with respect to the statue of Caius Marcellus. What is the meaning of it? Is it because he was the patron of the Sicilians? What then? What has that to do with it? Ought that fact to have had influence to procure assistance, or to bring disaster on his clients and friends? Was it your object to show that patrons were no protection against your violence? Who is there who would not be aware that there is greater power in the authority of a bad man who is present, than in the protection of good men who are absent? Or do you merely wish to prove by this conduct, your unprecedented insolence, and pride, and obstinacy? You thought, I imagine, that you were taking something from the dignity of the Marcelli? And therefore now the Marcelli are not the patrons of the Sicilians. Verres has been substituted in their place. What virtue or what dignity did you think existed in you, that you should attempt to transfer to yourself, and to take away from these most trusty and most ancient patrons, so illustrious a body of clients as that splendid province? Can you with your stupidity, and worthlessness, and laziness defend the cause, I will not say of all Sicily, but even of one, the very meanest of the Sicilians? Was the statue of Marcellus to serve you for a pillory for the clients of the Marcelli? Did you out of his honor seek for punishments for those very men who had held him in honor? What followed? What did you think would happen to your statues? was it that which did happen? For the people of Tyndaris threw down the statue of Verres, which he had ordered to be erected in his own honor near the Marcelli, and even on a higher pedestal, the very moment that they heard that a successor had been appointed to him.

XLII. The fortune of the Sicilians has then given you Caius Marcellus for a judge, so that we may now surrender you, fettered and bound, to appease the injured sanctity of him to whose statue Sicilians were bound while you were prætor. And in the first place, O judges, that man said that the people of Tyndaris had sold this statue to Caius Marcellus Æserninus, who is here present. And he hoped that Caius Marcellus himself would assert thus much for his sake, though it never seemed to me to be very likely that a young man born in that rank, the patron of Sicily, would lend his name to that fellow to enable him to transfer his guilt to another. But still I made such provision, and took such precaution against every possible bearing of the case, that if any one had been found who was ever so anxious to take the guilt and crime of Verres upon himself, still he would not have taken anything by his motion, for I brought down to court such witnesses, and I had with me such written documents, that it could not have been possible to have entertained a doubt about that man's actions. There are public documents to prove that that Mercury was transported to Messana at the expense of the state. They state at what expense; and that a man named Poleas was ordered by the public authority to superintend the business—what more would you have? Where is he? He is close at hand, he is a witness, by the command of Sopater the Proagorus.—Who is he? The man who was bound to the statue. What? where is he? He is a witness—you have seen the man, and you have heard his statement. Demetrius, the master of the gymnastic school, superintended the pulling down of the statue, because he was appointed to manage that business. What? is it we who say this? No, he is present himself; moreover, that Verres himself lately promised at Rome, that he would restore that statue to the deputies, if the evidence already given in the affair were removed, and if security were given that the Tyndaritans would not give evidence against him, has been stated before you by Zosippus and Hismenias, most noble men, and the chief men of the city of Tyndaris.

XLIII. What? did you not also at Agrigentum take away a monument of the same Publius Scipio, a most beautiful statue of Apollo, on whose thigh there was the name of Myron, inscribed in diminutive silver letters, out of that most holy temple of Æsculapius? And when, O judges, he had privily committed that atrocity, and when in that most nefarious crime and robbery he had employed some of the most worthless men of the city as his guides and assistants, the whole city was greatly excited. For the Agrigentines were regretting at the same time the kindness of Africanus, and a national object of their worship, and an ornament of their city, and a record of their victory, and an evidence of their alliance with us. And therefore a command is imposed on those men who were the chief men of the city, and a charge is given to the quæstors and ædiles to keep watch by night over the sacred edifices. And, indeed, at

Agrigentum, (I imagine, on account of the great number and
virtue of these men, and because great numbers of Roman citizens, gallant and intrepid and honorable men, live and trade in
that town among the Agrigentines in the greatest harmony,)
he did not dare openly to carry off, or even to beg for the things
that took his fancy. There is a temple of Hercules at Agrigentum, not far from the forum, considered very holy and greatly
reverenced among the citizens. In it there is a brazen image of
Hercules himself, than which I cannot easily tell where I have
seen anything finer; (although I am not very much of a judge
of those matters, though I have seen plenty of specimens;) so
greatly venerated among them, O judges, that his mouth and
his chin are a little worn away, because men in addressing their
prayers and congratulations to him, are accustomed not only to
worship the statue, but even to kiss it. While Verres was at
Agrigentum, on a sudden, one stormy night, a great assemblage
of armed slaves, and a great attack on this temple by them,
takes place, under the leading of Timarchides. A cry is raised
by the watchmen and guardians of the temple. And, at first,
when they attempted to resist them and to defend the temple,
they are driven back much injured with sticks and bludgeons.
Afterwards, when the bolts were forced open, and the doors
dashed in, they endeavor to pull down the statue and to overthrow it with levers; meantime, from the outcries of the keepers, a report got abroad over the whole city, that the national
gods were being stormed, not by the unexpected invasion of
enemies, or by the sudden irruption of pirates, but that a well
armed and fully equipped band of fugitive slaves from the
house and retinue of the prætor had attacked them. No one
in Agrigentum was either so advanced in age, or so infirm in
strength, as not to rise up on that night, awakened by that
news, and to seize whatever weapon chance put into his hands.
So in a very short time men are assembled at the temple from
every part of the city. Already, for more than an hour, numbers
of men had been laboring at pulling down that statue; and all
that time it gave no sign of being shaken in any part; while
some, putting levers under it, were endeavoring to throw it
down, and others, having bound cords to all its limbs, were trying to pull it towards them. On a sudden all the Agrigentines
collect together at the place; stones are thrown in numbers;

the nocturnal soldiers of that illustrious commander run away
—but they take with them two very small statues, in order not
to return to that robber of all holy things entirely empty-
handed. The Sicilians are never in such distress as not to be
able to say something facetious and neat; as they did on this
occasion. And so they said that this enormous boar had a right
to be accounted one of the labors of Hercules, no less than the
other boar of Erymanthus.

XLIV. The people of Assorum, gallant and loyal men, afterwards imitated this brave conduct of the Agrigentines, though
they did not come of so powerful or so distinguished a city.
There is a river called Chrysas, which flows through the territories of Assorum. Chrysas, among that people, is considered a
god, and is worshipped with the greatest reverence. His temple
is in the fields, near the road which goes from Assorum to
Enna. In it there is an image of Chrysas, exquisitely made of
marble. He did not dare to beg that of the Assorians on account of the extraordinary sanctity of that temple; so he en-
trusts the business to Tlepolemus and Hiero. They, having prepared and armed a body of men, come by night; they break in
the doors of the temple; the keepers of the temple and the
guardians hear them in time. A trumpet, the signal of alarm
well known to all the neighborhood, is sounded; men come in
from the country, Tlepolemus is tourned out and put to flight;
nor was anything missed out of the temple of Chrysas except
one very diminutive image of brass. There is a temple of the
mighty mother Cybele at Enguinum, for I must now not only
mention each instance with the greatest brevity, but I must
even pass over a great many, in order to come to the greater
and more remarkable thefts and atrocities of this sort which
this man has committed. In this temple that same Publius
Scipio, a man excelling in every possible good quality, had
placed breastplates and helmets of brass of Corinthian workmanship, and some huge ewers of a similar description, and
wrought with the same exquisite skill, and had inscribed his
own name upon them. Why should I make any more statements
or utter any further complaints about that man's conduct? He
took away, O judges, every one of those things. He left nothing
in that most holy temple except the traces of the religion he
had trampled on, and the name of Publius Scipio. The spoils

won from the enemy, the memorials of our commanders, the ornaments and decorations of our temples, will hereafter, when these illustrious names are lost, be reckoned in the furniture and appointments of Caius Verres. Are you, forsooth, the only man who delights in Corinthian vases? Are you the best judge in the world of the mixture of that celebrated bronze, and of the delicate tracery of that work? Did not the great Scipio, that most learned and accomplished man, understand it too? But do you, a man without one single virtue, without education, without natural ability, and without any information, understand them and value them? Beware lest he be seen to have surpassed you and those other men who wished to be thought so elegant, not only in temperance, but in judgment and taste; for it was because he thoroughly understood how beautiful they were, that he thought that they were made, not for the luxury of men, but for the ornamenting of temples and cities, in order that they might appear to our posterity to be holy and sacred monuments.

XLV. Listen, also, O judges, to the man's singular covetousness, audacity and madness, especially in polluting those sacred things, which not only may not be touched with the hands, but which may not be violated even in thought. There is a shrine of Ceres among the Catenans of the same holy nature as the one at Rome, and worshipped as the goddess is worshipped among foreign nations, and in almost every country in the world. In the inmost part of that shrine there was an extremely ancient statue of Ceres, as to which men were not only ignorant of what sort it was, but even of its existence. For the entrance into that shrine does not belong to men, the sacred ceremonies are accustomed to be performed by women and virgins. Verres's slaves stole this statue by night out of that most holy and most ancient temple. The next day the priestesses of Ceres, and the female attendants of that temple, women of great age, noble and of proved virtue, report the affair to their magistrates. It appeared to all a most bitter, and scandalous, and miserable business. Then that man, influenced by the atrocity of the action, in order that all suspicion of that crime might be removed from himself, employs some one connected with him by ties of hospitality to find a man whom he might accuse of having done it, and bids him take care that he be convicted of the accusation, so that he himself might not be subject to the charge. The matter is not delayed. For when he had departed from Catina, an information is laid against a certain slave. He is accused; false witnesses are suborned against him; the whole senate sits in judgment on the affair, according to the laws of the Catenans. The priestesses are summoned; they are examined secretly in the senate-house, and asked what had been done, and how they thought that the statue had been carried off. They answer that the servants of the prætor had been seen in the temple. The matter, which previously had not been very obscure, began to be clear enough by the evidence of the priestesses. The judges deliberate; the innocent slave is acquitted by every vote, in order that you may the more easily be able to condemn this man by all your votes. For what is it that you ask, O Verres? What do you hope for? What do you expect? What god or man do you think will come to your assistance? Did you send slaves to that place to plunder a temple, where it was not lawful for free citizens to go, not even for the purpose of praying? Did you not hesitate to lay violent hands on those things from which the laws of religion enjoined you to keep even your eyes? Although it was not even because you were charmed by the eye that you were led into this wicked and nefarious conduct; for you coveted what you had never seen. You took a violent fancy, I say, to that which you had not previously beheld. From your ears did you conceive this covetousness, so violent that no fear, no religious scruple, no power of the gods, no regard for the opinion of men could restrain it. Oh! but you had heard of it, I suppose, from some good man, from some good authority. How could you have done that, when you could never have heard of it from any man at all? You heard of it, therefore, from a woman; since men could not have seen it, nor known of it. What sort of woman do you think that she must have been, O judges? What a modest woman must she have been to converse with Verres! What a pious woman, to show him a plan for robbing a temple! But it is no great wonder if those sacred ceremonies which are performed by the most extreme chastity of virgins and matrons were violated by his adultery and profligacy.

XLVI. What, then, are we to think? Is this the only thing that he began to desire from mere hearing, when he had never

seen it himself? No, there were many other things besides; of
which I will select the plundering of that most noble and
ancient temple, concerning which you heard witnesses give
their evidence at the former pleading. Now, I beseech you, listen to the same story once more, and attend carefully as you
hitherto have done. There is an island called Melita, O judges,
separated from Sicily by a sufficiently wide and perilous navigation, in which there is a town of the same name, to which
Verres never went, though it was for three years a manufactory
to him for weaving women's garments. Not far from that town,
on a promontory, is an ancient temple of Juno, which was always considered so holy, that it was not only always kept inviolate and sacred in those Punic wars, which in those regions
were carried on almost wholly by the naval forces, but even by
the bands of pirates which ravage those seas. Moreover, it has
been handed down to us by tradition, that once, when the fleet
of King Masinissa was forced to put into these ports, the king's
lieutenant took away some ivory teeth of an incredible size out
of the temple, and carried them into Africa, and gave them to
Masinissa; that at first the king was delighted with the present,
but afterwards, when he heard where they had come from, he
immediately sent trustworthy men in a quinquereme to take
those teeth back; and that there was engraved on them in Punic
characters, "that Masinissa the king had accepted them igno-
rantly; but that, when he knew the truth, he had taken care
that they should be replaced and restored." There was besides
an immense quantity of ivory, and many ornaments, among
which were some ivory victories of ancient workmanship, and
wrought with exquisite skill. Not to dwell too long on this, he
took care to have all these things taken down and carried off
at one swoop by means of the slaves of the Venus whom he
had sent thither for that purpose.

XLVII. O ye immortal gods! what sort of man is it that I
am accusing? Who is it that I am prosecuting according to our
laws, and by this regular process? Concerning whom is it that
you are going to give your judicial decision? The deputies from
Melita sent by the public authority of their state, say that the
shrine of Juno was plundered; that that man left nothing in
that most holy temple; that that place, to which the fleets of
enemies often came, where pirates are accustomed to winter

almost every year, and which no pirate ever violated, no enemy
ever attacked before, was so plundered by that single man,
that nothing whatever was left in it. What, then, now are we to
say of him as a defendant, of me as an accuser, of this tribunal?
Is he proved guilty of grave crimes, or is he brought into this
court on mere suspicion? Gods are proved to have been carried
off, temples to have been plundered, cities to have been
stripped of everything. And of those actions he has left himself
no power of denying one, no plea for defending one. In every-
particular he is convicted by me; he is detected by the witnesses; he is overwhelmed by his own admissions; he is caught
in the evident commission of guilt; and even now he remains
here, and in silence recognizes his own crimes as I enumerate
them.

I seem to myself to have been too long occupied with one
class of crime. I am aware, O judges, that I have to encounter
the weariness of your ears and eyes at such a repetition of
similar cases; I will, therefore, pass over many instances. But I
entreat you, O judges, in the name of the immortal gods, in the
name of these very gods of whose honor and worship we have
been so long speaking, refresh your minds so as to attend to
what I am about to mention, while I bring forward and detail
to you that crime of his by which the whole province was
roused, and in speaking of which you will pardon me if I appear to go back rather far, and trace the earliest recollections
of the religious observances in question. The importance of
the affair will not allow me to pass over the atrocity of his guilt
with brevity.

XLVIII. It is an old opinion, O judges, which can be proved
from the most ancient records and monuments of the Greeks,
that the whole island of Sicily was consecrated to Ceres and
Libera. Not only did all other nations think so, but the Sicilians
themselves were so convinced of it, that it appeared a deeply
rooted and innate belief in their minds. For they believe that
these goddesses were born in these districts, and that corn was
first discovered in this land, and that Libera was carried off,
the same goddess whom they call Proserpine, from a grove in
the territory of Enna, a place which, because it is situated in
the centre of the island, is called the navel of Sicily. And when
Ceres wished to seek her and trace her out, she is said to have

lit her torches at those flames which burst out at the summit of
Ætna, and carrying these torches before her, to have wandered
over the whole earth. But Enna, where those things which I
am speaking of are said to have been done, is in a high and
lofty situation, on the top of which is a large level plain, and
springs of water which are never dry. And the whole of the
plain is cut off and separated, so as to be difficult of approach.
Around it are many lakes and groves, and beautiful flowers at
every season of the year; so that the place itself appears to tes-
tify to that abduction of the virgin which we have heard of
from our boyhood.[6] Near it is a cave turned towards the north,
of unfathomable depth, where they say that Father Pluto suddenly rose out of the earth in his chariot, and carried the virgin
off from that spot, and that on a sudden, at no great distance
from Syracuse, he went down beneath the earth, and that immediately a lake sprang up in that place; and there to this day
the Syracusans celebrate anniversary festivals with a most numerous assemblage of both sexes.

XLIX. On account of the antiquity of this belief, because in
those places the traces and almost the cradles of those gods
are found, the worship of Ceres of Enna prevails to a wonderful extent, both in private and in public over all Sicily. In truth,
many prodigies often attest her influence and divine powers.
Her present help is often brought to many in critical circumstances, so that this island appears not only to be loved, but
also to be watched over and protected by her. Nor is it the
Sicilians only, but even all other tribes and nations greatly worship Ceres of Enna. In truth, if initiation into those sacred
mysteries of the Athenians is sought for with the greatest
avidity, to which people Ceres is said to have come in that long
wandering of hers, and then she brought them corn. How much
greater reverence ought to be paid to her by those people
among whom it is certain that she was born, and first discovered corn. And, therefore, in the time of our fathers, at a most
disastrous and critical time to the republic, when, after the
death of Tiberius Gracchus, there was a fear that great dan-

---

[6] We have the same advantage as, or rather greater advantages than
Cicero in this respect; for we have heard the story from our boyhood told,
far more beautifully than any Sicilian ever imagined it. See Ovid, Fasti
iv. 419.

gers were portended to the state by various prodigies, in the consulship of Publius Mucius and Lucius Calpurnius, recourse was had to the Sibylline books, in which it was found set down, "that the most ancient Ceres ought to be appeased." Then, priests of the Roman people, selected from the most honorable college of decemvirs, although there was in our own city a most beautiful and magnificent temple of Ceres, nevertheless went as far as Enna. For such was the authority and antiquity of the reputation for holiness of that place, that when they went thither, they seemed to be going not to a temple of Ceres, but to Ceres herself. I will not din this into your ears any longer. I have been some time afraid that my speech may appear unlike the usual fashion of speeches at trials, unlike the daily method of speaking. This I say, that this very Ceres, the most ancient, the most holy, the very chief of all sacred things which are honored by every people, and in every nation, was carried off by Caius Verres from her temple and her home. Ye who have been to Enna, have seen a statue of Ceres made of marble, and in the other temple a statue of Libera. They are very colossal and very beautiful, but not exceedingly ancient. There was one of brass, of moderate size, but extraordinary workmanship, with the torches in its hands, very ancient, by far the most ancient of all those statues which are in that temple; that he carried off, and yet he was not content with that. Before the temple of Ceres, in an open and an uncovered place, there are two statues, one of Ceres, the other of Triptolemus, very beautiful, and of colossal size. Their beauty was their danger, but their size their safety; because the taking of them down and carrying them off appeared very difficult. But in the right hand of Ceres there stood a beautifully wrought image of victory; and this he had wrenched out of the hand of Ceres and carried off.

L. What now must be his feelings at the recollection of his crimes, when I, at the mere enumeration of them, am not only roused to indignation in my mind, but even shudder over my whole body? For thoughts of that temple, of that place, of that holy religion come into my mind. Everything seems present before my eyes,—the day on which, when I had arrived at Enna, the priests of Ceres came to meet me with garlands of vervain, and with fillets; the concourse of citizens, among whom, while I was addressing them, there was such weeping and groaning that the most bitter grief seemed to have taken possession of the whole. They did not complain of the absolute way in which the tents were levied, nor of the plunder of property, nor of the iniquity of tribunals, nor of that man's unhallowed lusts, nor of his violence, nor of the insults by which they had been oppressed and overwhelmed. It was the divinity of Ceres, the antiquity of their sacred observances, the holy veneration due to their temple, which they wished should have atonement made to them by the punishment of that most atrocious and audacious man. They said that they could endure everything else; that to everything else they were indifferent. This indignation of theirs was so great, that you might suppose that Verres, like another king of hell, had come to Enna and had carried off, not Proserpine, but Ceres herself. And, in truth, that city does not appear to be a city, but a shrine of Ceres. The people of Enna think that Ceres dwells among them; so that they appear to me not to be citizens of that city, but to be all priests, to be all ministers and officers of Ceres. Did you dare to take away out of Enna the statue of Ceres? Did you attempt at Enna to wrench Victory out of the hand of Ceres? to tear one goddess from the other?—nothing of which those men dared to violate, or even to touch, whose qualities were all more akin to wickedness than to religion. For while Publius Popillius and Publius Rupilius were consuls, slaves, runaway slaves, and barbarians, and enemies, were in possession of that place; but yet the slaves were not so much slaves to their own masters, as you are to your passions; nor did the runaways flee from their masters as far as you flee from all laws and from all right; nor were the barbarians as barbarous in language and in race as you are in your nature and your habits; nor were the enemies as much enemies to men as you are to the immortal gods. How, then, can a man beg for any mercy who has surpassed slaves in baseness, runaway slaves in rashness, barbarians in wickedness, and enemies in inhumanity?

LI. You heard Theodorus and Numinius and Nicasio, deputies from Enna, say, in the name of their state, that they had this commission from their fellow-citizens, to go to Verres, and to demand from him the restoration of the statues of Ceres and of Victory. And if they obtained it, then they were to adhere

to the ancient customs of the state of Enna, not to give any
public testimony against him, although he had oppressed
Sicily, since these were the principles which they had received
from their ancestors. But if he did not restore them, then they
were to go before the tribunal, to inform the judges of the injuries they had received, but, far above all things, to complain
of the insults to their religion. And, in the name of the immortal gods, I entreat you, O judges, do not you despise, do not you
scorn or think lightly of their complaints. The injuries done to
our allies are the present question; the authority of the laws
is at stake; the reputation and the honesty of our courts of justice is at stake. And though all these are great considerations,
yet this is the greatest of all,—the whole province is so imbued
with religious feeling, such a superstitious dread arising out of
that man's conduct has seized upon the minds of all the Sicilians, that whatever public or private misfortunes happen, appear to befall them because of that man's wickedness. You have
heard the Centuripans, the Agyrians, the Catenans, the Herbi-
tans, the Ennans, and many other deputies say, in the name of
their states, how great was the solitude in their district, how
great the devastation, how universal the flight of the cultiva-
tors of the soil; how deserted; how uncultivated, how desolate
every place was. And although there are many and various injuries done by that man to which these things are owing, still
this one cause, in the opinion of the Sicilians, is the most
weighty of all; for, because of the insults offered to Ceres, they
believe that all the crops and gifts of Ceres have perished in
these districts. Bring remedies, O judges, to the insulted religion of the allies; preserve your own, for this is not a foreign
religion, nor one with which you have no concern. But even if
it were, if you were unwilling to adopt it yourselves, still you
ought to be willing to inflict heavy punishment on the man who
had violated it. But now that the common religion of all nations is attacked in this way, now that these sacred observances
are violated which our ancestors adopted and imported from
foreign countries, and have honored ever since,—sacred observances, which they called Greek observances, as in truth
they were,—even if we were to wish to be indifferent and cold
about these matters, how could we be so?

LII. I will mention the sacking of one city, also, and that the most beautiful and highly decorated of all, the city of Syracuse. And I will produce my proofs of that, O judges, in order at length to conclude and bring to an end the whole history of offences of this sort. There is scarcely any one of you who has not often heard how Syracuse was taken by Marcus Marcellus, and who has not sometimes also read the account in our annals. Compare this peace with that war; the visit of this prætor with the victory of that general; the debauched retinue of the one with the invincible army of the other; the lust of Verres with the continence of Marcellus;—and you will say that Syracuse was built by the man who took it; was taken by the man who received it well established and flourishing. And for the present I omit those things which will be mentioned, and have been already mentioned by me in an irregular manner in different parts of my speech—that the market-place of the Syracusans, which at the entrance of Marcellus was preserved unpolluted by slaughter, on the arrival of Verres overflowed with the blood of innocent Sicilians; that the harbor of the Syracusans, which at that time was shut against both our fleets and those of the Carthaginians, was, while Verres was prætor, open to Sicilian pirates, or even to a single piratical galley. I say nothing of the violence offered to people of noble birth, of the ravishment of matrons, atrocities which then, when the city was taken, were not committed, neither through the hatred of enemies, nor through military licence, nor through the customs of war or the rights of victory. I pass over, I say, all these things which were done by that man for three whole years. Listen rather to acts which are connected with those matters of which I have hitherto been speaking. You have often heard that the city of Syracuse is the greatest of the Greek cities, and the most beautiful of all. It is so, O judges, as it is said to be; for it is so by its situation, which is strongly fortified, and which is on every side by which you can approach it, whether by sea or land, very beautiful to behold. And it has harbors almost enclosed within the walls, and in the sight of the whole city; harbors which have different entrances, but which meet together, and are connected at the other end. By their union a part of the town, which is called the island, being separated from the rest by a narrow arm of the sea, is again joined to and connected with the other by a bridge.

LIII. That city is so great that it may be said to consist of
four cities of the largest size; one of which, as I have said, is
that "Island," which, surrounded by two harbors, projects out
towards the mouth and entrance of each. In it there is a palace
which did belong to king Hiero, which our prætors are in the
habit of using; in it are many sacred buildings, but two, which
have a great pre-eminence over all the others,—one a temple
of Diana, and the other one, which before the arrival of that
man was the most ornamented of all, sacred to Minerva. At the
end of this island is a fountain of sweet water, the name of
which is Arethusa, of incredible size, very full of fish, which
would be entirely overwhelmed by the waves of the sea, if it
were not protected from the sea by a rampart and dam of stone.
There is also another city at Syracuse, the name of which is
Achradina, in which there is a very large forum, most beautiful
porticoes, a highly decorated town-hall, a most spacious senate-
house, and a superb temple of Jupiter Olympius; and the other
districts of the city are joined together by one broad unbroken
street, and divided by many cross streets, and by private
houses. There is a third city, which, because in that district
there is an ancient temple of Fortune, is called Tyche, in which
there is a spacious gymnasium, and many sacred buildings,
and that district is the most frequented and the most populous.
There is also a fourth city, which, because it is the last built,
is called Neapolis,[7] in the highest part of which there is a very
large theatre, and, besides that, there are two temples of great
beauty, one of Ceres, the other of Libera, and a statue of
Apollo, which is called Temenites, very beautiful and of colossal size which, if he could have moved them, he would not
have hesitated to carry off.

LIV. Now I will return to Marcellus, that I may not appear to have entered into this statement without any reason.
He, when with his powerful army he had taken this splendid
city, did not think it for the credit of the Roman people to
destroy and extinguish this splendor, especially as no danger
could possibly arise from it, and therefore he spared all the

---

[7] Neapolis meaning, "new city," or as we might say, Newtown, from
the Greek words Νέα πόλις. as Tyche is the Greek name of Fortune—
Τύχη. Compare with this passage the description of Syracuse given by
Thucydides in his sixth and seventh books.

buildings, public as well as private, sacred as well as ordinary, as if he had come with his army for the purpose of defending them, not of taking them by storm. With respect to the decorations of the city, he had a regard to his own victory, and a regard to humanity; he thought it was due to his victory to transport many things to Rome which might be an ornament to this city, and due to humanity not utterly to strip the city, especially as it was one which he was anxious to preserve. In this division of the ornaments, the victory of Marcellus did not covet more for the Roman people than his humanity reserved to the Syracusans. The things which were transported to Rome we see before the temples of Honor and of Virtue, and also in other places. He put nothing in his own house, nothing in his gardens, nothing in his suburban villa; he thought that his house could only be an ornament to the city if he abstained from carrying the ornaments which belonged to the city to his own house. But he left many things of extraordinary beauty at Syracuse; he violated not the respect due to any god; he laid hands on none. Compare Verres with him; not to compare the man with the man,—no such injury must be done to such a man as that, dead though he be; but to compare a state of peace with one of war, a state of law and order, and regular jurisdiction, with one of violence and material law, and the supremacy of arms; to compare the arrival and retinue of the one with the victory and army of the other.

LV. There is a temple of Minerva in the island, of which I have already spoken, which Marcellus did not touch, which he left full of its treasures and ornaments, but which was so stripped and plundered by Verres, that it seems to have been in the hands, not of any enemy,—for enemies, even in war, respect the rites of religion, and the customs of the country,— but of some barbarian pirates. There was a cavalry battle of their king Agathocles, exquisitely painted in a series of pictures, and with these pictures the inside walls of the temple were covered. Nothing could be more noble than those paintings; there was nothing at Syracuse that was thought more worthy going to see. These pictures, Marcus Marcellus, though by that victory of his he had divested everything of its sacred inviolability of character, still, out of respect for religion, never touched; Verres, though in consequence of the long peace, and the loyalty of the Syracusan people, he had received them as sacred and under the protection of religion, took away all those pictures, and left naked and unsightly those walls whose decorations had remained inviolate for so many ages, and had escaped so many wars: Marcellus, who had vowed that if he took Syracuse he would erect two temples at Rome, was unwilling to adorn the temple which he was going to build with these treasures which were his by right of capture; Verres, who was bound by no vows to Honor or Virtue, as Marcellus was, but only to Venus and to Cupid, attempted to plunder the temple of Minerva. The one was unwilling to adorn gods in the spoil taken from gods, the other transferred the decorations of the virgin Minerva to the house of a prostitute. Besides this, he took away out of the same temple twenty-seven more pictures beautifully painted; among which were likenesses of the kings and tyrants of Sicily, which delighted one, not only by the skill of the painter, but also by reminding us of the men, and by enabling us to recognize their persons. And see now, how much worse a tyrant this man proved to the Syracusans than any of the old ones, as they, cruel as they were, still adorned the temples of the immortal gods, while this man took away the monuments and ornaments from the gods.

LVI. But now what shall I say of the folding-doors of that temple? I am afraid that those who have not seen these things may think that I am speaking too highly of, and exaggerating everything, though no one ought to suspect that I should be so inconsiderate as to be willing that so many men of the highest reputation, especially when they are judges in this cause, who have been at Syracuse, and who have seen all these things themselves, should be witnesses to my rashness and falsehood. I am able to prove this distinctly, O judges, that no more magnificent doors, none more beautifully wrought of gold and ivory, ever existed in any temple. It is incredible how many Greeks have left written accounts of the beauty of these doors: they, perhaps, may admire and extol them too much; be it so, still it is more honorable for our republic, O judges, that our general, in a time of war, should have left those things which appeared to them so beautiful, than that our prætor should have carried them off in a time of peace. On the folding-doors were some subjects most minutely executed in ivory; all these he caused to be taken out; he tore off and took away a very fine head of the Gorgon with snakes for hair; and he showed, too, that he was influenced not only by admiration for the workmanship, but by a desire of money and gain; for he did not hesitate to take away also all the golden knobs from these folding-doors, which were numerous and heavy; and it was not the workmanship of these, but the weight which pleased him. And so he left the folding-doors in such state, that, though they had formerly contributed greatly to the ornament of the temple, they now seemed to have been made only for the purpose of shutting it up. Am I to speak also of the spears made of grass? for I saw that you were excited at the name of them when the witnesses mentioned them. They were such that it was sufficient to have seen them once, as there was neither any manual labor in them nor any beauty, but simply an incredible size, which it would be quite sufficient even to hear of, and too much to see them more than once. Did you covet even those?

LVII. For the Sappho which was taken away out of the town-hall affords you so reasonable an excuse, that it may seem almost allowable and pardonable. That work of Silanion, so perfect, so elegant, so elaborate, (I will not say what private man, but) what nation could be so worthy to possess, as the most elegant and learned Verres? Certainly, nothing can be said against it. If any one of us, who are not as happy, who cannot be as refined as that man, should wish to behold anything of the sort, let him go to the temple of Good Fortune, to the monument of Catulus, to the portico of Metullus; let him take pains to get admittance into the Tusculan villa of any one of those men; let him see the forum when decorated, if Verres is ever so kind as to lend any of his treasures to the ædiles. Shall Verres have all these things at home? shall Verres have his house full of, his villas crammed with, the ornaments of temples and cities? Will you still, O judges, bear with the hobby, as he calls it, and pleasures of this vile artisan? a man who was born in such a rank, educated in such a way, and who is so formed, both in mind and body, that he appears a much fitter person to take down statues than to appropriate them. And how great a regret this Sappho which he carried off left behind her, can scarcely be told; for in the first place it was admirably made, and, besides, it had a very noble Greek epigram engraved upon the pedestal; and would not that learned man, that Grecian, who is such an acute judge of these matters, who is the only man who understands them, if he had understood one letter of Greek, have taken that away too? for now, because it is engraved on an empty pedestal, it both declares what was once on the pedestal, and proves that it has been taken away. What shall I say more? Did you not take away the statue of Pæan from out of the temple of Æsculapius, beautifully made, sacred, and holy as it was? a statue which all men went to see for its beauty, and worshipped for its sacred character. What more? was not the statue of Aristæus openly taken away by your command out of the temple of Bacchus? What more? did you not take away out of the temple of Jupiter that most holy statue of Jupiter Imperator, which the Greeks call οὔριος most beautifully made? What next? did you hesitate to take away out of the temple of Libera, that most exquisite bust of Parian marble, which we used to go to see? And that Pæan used to be worshipped among that people together with Æsculapius, with anniversary sacrifices. Aristæus, who being, as the Greeks report, the son of Bacchus, is said to have been the inventor of oil, was consecrated among them together with his father Bacchus, in the same temple.

LVIII. But how great do you suppose was the honor paid to Jupiter Imperator in his own temple? You may collect it from this consideration, if you recollect how great was the religious reverence attached to that statue of the same appearance and form which Flaminius brought out of Macedonia, and placed in the Capitol. In truth, there were said to be in the whole world three statues of Jupiter Imperator, of the same class, all beautifully made; one was that one from Macedonia, which we have seen in the Capitol; a second was the one at the narrow straits, which are the mouth of the Euxine Sea; the third was that which was at Syracuse, till Verres came as prætor. Flaminius removed the first from its habitation, but only to place it in the Capitol, that is to say, in the house of Jupiter upon earth; but as to the one that is at the entrance of the Euxine, that though so many wars have proceeded from the shores of that sea, and though so many have been poured into Pontus, has still remained inviolate and untouched to this day. This third one, which was at Syracuse, which Marcus

Marcellus, when in arms and victorious, had seen, which he had spared to the religion of the place, which both the citizens of, and settlers in Syracuse were used to worship, and strangers not only visited, but often venerated, Caius Verres took away from the temple of Jupiter. To return again to Marcellus. Judge of the case, O judges, in this way; think that more gods were lost to the Syracusans owing to the arrival of Verres, than even were owing to the victory of Marcellus. In truth, he is said to have sought diligently for the great Archimedes, a man of the highest genius and skill, and to have been greatly concerned when he heard that he had been killed; but that other man sought for everything which he did seek for, not for the purpose of preserving it, but of carrying it away.

LIX. At present, then, all those things which might appear more insignificant, I will on that account pass over—how he took away Delphic tables made of marble, beautiful goblets of brass, an immense number of Corinthian vases, out of every sacred temple at Syracuse; and therefore, O judges, those men who are accustomed to take strangers about to all those things which are worth going to see, and to show them every separate thing, whom they call mystagogi, (or cicerones), now have their description of things reserved; for as they formerly used to show what there was in every place, so now they show what has been taken from every place.

What do you think, then? Do you think that those men are affected with but a moderate indignation? Not so, O judges; in the first place, because all men are influenced by religious feeling, and think that their paternal gods, whom they have received from their ancestors, are to be carefully worshipped and retained by themselves; and secondly, because this sort of ornament, these works and specimens of art, these statues and paintings, delight men of Greek extraction to an excessive degree; therefore by their complaints we can understand that these things appear most bitter to those men, which perhaps may seem trifling and contemptible to us. Believe me, O judges, although I am aware to a certainty that you yourselves hear the same things; that though both our allies and foreign nations have during these past years sustained many calamities and injuries, yet men of Greek extraction have not been, and are not, more indignant at any than at this ruthless plundering of their temples and altars. Although that man may say that he bought these things, as he is accustomed to say, yet, believe me in this, O judges,—no city in all Asia or in all Greece has ever sold one statue, one picture, or one decoration of the city, of its own free will to anybody. Unless, perchance, you suppose that, after strict judicial decisions had ceased to take place at Rome, the Greeks then began to sell these things, which they not only did not sell when there were courts of justice open, but which they even used to buy up; or unless you think that Lucius Crassus, Quintus Scævola, Caius Claudius, most powerful men, whose most splendid ædileships we have seen, had no dealings in those sort of matters with the Greeks, but that those men had such dealings who became ædiles after the destruction of the courts of justice.

LX. Know also that that false pretense of purchase was more bitter to the cities than if any one were privily to filch things, or boldly to steal them and carry them off. For they think it the most excessive baseness, that it should be entered on the public records that the city was induced by a price, and by a small price too, to sell and alienate those things which it had received from men of old. In truth, the Greeks delight to a marvelous degree in those things, which we despise. And therefore our ancestors willingly allowed those things to remain in numbers among the allies, in order that they might be as splendid and as flourishing as possible under our dominion; and among those nations whom they rendered taxable or tributary,[8] still they left these things, in order that they who take delight in those things which to us seem insignificant, might have them as pleasures and consolations in slavery. What do you think that the Rhegians, who now are Roman citizens, would take to allow that marble Venus to be taken from them? What would the Tarentines take to lose the Europa sitting on the Bull? or the Satyr which they have in the temple of Vesta? or their other monuments? What would the Thespians take to lose the statue of Cupid, the only object for which any one ever goes to see Thespiæ? What would the men of Cnidos take

---

[8] The Latin is "quos vectigales aut stipendiarius fuerant"—"*Stipendiarii* and *vectigales* are thus distinguished: *Stipendiarii* are those who pay annually a fixed sum as tribute; *vectigales*, those who pay in proportion to their property or income."—Riddle's Dict. v. *Stipendiarius*.

for their marble Venus? or the Coans for their picture of her? or the Ephesians for Alexander? the men of Cyzicus for their Ajax or Medea? What would the Rhodians take for Ialysus? the Athenians for their marble Bacchus, or their picture of Paralus, or their brazen Heifer, the work of Myron? It would be a long business and an unnecessary one, to mention what is worth going to see among all the different nations in all Asia and Greece; but that is the reason why I am enumerating these things, because I wish you to consider that an incredible indignation must be the feeling of those men from whose cities these things are carried away.

LXI. And to say nothing of other nations, judge of the Syracusans themselves. For when I went to Syracuse, I originally believed what I had heard at Rome from that man's friends, that the city of Syracuse, on account of the inheritance of Heraclius, was no less friendly to him than the city of the Mamertines, because of their participation in all his booty and robberies. And at the same time I was afraid that, owing to the influence of the high-born and beautiful women at whose will he had directed all the measures of his prætorship for three years, and of the men to whom they were married, I should be opposed not only by an excessive lenity, but even by a feeling of liberality towards that man, if I were to seek for any evidence out of the public records of the Syracusans. Therefore when at Syracuse I was chiefly with Roman citizens; I copied out their papers; I inquired into their injuries. As I was a long time occupied by that business, in order to rest a little and to give my mind a respite from care, I returned to those fine documents of Carpinatius; in which, in company with some of the most honorable knights of the body of Roman settlers, I unraveled the case of those Verrutii, whom I have mentioned before, but I expected no aid at all, either publicly or privately, from the Syracusans, nor had I any idea of asking for any. While I was doing this, on a sudden Heraclius came to me, who was in office at Syracuse, a man of high birth, who had been priest of Jupiter, which is the highest honor among the Syracusans; he requests of me and of my brother, if we have no objection, to go to their senate; that they were at that moment assembled in full numbers in the senate-house, and he said that he made this request to us to attend by command of the senate. At first we were in doubt what to do; but afterwards it soon occurred to us that we ought not to shun that assembly or that place.

LXII. Therefore we came to the senate-house; they all rise at our entry to do us honor. We sat down at the request of the magistrates. Diodorus the son of Timarchides, who was the first man in that body both in influence and in age, and also as it seemed to me in experience and knowledge of business, began to speak; and the first sentence of his speech was to this effect—That the senate and people of Syracuse were grieved and indignant, that, though in all the other cities of Sicily I had informed the senate and people of what I proposed for their advantage or for their safety, and though I had received from them all commissions, deputies, letters and evidence, yet in that city I had done nothing of that sort. I answered, that deputies from the Syracusans had not been present at Rome in that assembly of the Sicilians when my assistance was entreated by the common resolution of all the deputations, and when the cause of the whole of Sicily was entrusted to me; and that I could not ask that any decree should be passed against Caius Verres in that senate-house in which I saw a gilt statue of Caius Verres. And after I said that, such a groaning ensued at the sight and mention of the statue, that it appeared to have been placed in the senate-house as a monument of his wickedness and not of his services. Then every one for himself, as fast as each could manage to speak, began to give me information of those things which I have just now mentioned; to tell me that the city was plundered—the temples stripped of their treasures—that of the inheritance of Heraclius, which he had adjudged to the men of the palæstra, he had taken by far the greatest share himself; and indeed, that they could not expect that he should care for the men of the palæstra, when he had taken away even the god who was the inventor of oil; that that statue had neither been made at the public expense, nor erected by public authority, but that those men who had been the sharers in the plunder of the inheritance of Heraclius, had had it made and placed where it was; and that those same men had been the deputies at Rome, who had been his assistants in dishonesty, his partners in his thefts, and the witnesses of his debaucheries; and that therefore I ought the less to wonder if they were wanting to the unanimity of the deputies and to the safety of Sicily.

LXIII. When I perceived that their indignation at that man's injuries was not only not less, but almost greater than that of the rest of the Sicilians, then I explained my own intentions to them, and my whole plan and system with reference to the whole of the business which I had undertaken; then I exhorted them not to be wanting to the common cause and the common safety, and to rescind that panegyric which they had voted a few days before, being compelled, as they said, by violence and fear. Accordingly, O judges, the Syracusans, that man's clients and friends, do this. First of all, they produce to me the public documents which they had carefully stored up in the most sacred part of the treasury; in which they show me that everything, which I have said had been taken away, was entered, and even more things than I was able to mention. And they were entered in this way. "What had been taken out of the temple of Minerva . . . This, . . . and that." "What was missing out of the temple of Jupiter." "What was missing out of the temple of Bacchus." As each individual had had the charge of protecting and preserving those things, so it was entered; that each, when according to law he gave in his accounts, being bound to give up what he had received, had begged that he might be pardoned for the absence of these things, and that all had accordingly been released from liability on that account, and that it was kept secret; all which documents I took care to have sealed up with the public seal and brought away. But concerning the public panegyric on him this explanation was given: that at first, when the letters arrived from Verres about the panegyric, a little while before my arrival, nothing had been decreed; and after that, when some of his friends urged them that it ought to be decreed, they were rejected with the greatest outcry and the bitterest reproaches; but when I was on the point of arriving, then he who at that time was the chief governor had commanded them to decree it, and that it had been decreed in such a manner that the panegyric did him more damage than it could have done him good. So now, judges, do you receive the truth of that matter from me just as it was shown to me by them.

LXIV. It is a custom at Syracuse, that, if a motion on any

subject is brought before the senate, whoever wishes, gives his opinion on it. No one is asked by name for his sentiments; nevertheless, those are accustomed to speak first of their own accord, and naturally, according as they are superior in honor or in age; and that precedence is yielded to them by the rest; but, if at any time all are silent, then they are compelled to speak by lot. This was the custom when the motion was made respecting the panegyric of Verres. On which subject at first great numbers speak, in order to delay coming to any vote, and interpose this objection, that formerly, when they had heard that there was a prosecution instituted against Sextus Peducæus, who had deserved admirably well of that city and of the whole province, and when, in return for his numerous and important services, they wished to vote a panegyric on him, they had been prohibited from doing so by Caius Verres; and that it would be an unjust thing, although Peducæus had now no need of their praise, still not to vote that which at one time they had been eager to vote, before decreeing what they would only decree from compulsion. All shout in assent, and say approvingly that that is what ought to be done. So the question about Peducæus is put to the senate. Each man gave his opinion in order, according as he had precedence in age and honor. You may learn this from the resolution itself; for the opinions delivered by the chief men are generally recorded. Read

[*The list of speeches made on the subject of Sextus Peducæus is read.*]

It says who were the chief supporters of the motion. The vote is carried. Then the question about Verres is put. Tell me, I pray, what happened.

[*The list of speeches made on the subject of Caius Verres ....*]

Well what comes next?

[*As no one rose, and no one delivered his opinion . . . .*]

What is this?

[*They proceed by lot.*]

Why was this? Was no one a willing praiser of your prætorship, or a willing defender of you from danger, especially
when by being so he might have gained favor with the prætor?
No one. Those very men who used to feast with you, your
advisers and accomplices, did not venture to utter a word. In
that very senate-house in which a statue of yourself and a naked
statue of your son were standing, was there no one whom even
your naked son in a province stripped naked could move to
compassion? Moreover they inform me also of this, that they
had passed the vote of panegyric in such a form that all men
might see that it was not a panegyric, but rather a satire, to
remind every one of his shameful and disastrous prætorship.
For in truth it was drawn up in these words. "Because he had
scourged no one." From which you are to understand, that he
had caused most noble and innocent men to be executed. "Because he had administered the affairs of the province with
vigilance," when all his vigils were well known to have been
devoted to debauchery and adultery; moreover, there was this
clause added, which the defendant could never venture to
produce, and the accuser would never cease to dwell upon;
"Because Verres had kept all pirates at a distance from the
island of Sicily;" men who in his time had entered even into
the "island" of Syracuse. And after I had received this information from them, I departed from the senate-house with my
brother, in order that they might decree what they chose.

LXV. Immediately they pass a decree. First. "That my
brother Lucius should be connected with the city by ties of
hospitality;" because he had shown the same goodwill to the
Syracusans that I had always felt myself. That they not only
wrote at that time, but also had engraved on brazen tablets
and presented to us. Truly very fond of you are your Syracusans whom you are always talking of, who think it quite a
sufficient reason for forming an intimate connection with your
accuser, that he is going to be your accuser, and that he has
come among them for the purpose of prosecuting inquiries
against you. After that, a decree is passed, not with any difference of opinion, but almost unanimously, "That the panegyric
which had been decreed to Caius Verres, be rescinded." But,
when not only the vote had been come to, but when it had
even been drawn up in due form and entered in the records,

an appeal is made to the prætor. But who makes this appeal? Any magistrate? No. Any senator? Not even that. Any Syracusan? Far from it. Who, then, appeals to the prætor? The man who had been Verres's quæstor, Cæsetius. Oh, the ridiculous business! Oh, the deserted man! O man despaired of and abandoned by the Sicilian magistracy! In order to prevent the Sicilians passing a resolution of the senate, or from obtaining their rights according to their own customs and their own laws, an appeal is made to the prætor, not by any friend of his, not by any connection, not, in short, by any Sicilian, but by his own quæstor. Who saw this? Who heard it? That just and wise prætor orders the senate to be adjourned. A great multitude flocks to me. First of all, the senators cry out that their rights are being taken away; that their liberty is being taken away. The people praise the senate and thank them. The Roman citizens do not leave me. And on that day I had no harder task, than with all my exertions to prevent violent hands being laid on the man who made that appeal. When we had gone before the prætor's tribunal, he deliberates, forsooth, diligently and carefully what decision he shall give; for, before I say one word, he rises from his seat, and departs. And so we departed from the forum when it was now nearly evening.

LXVI. The next day, the first thing in the morning, I beg of him to allow the Syracusans to give me a copy of the resolution which they had passed the day before. But he refuses, and says that it is a great shame for me to have made a speech in a Greek senate; and that, as for my having spoken in the Greek language to Greeks, that was a thing which could not be endured at all. I answered the man as I could, as I chose, and as I ought. Among other things, I recollect that I said that it was easy to be seen how great was the difference between him and the great Numidicus, the real and genuine Metellus. That that Metellus had refused to assist with his panegyric Lucius Lucullus, his sister's husband, with whom he was on the very best terms, but that he was procuring panegyrics from cities for a man totally unconnected with himself, by violence and compulsion. But when I understood that it was many recent messengers, and many letters, not of introduction but of credit, that had had so much influence over him, at the suggestion of the Syracusans themselves I make a seizure of those documents in which the resolutions of the senate were recorded. And now behold a fresh confusion and strife. That, however, you may not suppose that he was without any friends or connections at Syracuse, that he was entirely desolate and forsaken, a man of the name of Theomnastus, a man ridiculously crazy, whom the Syracusans call Theoractus,[9] attempted to detain those documents; a man in such a condition, that the boys follow him, and that every one laughs at him every time he opens his mouth. But his craziness, which is ridiculous to others, was then in truth very troublesome to me. For while he was foaming at the mouth, his eyes glaring, and he crying out as loud as he could that I was attacking him with violence, we came together before the tribunal. Then I began to beg to be allowed to seal up and carry away the records. He spoke against me; he denied that there had been any regular resolution of the senate passed, since an appeal had been made to the prætor. He said that a copy of it ought not to be given to me. I read the act, that I was to be allowed all documents and records. He, like a crazy man as he was, urged that our laws had nothing to do with him. That intelligent prætor decided that he did not choose, as the resolution of the senate had no business ever to be ratified, to allow me to take a copy of it to Rome. Not to make a long story of it, if I had not threatened the man vigorously, if I had not read to him the provisions of the act passed in this case, and the penalties enacted by it, I should not have been allowed to have the documents. But that crazy fellow, who had declaimed against me most violently on behalf of Verres, when he found he did not succeed, in order I suppose to recover my favor, gives me a book in which all Verres's Syracusan thefts were set down, which I had already been informed of by, and had a list of from them.

LXVII. Now, then, let the Mamertines praise you, who are the only men of all that large province who wish you to get off; but let them praise you on condition that Heius, who is the chief man of that deputation, is present; let them praise you on condition that they are here, ready to reply to me on those points concerning which they are questioned. And that they

---

[9] Theoractus seems a sort of nickname, to indicate his insanity, being derived from Θεὸs, God, and ῥήγνυμι, to break; while Theomnastus is derived from Θεὸs and μέμνημαι to remember.

may not be taken by surprise on a sudden, this is what I shall ask them:—Are they bound to furnish a ship to the Roman people? They will admit it. Have they supplied it while Verres was prætor? They will say, No. Have they built an enormous transport at the public expense which they have given to Verres? They will not be able to deny it. Has Verres taken corn from them to send to the Roman people, as his predecessor did? They will say, No. What soldiers or sailors have they furnished during those three years? They will say they furnished none at all. They will not be able to deny that Messana has been the receiver of all his plunder and all his robberies. They will confess that an immense quantity of things were exported from that city; and besides that, that this large vessel given to him by the Mamertines, departed loaded when the prætor left Sicily. You are welcome, then, to that panegyric of the Mamertines. As for the city of Syracuse, we see that that feels towards you as it has been treated by you; and among them that infamous Verrean festival, instituted by you, has been abolished. In truth, it was a most unseemly thing for honors such as belong to the gods to be paid to the man who had carried off the images of the gods. In truth, that conduct of the Syracusans would be deservedly reproached, if when they had struck a most celebrated and solemn day of festival games out of their annals, because on that day Syracuse was said to have been taken by Marcellus, they should, notwithstanding, cele- brate a day of festival in the name of Verres; though he had plundered the Syracusans of all which that day of disaster had left them. But observe the shamelessness and arrogance of the man, O judges, who not only instituted this disgraceful and ridiculous Verrean festival out of the money of Heraclius, but who also ordered the Marcellean festival to be abolished, in order that they might every year offer sacrifices to the man by whose means they had lost the sacred festivals which they had ever observed, and had lost their national deities, and that they might take away the festival days in honor of that family by whose means they had recovered all their other festivals.

IN DEFENSE OF QUINTUS LIGARIUS

THE ARGUMENT

Quintus Ligarius was a Roman knight, who had been one of the
lieutenants of Considius, the proconsul of Africa, and one of
Pompey's partisans, and as such had borne arms against Cæsar in
Africa, on which account he had gone into voluntary exile, to
get out of the reach of the conqueror. But his two brothers had
been on Cæsar's side, and had joined Pansa and Cicero in inter-
ceding with Cæsar to pardon him. While Cæsar was hesitating,
Quintus Tubero, who was an ancient enemy of his, knowing that
Cæsar was very unwilling to restore him, (for Ligarius was a
great lover of liberty,) impeached him as having behaved with
great violence in the prosecution of the African war against
Cæsar, who privately encouraged this proceeding, and ordered
the action to be tried in the forum, where he sat in person as
judge to decide it; and so determined was he against Ligarius,
that he is said to have brought the sentence of condemnation with
him into court, already drawn up and formally signed and sealed.
But he was prevailed upon by Cicero's eloquence, which extorted
from him a verdict of acquittal against his will; and he afterwards
pardoned Ligarius and allowed him to return to Rome. Ligarius
afterwards became a great friend of Brutus, and joined him in
the conspiracy against Cæsar.

I. It is a new crime, and one never heard of before this day,
O Caius Cæsar, which my relation Quintus Tubero has brought
before you, when he accuses Quintus Ligarius with having
been in Africa; and that charge Caius Pansa, a man of eminent
genius, relying perhaps on that intimacy with you which he
enjoys, has ventured to confess. Therefore I do not know which
way I had best proceed. For I had come prepared, as you did
not know that fact of your own knowledge, and could not have
heard it from any other quarter, to abuse your ignorance in
order to further the safety of a miserable man. But, however,
since that which was previously unknown has been ferreted

out by the diligence of his enemy we must, I suppose, confess the truth; especially as my dear friend Caius Pansa has so acted that it would not now be in my power to deny it. Therefore, abandoning all dispute of the fact, all my speech must be addressed to your mercy; by which many have already been preserved, having besought of you, not a release from all guilt, but pardon from admitted error.

You, therefore, O Tubero, have that which is of all things most desirable for a prosecutor, a defendant who confesses his fault; but still, one who confesses it only so far as he admits that he was of the same party as you yourself, O Tubero, were, and as that man worthy of all praise, your father, also was. Therefore you must inevitably confess yourselves also to be guilty, before you can find fault with any part of the conduct of Ligarius.

Quintus Ligarius, then, at a time when there was no suspicion of war, went as lieutenant into Africa with Caius Considius, in which lieutenancy he made himself so acceptable, both to our citizens there and to our allies, that Considius on departing from the province could not have given satisfaction to those men if he had appointed any one else to govern it. Therefore, Quintus Ligarius, after refusing it for a long time without effect, took upon himself the government of the province against his will. And while peace lasted, he governed it in such a manner, that his integrity and good faith were most acceptable both to our citizens and to our allies. On a sudden, war broke out, which those who were in Africa heard of as being actually raging before any rumor of its preparation had reached them. But when they did hear of it, partly out of an inconsiderate eagerness, partly out of some blind apprehension, they sought for some one as a leader, at first only with the object of securing their safety, and afterwards with that of indulging their party-spirit; while Ligarius, keeping his eyes fixed on home, and wishing to return to his friends, would not allow himself to be implicated in any business of the sort. In the mean time, Publius Attius Varus, who as prætor had obtained the province of Africa, came to Utica. Every one immediately flocked to him, and he seized on the government with no ordinary eagerness, if that may be called government which was conferred on him, while a private individual, by the clamor of an ignorant mob, without the sanction of any public council. Therefore, Ligarius, who was anxious to avoid being mixed up in any transactions of the sort, remained quiet for some time on the arrival of Varus.

II. Up to this point, O Caius Cæsar, Quintus Ligarius is free from all blame. He left his home, not only not for the purpose of joining in any war, but when there was not even the slightest suspicion of war. Having gone as lieutenant in time of peace, he behaved himself in a most peaceable province in such a manner, that it wished that peace might last for ever. Beyond all question, his departure from Rome with such an object ought not to be and cannot be offensive to you. Was, then, his remaining there offensive? Much less. For if it was no discreditable inclination that led to his going thither, it was even an honorable necessity which compelled him to remain. Both these times, then, are free from all fault—the time when he first went as lieutenant, and the time when, having been demanded by the province, he was appointed governor of Africa.

There is a third time: that during which he remained in Africa after the arrival of Varus; and if that is at all criminal, the crime is one of necessity, not of inclination. Would he, if he could possibly have escaped thence by any means whatever, would he rather have been at Utica than at Rome,—with Publius Attius, in preference to his own most united brothers? would he rather have been among strangers, than with his own friends? When his lieutenancy itself had been full of regret and anxiety on account of the extraordinary affection subsisting between him and his brothers, could he possibly remain there with any equanimity when separated from those brothers by the discord of war?

You have, therefore, O Cæsar, no sign as yet of the affections of Quintus Ligarius being alienated from you. And observe, I entreat you, with what good faith I am defending his cause. I am betraying my own by so doing. O the admirable clemency, deserving to be celebrated by all possible praise, and publicity, and writings and monuments! Marcus Cicero is urging in Ligarius's defence before you, that the inclinations of another were not the same as he admits his own to have been; nor does he fear your silent thoughts, nor is he under any apprehension as to what, while you are hearing of the conduct of another, may occur to you respecting his own.

III. See how entirely free from fear I am. See how brilliantly the light of your liberality and wisdom rises upon me while speaking before you! As far as I can, I will lift up my voice so that the Roman people may hear me. When the war began, O Cæsar, when it was even very greatly advanced towards its end, I, though compelled by no extraneous force, of my own free judgment and inclination went to join that party which had taken up arms against you. Before whom now am I saying this? Forsooth, before the man who, though he was acquainted with this, nevertheless restored me to the republic before he saw me; who sent letters to me from Egypt, to desire me to behave as I always had behaved; who, when he himself might have been the sole leader of the Roman people in the whole empire, still permitted me to be the other; by whose gift it was, (this very Caius Pansa, who is here present, bringing me the news,) that I retained the fasces wreathed with laurel, as long as I thought it becoming to retain them at all, and who would not have considered that he was giving me safety at all, if he did not give it me without my being stripped of any of my previous distinctions.

Observe, I pray you, O Tubero, how I, who do not hesitate to speak of my own conduct, do not venture to make any confession with respect to Ligarius: and I have said thus much respecting myself, to induce Tubero to excuse me when I say the same things of him. For I look in the forum on his industry and desire of glory, either on account of the nearness of our relationship, or because I am delighted with his genius and with his earnestness, or because I think that the praises of a young man who is my relative redound somewhat to my own credit. But I ask this—Who is it who thinks that it was any crime in Ligarius to have been in Africa? Why, the very man who himself also wished to be in Africa, and who complains that he was prevented by Ligarius from going there, and who certainly was in arms and fought against Cæsar. For, O Tubero, what was that drawn sword of yours doing in the battle of Pharsalia? against whose side was that sword-point of yours aimed? What was the feeling with which you took up arms? What was your intention? Where were your eyes? your hands?

your eagerness of mind? What were you desirous of? What were you wishing for? I am pressing you too hard. The young man appears to be moved. I will return to myself. I also was in arms in the same camp.

IV. But what other object had we, O Tubero, except to be able to do what this man can do now? Shall, then, O Cæsar, the speech of those men spur you on to deeds of cruelty, whose impunity is the great glory of your clemency? And in this cause, in truth, O Tubero, I am somewhat at a loss to discern your usual prudence, but much more so to see the sagacity of your father, since that man, eminent both for genius and erudition, did not perceive what sort of case this was. For if he had perceived it, he would, I doubt not, have preferred that you should conduct it in any manner in the world, rather than as you did.

You are accusing one who confesses the facts which you allege against him. That is not enough. You are accusing one who has a case, as I say, better than your own, or, as you yourself allow, at least as good as yours. This is strange enough; but what I am about to say is a perfect miracle. That accusation of yours does not tend to the point of procuring the condemnation of Quintus Ligarius, but of causing his death. And this is an object which no Roman citizen has ever pursued before you. That way of acting is quite foreign. It is the hatred of fickle Greeks or of savage barbarians that is usually excited to the pitch of thirsting for blood. For what else is your object? To prevent him from being at Rome? To deprive him of his country? To hinder him from living with his excellent brothers, with this Titus Brocchus, whom you see in court, his uncle, or with Brocchus's son, his cousin? To prevent his appearing in his country? Is that it? Can he be more deprived of all these things than he is already? He is prevented from approaching Italy; he is banished. You, therefore, do not wish to deprive him of his country, of which he already is deprived, but of his life.

But even in time of that dictator who punished with death every one whom he disliked, no one ever proceeded in that manner to accomplish such an end. He himself ordered men to be slain, without any one asking him; he even invited men to slay them by rewards; and that cruelty of his was avenged some years afterwards by this selfsame man whom you now wish to become cruel!

V. "But I am not asking for his death," you will say. I think indeed that you do not intend to do so, O Tubero. For I know you, I know your father, I know your birth and your name, and the pursuits of your race and family; your love of virtue, and civilization, and learning; your many admirable qualities, —all are known to me. Therefore I know for a certainty that you are not thirsting for blood, but you give no heed to the effect of your prosecution. For the transaction has this tendency, to make you seem not contented with that punishment under which Quintus Ligarius is at present suffering. What further punishment then is there but death? For if he be in exile, as he is, what more do you require? That he may never be pardoned? But this is much more bitter and much harsher. That which we begged for at his house with prayers and tears, throwing ourselves at his feet, trusting not so much to the strength of our cause as to his humanity, will you now struggle to prevent our obtaining? Will you interrupt our weeping? and will you forbid us to speak, lying at his feet, with the voice of suppliants? If, when we were doing this at his house, as we did, and as I hope we did not do in vain, you had all on a sudden burst in, and had begun to cry out, "O Caius Cæsar, beware how you pardon, beware how you pity brothers entreating you for the safety of their brother," would you not have renounced all humanity by such conduct? How much harder is this, for you to oppose in the forum what we begged of him in his own house! and while numbers are in this distress, to take away from them the refuge which they might find in his clemency!

I will speak plainly, O Caius Cæsar, what I feel. If in this splendid fortune of yours your lenity had not been as great as you of your own accord—of your own accord, I say, (I know well what I am saying,) make it, that victory of yours would have been pregnant with the bitterest grief to the state. For how many of the conquering party must have been found who would have wished you to be cruel, when some of even the conquered party are found to wish it! how many who, wishing no one to be pardoned by you, would have thrown obstacles in the way of your clemency, when even those men whom you yourself have pardoned are unwilling that you should be merciful to others!

But if we could prove to Cæsar that Ligarius was actually not in Africa at all, if we wished to save an unfortunate citizen by an honorable and merciful falsehood; still it would not be the act of man, in a case of such danger and peril to a fellow-citizen, to contradict and refute our falsehood; and if it were decent for any one to do so, it would certainly not be so for one who had himself been in the same case and condition. But, however, it is one thing to be unwilling that Cæsar should make a mistake, and another to be unwilling that he should be merciful. Then you would say, "Beware, O Cæsar, of believing all this—Ligarius was in Africa. He did bear arms against you." But now what is it that you say? "Take care you do not pardon him." This is not the language of a man; but he who uses it to you, O Caius Cæsar, will find it an easier matter to abjure his own humanity than to strip you of yours.

VI. And the first beginning, and the first proposition of Tubero, I imagine, was this; that he intended to speak of the wickedness of Quintus Ligarius. I make no doubt that you wondered how it was that no one made this statement respecting some one else, or how it was that he made it who had been in the same condition himself, or what new crime it was which he was bringing forward. Do you call that wickedness, Tubero? Why so? For that cause has not as yet been attacked by that name. Some call it mistake; some call it fear; those who give it a harder name term it hope, ambition, hatred, obstinacy; those who use the hardest language style it rashness. But up to this time no one except you has ever called it wickedness. My own opinion is, if any one seeks for a proper and accurate name for our misfortune, that some disaster sent by destiny descended upon and occupied the improvident minds of men; so that no one ought to wonder that human counsels were overruled by divine necessity.

Let it be allowed to us to be miserable, although that we cannot be when this man is our conqueror. But I am not speaking of those who have perished. Grant that they were ambitious, that they were angry, that they were obstinate men; but still let Cnæus Pompeius, for he is dead, and let many others with him, be free from the imputation of wickedness, of insanity, of parricide. When did any one hear such an expression from you, O Caius Cæsar? or what other object did your arms propose to themselves except the repelling insult from yourself? What was it that was accomplished by that invincible army of yours, beyond the preservation of its own rights, and of your dignity? What? when you were anxious for peace, was it your object to be able to come to terms of agreement with the wicked, or with the virtuous part of the citizens? To me, of a truth, O Cæsar, your services towards me, immense as they are, would certainly not appear so great, if I thought that I had been preserved by you while you considered me a wicked man. And how could you possibly have deserved well of the republic, if you had wished so many wicked men to remain with all their dignity unimpaired? Originally, O Cæsar, you considered that as a secession, not as a declaration of war; you considered it as a demonstration not of hostile hatred, but of civil dissension, in which both parties desired the safety of the republic, but some departed from measures calculated for the general welfare out of an error of judgment, and some out of party spirit. The dignity of the leaders was nearly on a par; but that of those who followed them was perhaps not quite equal; the justice of the cause, too, was at that time doubtful, because there was something on each side which deserved to be approved of; but now that is unquestionably entitled to be thought the better cause which even the gods assisted. But now that your clemency is known, who is there who does not think well of that victory, in which no one has fallen except those who fell with arms in their hands?

VII. But to say no more of the general question, let us come to our own individual case. Which do you think was easiest, O Tubero, for Ligarius to depart from Africa, or for you to abstain from coming into Africa? "Could we so abstain," you will say, "after the senate had voted that we should do so?" If you ask me, I say, Certainly not. But still the same senate had appointed Ligarius lieutenant. And he obeyed them at a time when men were forced to obey the senate; but you obeyed at a time when no one obeyed them who did not like it. Do I then find fault with you? By no means;—for a man of your family, of your name, of your race, of your hereditary principles, could not act otherwise. But I do not grant that you have a right to reprove in others the very same conduct which you boast of in yourselves.

Tubero's lot was drawn in pursuance of a resolution of the senate when he himself was not present, when he was even hindered by sickness from being present. He had made up his mind to excuse himself. I know all this from the great intimacy which exists between Lucius Tubero and myself: we were brought up together, in our campaigns we were comrades, afterwards we became connected by marriage, and throughout the whole of our lives, in short, we have been friends; it has been, moreover, a great bond between us, that we have been devoted to the same studies. I know, therefore, that Tubero wished to remain at home; but there was a person who contrived matters in such a way, who put forth that most holy name of the republic so artfully, that even had his sentiments been different from what they were, he would not have been able to support the weight of his language. He submitted to the authority of a most distinguished man, or, I should rather say, he obeyed him. He went off at the same time with those men who were already embarked in the same cause, but he made his journey slower than they. Therefore, he arrived in Africa when it was already occupied; and from this it is that the charge against Ligarius, or rather the enmity against him, has its rise. For if it be a crime in him to have wished to hinder you, it is a no less serious one for you to have wished to obtain Africa, the citadel of all the provinces, a land created for the purpose of waging war against this city, than for somebody else to have preferred obtaining it himself,—and that somebody was not Ligarius. Varus kept saying, that he had the command there; the fasces he certainly had. But however the case, as to that part of it, may be, what weight is there, O Tubero, in this complaint of yours? "We were admitted into the province." Well, suppose you had been admitted? was it your object to deliver it up to Cæsar, or to hold it against Cæsar?

VIII. See, O Cæsar, what licence, or rather what audacity, your liberality gives us. If Tubero replies that his father would have given up to you that province to which the senate and the lot which he drew had sent him, I will not hesitate in severe language to reprove that design of his before you yourself, to whose advantage it was that he should do so. For even if the action had been an acceptable one to you, it would not have been thought an honest one by you. But, however, all these topics I will pass over, not so much for fear of offending your most patient ears, as because that I do not wish that Tubero should appear to have been likely to do what he never thought of.

You two came, then, into the province of Africa,—the province of all others that was most hostile to the views of this victorious party, in which there was a most powerful king, an enemy to this cause, and in which the inclinations of a large and powerful body of Roman settlers were entirely adverse to it. I ask what you intended to do? Though I do not really doubt what you intended to do, when I see what you have done. You were forbidden to set foot in your province, and forbidden, as you state yourselves, with the greatest insults. How did you bear that? To whom did you carry your complaints of the insults which you had received? Why, to that man whose authority you had followed when you came to join his party in the war. If it had been in Cæsar's cause that you were coming to the province, unquestionably, when excluded from the province, it was to him that you would have gone. But you came to Pompeius. What is the meaning, then, of this complaint which you now urge before Cæsar, when you accuse that man by whom you complain that you were prevented from waging war against Cæsar? And as to this part of the business you may boast, for all I care, even though it will be falsely, that you would have given the province up to Cæsar, even if you had been forbidden by Varus, and by some others. But I will confess that the fault was all Ligarius's, who deprived you of an opportunity of acquiring so much glory.

IX. But observe, I pray you, O Caius Cæsar, the consistency of that most accomplished man, Lucius Tubero, which even though I thought as highly of it as I do, I still would not mention, if I were not aware that that is a virtue which you are in the habit of praising as much as any. Where, then, was there ever an example of such great consistency in any man? Consistency, do I say? I do not know whether I might not more fitly call it patience. For how few men would have acted in such a manner as to return to the same party by which he had been rejected in a time of civil dissension, and rejected even with cruelty! That is the act of a great mind, and of a man whom no contumely, no violence, and no danger can turn from a side which he has espoused, and from an opinion which he has adopted. Grant that in all other respects Tubero and Varus were on a par, as to honor, that is, and nobleness of birth, and respectability, and genius,—which, however, was by no means the case; at all events, Tubero had this great advantage that he had come to his own province with a legitimate command, in pursuance of a resolution of the senate. When he was prevented from entering it, he did not betake himself to Cæsar, lest he should appear to be in a passion,—he did not go home, lest he should be thought inactive,—he did not go into any other district, lest he might seem to condemn that cause which he had espoused. He came into Macedonia to the camp of Cnæus Pompeius, to join that very party by whom he had been repulsed with every circumstance of insult.

What? when that affair had had no effect on the mind of the man to whom you came, you behaved, after that, with a more languid zeal, I suppose, in his cause? You only stayed in some garrison? But your affections were alienated from his cause? Or were we all, as is the case in a civil war, and not more with respect to you two, than with respect to others,—were we all wholly occupied with a desire of victory? I, indeed, was at all times an advocate of peace, but that time I was too late. For it was the part of a madman to think of peace when he saw the hostile army in battle array. We all, every one of us, I say, were eager for victory; you most especially, as you had come into a place where you must inevitably perish if your side were not victorious. Although, as the result now turns out, I make no doubt that you consider your present safety preferable to what would have been the consequences of victory.

X. I would not say these things, O Tubero, if you had any reason to repent of your consistency, or Cæsar of his kindness. I ask now whether you are seeking to avenge your own injuries, or those of the republic? If those of the republic, what reply can you make with respect to your perseverance in the cause of that other party? If your own, take care that you are not making a great mistake in thinking that Cæsar will be angry with your enemies, after he has pardoned his own.

Do I, then, appear to you, O Cæsar, to be occupied in the

cause of Ligarius? Do I appear to be speaking of his conduct? In whatever I have said, I have endeavored to refer everything to the leading idea of your humanity, or clemency, or mercy, whichever may be its most proper name. I have indeed, O Caius Cæsar, pleaded many causes with you, while your pursuit of honors detained you in the forum; but certainly I never pleaded in this way, "Pardon my client, O judges; he has erred, he has tripped, he did not think. * * * If ever hereafter * * " This is the sort of way in which one pleads with a parent; to judges one says, "He never did it, he never thought of it, the witnesses are false, the accusation is false." Say, O Cæsar, that you are sitting as judge on the conduct of Ligarius. Ask me in what garrisons he was. I make no reply. I do not even adduce these arguments, which, perhaps, might have weight even with a judge.—"He went as a lieutenant before the war broke out; he was left there in time of peace; he was overtaken by the war; in the war itself he was not cruel; he was in disposition and zeal wholly yours." This is the way in which men are in the habit of pleading before a judge. But I am addressing a parent. "I have erred; I have acted rashly; I repent; I flee to your clemency; I beg pardon for my fault; I entreat you to pardon me." If no one has gained such indulgence from you, it is an arrogant address. But if many have, then do you give us assistance who have already given us hope. Is it possible that Ligarius should have no reason for hope, when I am allowed to approach you even for the purpose of entreating mercy for another? Although the hope which we entertain in this cause does not rest upon this oration of mine, nor on the zeal of those who entreat you for Ligarius, intimate friends of your own.

XI. For I have seen and known what it was that you mainly considered when many men were exerting themselves for any one's safety; I have seen that the causes of those who were entreating you had more weight with you than the persons of the advocates, and that you considered, not how much the man who was entreating you was your friend, but how much he was the friend of him for whom he was exerting himself. Therefore, you grant your friends so many favors, that they who enjoy your liberality appear to me sometimes to be happier than you yourself who give them so much. But, however, I see, as I said before, that the causes of those who entreat your mercy have more weight with you than the entreaties themselves; and that you are most moved by those men whose grief, which they display in their petitions to you, is the most genuine.

In preserving Quintus Ligarius you will do what will be acceptable to numbers of your intimate friends; but, I entreat you, give weight to the considerations which are accustomed to influence you. I can mention to you most brave men, Sabines, men most highly esteemed by you; and the whole of the Sabine district, the flower of Italy and the chief strength of the republic. You are well acquainted with the men. Observe the sadness and grief of all these men. You see yourself the tears and mourning attire of Titus Brocchus, who is here present, and I am in no doubt as to what your opinion of him is: you see the grief of his son. Why need I speak of the brothers of Ligarius? Do not fancy, O Cæsar, that we are pleading for the life of one individual only. You must either retain all three of the Ligarii in the city, or banish them all three from the city. Any exile is more desirable for them than their own country, their own house, and their own household gods will be, if this their brother is banished by himself. If they act as brothers should,—if they behave with affection and with genuine grief, then let their tears, their affection, and their relationship as brothers move you. Let that expression of yours have weight now which gained the victory; for we heard that you said that we thought all men our enemies, but those who were with us; but that you considered all men as your friends who were not actually arrayed against you. Do you see, then, this most respectable band; do you see the whole house of the Brocchi here present, and Lucius Marcius, and Caius Cæsetius, and Lucius Corfidius, and all these Roman knights, who are present here in mourning garments,—men who are not only well known to, but highly esteemed by you? They all were with you, then; and we were full of anger against them,—we were attacking them; some even personally threatened them. Preserve, therefore, their friends to your friends; so that, like everything else which has been said by you, this, too, may be found to be strictly true.

XII. But if you were able to look into the hearts of the Ligarii, so as to see the perfect unanimity which subsists between them, you would think that all the brothers were on your side. Can any one entertain a doubt that, if Quintus Ligarius had been able to be in Italy, he would also have adopted the same opinions as his brothers adopted? Who is there who is not acquainted with the harmony existing between them, united and molten together, as I may say, by their nearness of age to one another? Who does not feel that anything in the world was more likely than that these brothers should adopt different opinions and embrace different parties? By inclination, therefore, they were all with you. Owing to the necessity of the times, one was separated from you; but he, even if he had done what he did deliberately, would still have been only like those men whom, nevertheless, you have shown yourself desirous to save.

However, grant that he went up of his own accord to the war, and that he departed, not only from you, but also from his brothers. These friends of your own entreat you to pardon him. I, indeed, at the time when I was present at, and mixed up in, all your affairs, remember well what was the behavior of Titus Ligarius at that time, when he was city quæstor, with reference to you and your dignity. But it is of no importance for me to remember this. I hope that you, too, who are not in the habit of forgetting anything, except the injuries which have been done to you, since it is a part of your character, a part of your natural disposition, to do so, while you are thinking of the manner in which he conducted himself [1] in the discharge of his duty as quæstor, and while you remember, too, how some other quæstors behaved,—I hope, I say, that you will also recollect this.

This Titus Ligarius, then, who had at that time no other object except to induce you to think him attached to your interests, and a virtuous man also, (for he could never foresee

[1] There is some uncertainty as to what Cicero alludes to here. Most of the commentators think that Ligarius must have been quæstor when Metellus and the rest of his colleagues endeavored to prevent Cæsar from taking the money from the public treasury; but Fabritius objects to this view, that at that time Cicero had no connection with Cæsar's affairs, which is certainly true, while he says here that he had at the time that he alludes to. He thinks, therefore, that Cicero is alluding to what took place in the consulship of Lentulus and Philippus, (the year of Cicero's recal,) respecting the vote of pay to Cæsar's army in Gaul.

these present circumstances,) now as a suppliant begs the
safety of his brother from you. And when, urged by the recollection of his devotion to you, you have granted that safety to
these men, you will by so doing have made a present of three
most virtuous and upright brothers, not only to themselves,
nor to these men, numerous and respectable as they are, nor
to us who are their intimate friends, but also to the republic.
That, therefor, which in the case of that most noble and most
illustrious man, Marcus Marcellus, you lately did in the senate-
house, do now also in the forum with respect to these most
virtuous brothers, who are so highly esteemed by all the crowd
here present. As you granted him to the senate, so grant this
man to the people, whose affections you have always considered most important to you. And if that day was one most
glorious to you, and at the same time most acceptable to the
Roman people, do not, I entreat you,—do not hesitate to earn
the praise of a glory like that as frequently as possible.

For there is nothing so calculated to win the affections of
the people as kindness. Of all your many virtues, there is none
more admirable, none more beloved than your mercy. For
there is no action by which men make a nearer approach to
the gods, than by conferring safety on others. Fortune has no
greater gifts for you than when it bestows on you the ability—
nature has no better endowment for you than when it bestows
on you the will to save as many people as possible. The cause
of my client, perhaps, requires a longer speech than this: a
shorter one would certainly be sufficient for a man of your
natural disposition. Wherefore, as I think it more desirable for
you to converse, as it were, with yourself, than for me or any
one else to be speaking to you, I shall now make an end. This
only will I remind you of, that if you do grant this protection
to him who is absent, you will be giving it also to all these
men who are here present.

S